as a primary architectural vehicle
the concept of the sublime, both
istically and iconographically. The
, according to the author, accounts
the lingering taste up to our own
for simple, solid, and clear architec-
forms that produce an architecture
ch might best be described as
yptianizing".

HARD G. CARROTT is Professor
rt History, University of California,
erside.

The
Egyptian
Revival

*But concerning Egypt
I will now speak at length,
because nowhere are there
so many marvellous things,
nor in the whole world beside
are there to be seen so many works
of unspeakable greatness.*

HERODOTUS, II, 35

The Egyptian Revival

Its Sources, Monuments, and Meaning

1808-1858

Richard G. Carrott

University of California Press

Berkeley • Los Angeles • London

University of California Press
Berkeley and Los Angeles, California

University of California Press, Ltd.
London, England

Copyright © 1978 by
The Regents of the
University of California

ISBN 0-520-03324-8
Library of Congress
Catalog Card Number: 76-24579

Printed in the United States of America

1 2 3 4 5 6 7 8 9

To
Jane Carrott Boardman

Contents

Plates

Preface

The idea for this work, originally a dissertation for Yale University on the Egyptian Revival, did not grow out of a seminar. It occurred to me one noon in Vienne, France, upon my wandering into the Church (formerly Cathedral) of St. Maurice. Inside the sanctuary I was struck by the magnificent pyramid monument by Michelange Slodtz of 1740–1747. Five minutes earlier I had noted the Roman pyramid in the nearby public square. The juxtaposition of these two examples of Egyptian revivals 1600 years apart recalled another Egyptian revival, that of America, about which I had often been curious, but had found little material. Later, Dr. Eleanor Dodge Barton of the University of Hartford suggested the possibility of this as a dissertation topic. To her I am affectionately grateful for her realization that this could be a subject, and a subject for me. But my greatest debt of appreciation and gratitude is to the late Carroll L. V. Meeks who urged me to seriously investigate the Egyptian Revival and who agreed to be my advisor when I undertook the project. Without his knowledge, imagination, and practical advice I could never have completed this work. Nor could it have been accomplished if he had not alternately browbeaten and encouraged me with masterful timing and tolerant patience. But more than this, and more than the provocative insights on nineteenth-century architecture and criticism which he generously shared, I am deeply appreciative of his understanding and sensitivity as a teacher, and, I hope, friend.

To Harold Allen who is interested in this same field, although with a much broader scope, I am especially grateful for munificently providing me with photographs, and much information from his rich archives. I am particularly appreciative, not only of his eagerness to share information and ideas, but also for his friendly interest in the course of my work.

Preface

To Mrs. Elizabeth Kolowatt, Mrs. Joan Thill, Mrs. Judith Rodwell, Mrs. Connie Orlando-Greco, and Mrs. Katherine Coy, I cannot express sufficient gratitude. Not only have they typed this work; they have spelled it. Their calm patience, able efficiency, and conscientious craftsmanship have made this book possible. Their enthusiastic interest has been both flattering and encouraging.

I should also like to thank those at the University of California Press who have been so helpful, considerate and unflappable in their dealings with me. I am particularly grateful to Mr. Thomas McFarland for his encouragement and confidence. And I should also like to express my appreciation to Mr. Wolfgang Lederer, who has so skillfully designed this book, for his tolerant consideration of my own concerns and thoughts on the matter, as well as his sensitive understanding of the material.

These are the people without whom this book indeed could not have been realized. But any merits it may have must also be due to many others. Among them I would like to thank: Dr. John Hoag for attending me during the year's absence of Professor Meeks, kindly offering advice, and information, and always available when help was needed; Professor Henry-Russell Hitchcock of the Institute of Fine Arts, New York University, who during the same period advised me, sharing his vast knowledge of the field, and remaining a helpful, generous, and interested friend, even though he disagreed with my initial premise in this work; Dr. Matthew Baigell, who has written a dissertation at the University of Pennsylvania on John Haviland, for many helpful suggestions and friendly corrections; my friend Dr. Robert H. Rosenblum of the Institute of Fine Arts, New York University for several factual items and leads, and for critically reading and correcting the "Tombs" material; Dr. Sumner McK. Crosby of Yale University also for reading the "Tombs" material and making suggestions; Professor George Tatum of the University of Delaware for cordially sharing information, ideas, and photographs; Mr. John Cooney, formerly of the Egyptian Department of the Brooklyn Museum for information on early collections of Egyptian artifacts in America; Dr. Paul Norton of the University of Massachusetts, Amherst; and Dr. Robert

Alexander of the University of Iowa for various items on Latrobe, Godefroy, and Warren. In England Dr. S. Lang and Sir John Summerson were graciously attentive with their valuable time. Miss Janet Byrne lately of the Print Room of the Metropolitan Museum of Art has been of exceptional help, especially in providing material and information on A. J. Davis. I would also like to thank the staffs of the Municipal Archives and Records Center of New York City, the New-York Historical Society, the Library of the University of Pennsylvania, and the Royal Institute of British Architects for many cheerful, polite and helpful attentions.

And, finally, I must thank all those who, upon learning of my topic, have thoughtfully kept me in mind when they came upon some item or other that could have been of interest. Such a list would be of inordinate length, but I would single out particularly Miss Helen Chillman of Yale University and Dr. Colin Eisler of the Institute of Fine Arts.

It was Dr. Guido Schonberger of the Institute of Fine Arts who with modesty and humour gave sensitivity, incisiveness and imaginative scholarship to his lectures and seminars, thus first directing my interests to architectural history.

I must accept full responsibility for the ideas herein expressed unless they are otherwise credited. In all cases except one, which is so noted, italics within quotations are my own and have been indicated by the phrase "author's italics."

Introduction:
The Problem of Eclecticism

The earliest of civilizations was in the Valley of the Nile. It had the longest history of any, having flourished for 3000 years. During the two millennia since that time the shadowy presence of Egypt has been a recurrent vision in the mind and imagination of Western man, haunting him with the awesome age of a mummy, the mysterious riddle of a sphinx, the enduring secret of a pyramid, and the past glory of an Ozymandias. In succeeding ages the mention of Egypt conjured up dark notions of sepulchral solemnity, sublime grandeur, and occult knowledge. It was the civilization more antique than Antiquity; the cult of the immortality of mortals; the Land of Wisdom and Mystery.

As a sign of this fascination, European art and architecture adopted for their own such motifs as the obelisk, the pyramid, and the sphinx, so that these became repetitive international themes in much the same manner as Greece's contribution of the Three orders.[1] But whereas these elements evoked merely an echo of antique Egypt, it was not until the Age of Revivals, in the later eighteenth century, that more obvious and direct appeals were attempted. For the taste of that time, the picturesque eclectic aesthetic demanded a more literal and forceful connection to the original source. This was achieved through a wider vocabulary in which the entire architectural form called up an image of Egypt. This late-eighteenth-century Egyptian Revival developed within itself from an initial rococo stage to a more consciously archeological one which was a serious attempt at solving formal-aesthetic and symbolical-iconographic problems.[2] The earlier phase, in the second half of the eighteenth century in Europe, was part of that pre-Napoleonic movement which included

Introduction

Chinese pagodas, Greek temples, rustic cottages, and Gothic ruins. The Egyptian style was used because it was a picturesque style, or, at least, because it gave a picturesque effect. It was employed in precisely the same manner as the Chinese pavilion, or the Moorish boudoir, or any exotic-romantic structure. In other words, there were, then, few if any formal or iconographic reasons for the specific choice of the Egyptian mode.

The later, more profound, phase used the style for its visual and literary associations. Because of this, it has status as an independent movement worthy of consideration as a manifestation of the ideas and attitudes of a particular epoch and culture. It was an Egyptian renaissance as opposed to earlier renascences, and as such, occurred most significantly in the recently established United States of America. The subject of this work is this curious re-emergence of Ancient Egypt in the New World; the Egyptian Revival in American Architecture; its monuments, sources, and meaning.

The definition of the Egyptian Revival and its position in the overall fabric of nineteenth-century architecture is followed by a consideration of revivals in general. This involves an investigation of the differences between the principles of the originals and those of the revivals, as seen in the Classical ones as well as the Egyptian. Three different pre-nineteenth-century attitudes towards eclecticism are to be noted along with later Egyptian Revival parallels. There is a chapter on the sources and stimuli which provided the background for the movement. The principal section deals with the analysis of the American monuments organized in conceptual, iconographic, and formal groups. It is at this point that the documentation of each building is given in the notes. Following the concluding chapter, there is a short critical bibliography, a listing of the monuments, and a separate essay on the building history of the major monument of the movement, New York City's "Tombs."

The Egyptian Revival is that movement in nineteenth-century architecture dependent upon motifs of form and detail from ancient Egypt, which produced some major structures in a wide geographical range of American cities within the years 1808–1858. Although there are Egyptian Revival monuments from Ireland[3] to Tasmania (plate 89),[4] it is only in the United States that a significant number were constructed.[5] These were built during the half century beginning 1808, the date of the first comprehensive use of the style by Benjamin Latrobe (1764–1820) in his Library of Congress project (plate 97); to 1858, the completion of the last major structure erected in the series, J. Francis Rague's (1799–1877) Dubuque City Jail (plates 132, 133). Contemporary and earlier examples in Europe are also noted. That there were later ones both here and abroad is not denied. But these are merely a few isolated instances of the picturesque, or, at least, of the attention-attracting. They cannot be considered as a serious part of the Revival.

The preoccupation of the study of the history of art with what is progressive and forward-looking may tend to overshadow what is conservative and backward-looking. The fact remains, however, that these latter aspects, in their combinations with the former, are equally important. Often, the historian seems to emphasize the concept of developmental trends, and the changes which bring these about, to the relative exclusion of the links with the past. These links are, of course, a vital component of a style. This does not mean that art historical investigations have neglected sources and influences, nor that they should emphasize the unchanging and the constant. It does mean that the attitudes towards the past might be more carefully analyzed and evaluated. Pioneering works by such scholars as T. Bannister, H.-R. Hitchcock, and C. L. V. Meeks, among others, have opened the eyes of the intellectual public to an appreciation and understanding of eclecticism and revivalism by directing attention to their positive qualities and objectively reconsidering them in their own terms.

But if the case for eclecticism and revivalism has already been stated, there is a related area which suffers from neglect. The study of the history of art is not only the consideration of the chain of development forward, and the reversions backward in the cultural mainstream, but also the side eddies of that stream. Far from being muddy backwaters, or murky dead-ends leading nowhere, these branches may, through investigation and understanding, provide a clearer comprehension of the vagaries of the principal current. Knowledge of an era may be primarily dependent upon a familiarity with the major lines of development, but a consciousness of the significant minor forces allows for a more complete fabric of understanding. Indeed, it is the effect of these side tendencies which often explains otherwise puzzling phenomena in the dominant one.

In any case apologies need not be made in this day and age for serious scholarly consideration of these cultural aspects which lie somewhat outside the main arena. In the past decade or so historians have turned more and more attention to such areas as folk art, the art of minorities and women, as well as the art of the Third World. And these studies have not been without profit to our comprehension of the mainstream of the nature of man, nor even of "high art."

The Egyptian Revival is one of those side channels which, like an oxbow, indicates a former directional flow, now abandoned, but leaving its mark on the landscape. In this manner, although a revival, the Egyptian one is not major. But it did represent specific aesthetic ideals and symbolic ideas of a formative period in American architecture. If, among other accomplishments, it was to represent a final crystallization of Romantic Classicism through a hyper-simplicity, sharp geometry, and clear symmetry, these qualities were to fall from popular taste by mid-century. But they were not lost. They reappeared in works of later decades, be it McKim, Mead, and White, or Mies van der Rohe and Philip Johnson. If, on the other hand, certain forms of the Revival particularly suited practical, functional requirements, such requirements continued to be contained within the American tradition of architecture. And, finally, if the style was used to convey particular specialized meanings, this also has been a recurrent problem in all architecture; the case of the Egyptian Revival simply represents one attempt at a solution.

Before investigating the Egyptian Revival in detail, the question of architectural revivals should be considered generically. There are two aspects to this question: to what extent is a revival a matter of copying; and why is a particular style revived at a particular time? The answer to the first is provided by visual analysis, i.e., what motifs are borrowed from past monuments. The answer to the second is provided by literary analysis, i.e., what attitudes towards the past and its forms were expressed. This essay, in relation to the Egyptian Revival, deals primarily with the latter, while also indicating the relatively self-evident visual material. Nevertheless, it should not be felt that a simple listing of forms and details can answer the first question, the morphological one; for it does not take a prolonged investigation of the evidence to realize that revival design is not simply a copy of something from the original period. Specific motifs may be based on ancient details, but it can be said that exact replicas of entire structures hardly exist.[6]

With the availability of the archeological publications appearing from the mid-eighteenth century, the trained architects of the period could, even by the most unsympathetic judges, be considered competent to reproduce exact replicas. In view of their knowledge it would seem that the traditional criticism, "It's just a copy, and not a good one at that," is invalid. Nor would the arguments of lack of finances and loss of technique seem to apply for a period of enormous economic and engineering advances. It must be that the architects and patrons did not wish to recreate the past in its entirety. Thus the first question of what makes a revival building is in itself subdivided into the consideration of what parts are old and what elements are new. This is the meaning of Heinrich Wölfflin's "new wine in old bottles."[7] His point is made about Romantic Classicism, but this concept may be extended to revivals in general. What is especially significant is his comment that the newness of feeling is more important than the connection with the past. For Wölfflin, of course, formal values more than outweighed iconographical ones. As an introduction to some of the problems of this paper, it might be helpful to consider various aspects of the "new wine" in the revivals of this period, including the Egyptian. More time is spent in this work, however, on the meanings of the connections with the past.

In plan, the innovation is the increased importance of the interior which produces a greater freedom of arrangement. Religious buildings in Greece, Rome and Egypt were not conceived of in terms of interior areas to accommodate large groups of people, or in terms of complex and varied functions. They were sacred shrines of a restricted size and form to be visited only by the elect. Although late Roman civilization contributed great vaulted inner spaces, they were for secular purposes. Thus Pierre Vignon's (1762–1826) monumental Corinthian temple, the Madeleine (1808–1843), was to be given a Byzantine domed interior by J.-J.-M. Huvé (1783–1852). Actually the wall system of the inside recalls that the Baths of Caracalla. Similarly, Jefferson's (1743–1826) State Capitol at Richmond (1785–1789), for all its debt to the Maison Carrée, has a much more complicated inner arrangement than the single cella of the Nimes structure. The countless Greek and Roman "temples" which are the domestic houses of nineteenth-century America, as at Berry Hill (1835–1840) in Virginia, or A. J. Davis' (1803–1892) Russell House (1828) of Middletown, Connecticut, indicate the free use of the antique form which the revival employed. The revivals exploited the ancient religious building type for a vastly increased variety of purposes, e.g., government offices, banks, schools, and even domestic structures.

This same freedom of organization due to the greater importance of the interior is equally true of Egyptian Revival buildings. In Egypt the interior of a temple was a confined, minimal space, inserted into a forest of columns, serving a strictly ordained purpose, for the use of none but the elect few of the upper priestly hierarchy. John Haviland's (1792–1852) New York Halls of Justice and House of Detention, the "Tombs" (1835–1838), which was the most important of Egyptian Revival structures, was a sprawling complex whose interior space alone covered over half a city block. It served a wide variety of purposes, and was used by all classes of society (plates 111–128).

A corollary to the principle of the freedom of the plan is that the axial sequence of spaces in ancient Egyptian complexes is ignored in the Revival. The frontality of the pylon facade is maintained, while the longitudinality of the hypostyle hall is, in most instances, abandoned. Further, whereas in Egypt obelisks were usually in pairs flanking the axis of the ritualistic route between the first entrance and the final sacred shrine of a temple arrangement as at Karnac and

Luxor, in the nineteenth century this was not the case. Either new ones, as in Robert Mills' (1781–1855) Washington Monument (1833, 1848–1884),[8] or reerected ones, as in L.-H. Lebas' (1782–1867) Place de la Concorde obelisk (1836),[9] were placed as central focal points to define open Baroque spaces (plates 33, 136).

The case of cemetery gateways is similar. In Egypt, propylaea, usually in series, served as part of a clear linear progression, whereas in the Revival they mark the abrupt entrance to a burial ground, not at the end of an avenue, but alongside one, e.g., Mount Auburn (1831), Odd Fellows (1849) (see chapter on cemetery gates) (plates 57–58, 74). Once through the portal, there is no straight way leading directly into the distance, but an irregular diffusion of paths meandering off at all angles. In this case the gateway becomes a focal point, not to define Baroque space, but to bring order to the confluence of the chaos of one world, and the informality of the picturesque one.

There are changes in elevations, too. The most notable change is the subdivision into stories. The podium becomes the ground floor, while the attic becomes another usable floor, e.g., the Pantheon and the Library of the University of Virginia (1817–1826) or the Maison Carrée and the Virginia State Capitol. Also, in both these Jeffersonian examples there is an important change in the materials used. The revival architects did not hesitate to combine brick, stone, and wood in an obvious manner, as in the above-mentioned Library, whereas the ancients sought after visual unity. More striking is the variety of forms employed in the nineteenth century. The complicated mass of the Palais Bourbon passes as a neo-classical building only because of Bernard Poyet's (1742–1824) pedimental facade (1806–1808). Aside from this temple front, the building exhibits, in its various elevations, of other periods, the greatest freedom of organization. Often the antique motif is used to mask an otherwise awkward arrangement, as in this example. In any case, the rule appears to be one of archeological purity. As has been noted in the instance of the Madeleine, a classical temple may have a Byzantine interior dome system. Its Hellenistic exterior may cover later Imperial inner wall arrangements. The outside elevation of Town and Davis' New York

Customs House (1836) may be Greek Doric, but its inside with William Ross' dome is certainly Roman.

These same characteristics are true of Egyptian Revival buildings. They are divided into stories and exhibit a wide variety of forms which are archeologically eclectic, if not archeologically pure, in that they do not strictly adhere to the ancient canons of organization. The long axial temple arrangement is abandoned, the battered openings become windows, projecting porticoes and tower forms are employed (*vide*, the "Tombs," plates 111–128).

A study of the sculptural reliefs on the facing pediments of the Palais Bourbon and the Madeleine reveals the change in attitude towards decoration for in neither case is it integrated with the architecture as in antique prototypes. Further, as Emil Kaufmann pointed out, decoration and accents are more evenly distributed, often simpler, with the revival architects, as in the Paris *barrières*.[10] This subordinates the individuality of, or emphasis upon, a particular element.

In the Egyptian Revival, conversely, it is not a case of decoration being non-integrated, or more widely distributed, for the builders of the nineteenth-century examples did not aspire to the complete ornamental coverage of ancient Egyptian temples with their acres of hieroglyphic murals and descriptive reliefs.[11] But in the even spacing of the decorative accents, and by the widely distributed paucity of ornament, the same effect is achieved, as can be noted from the facade of the "Tombs" (plate 114), or A. J. Davis' design for a cemetery gate (plate 68).

As for the differences in three-dimensional concepts, the "new wine" is the principle of space enclosure, rather than sculptural mass in Greek and Roman buildings, or space-displacing mass in Egyptian structures. Even without the study of ground plans, the revival scheme is seen to be one of mural architecture. It has been noted that the purpose of the nineteenth-century buildings was to accommodate a variety of functions for a considerable number of people. Thus, although prepossessing on the exterior, it is the interior which is the more important. In Classical Revival architecture, using the Palais Bourbon as an illustration, this results in such changes as the colonnade as a stage scrim rather than a screen; a clear statement of the walls which includes schemes of fenestration; and a contraction of projecting elements which produces an unaccented rhythm of shading, rather than a stressed cadence of shadows. Cornices and moldings protrude less. Porches are shallower. Walls are pushed to the outer limits of the structure. The ebb and flow of "refinements" is replaced by the brittle astringency of sharper and more unyielding silhouettes. In sum, the geometric volume of the edifice is emphasized by the relatively unadorned mural areas, which in the antique prototypes had been broken up and pulled inward through the effects of columns, relief sculptures, and architectural decorations.

In Egyptian Revival architecture the contrast to the ancient prototypes is less subtle, although both the old and new forms are predicated upon a strong sense of geometry. Neo-Egyptian buildings, like Romantic Classical ones, are conceived of as space enclosures. The solid masses of Nilotic temple complexes, on the other hand, represent a series of space displacements. The great masonic bulk of the pylon form becomes, in the nineteenth-century reemergence, emptied out by means of long windows, projecting porticoes, recessed portals, and corbelled arches. The familiar Romantic Classical silhouette of hardness and clarity is given, but it is achieved not through the suppression of "refinements"—there was more of a sense of ponderous swelling and bulging in ancient Egyptian architecture—but through the deletion of the lavish use of polychrome mural and columnar relief which had a tendency to invite attention away from the precise edges of the forms. These forms in the Revival thus appear as encompassing outer shells whose geometric perimeters remain inviolate. If a principle of ancient Egyptian architecture is one of mass, that of the Revival is volume.

Thus the "new wine" symbolizes the sacrifice of the letter of archeological purity and strictness, and becomes the liberation of the spirit of architectural freedom, variety and reinterpretation. The law here is that of current needs and tastes. Wölfflin's metaphor might be reversed, if the question is considered in terms of the changes in form, to read "old wine in new bottles." The taste is the same, but the bottle

9

has changed its shape. Whichever way the metaphor reads, the point is: the new attitude is of greater significance than the links to the past.

Contrarily, an investigation of earlier, pre-nineteenth-century eclectic monuments would seem to indicate that there was a strong case for forms of revivalism based on the greater importance of past associations. Although not always direct copies, these examples evoke an image of earlier models. It is this evocation, rather than any new feeling, which is fundamental to the understanding of such structures. A selection will illustrate three basic principles of this traditional eclecticism: *viz.*, the concept of the symbol, the concept of unity, and the concept of the museum. Interestingly enough, there are nineteenth-century Egyptian Revival parallels to each of these. They are, significantly, almost exclusively found in Europe, the more traditional locale which produced the first phase of the Revival, that of the Rococo Picturesque.

The concept of eclecticism as symbolism has been stated by Richard Krautheimer in his notable articles on mediaeval architectural iconography.[12] His point is that a structure, although in a current style, may still refer to an earlier one for psychological or religious reasons. This may be achieved through the use of similar features such as the ground plan, the arrangement of the elevation, or motifs like the dome, ambulatory, or even the repetition of specific measurements such as the diameter of a circular building. He argues that direct copying is not needed. An octagonal building, for instance, may evoke an earlier round one, simply because it is similar in concept. An axial, or square, structure is based on entirely different principles. Thus he accounts for the persistence in the Middle Ages of the domed, centralized baptistry in its varying guises. It is a matter of free architectural evocation rather than strict archeological imitation.

That this was not a principle restricted to the Mediaeval period has been shown by Earl Rosenthal in his work on the Renaissance Cathedral of Granada.[13] He argues that because the church was planned as a royal mausoleum, and was dedicated to the Corpus Christi, its iconographic associations go back to the Holy Sepulchre in Jerusalem.

Clothed in a Classical-Roman Renaissance garb, the Spanish structure contains such features of the Anastasis as the circular ground-plan, dome, ambulatory, a similar elevation, an almost equal diameter, and a tall triumphal arch. Thus the church, "although Renaissance in style, . . . is a revival of a late Mediaeval form."

The most obvious parallel in the Egyptian Revival is the use of the pyramid form for funerary monuments (plates 25–27). The association of the pyramid with Egypt and its Cult of the Dead is a long one beginning in Rome with the Tomb of Cestius, and continuing to the present. Raphael (1515 ff.), Bernini (1652 ff.), J.-B. Tuby (1675), Michelange Slodtz (1740–1747), N.S. Adam (1747), L.F. Roubiliac (1748), J.-B. Pigalle (1753–1776), E.-L. Boullée (ca. 1785), J.-N.-L. Durand (1805), and A. Canova (1805) designed a notable series of pyramid tombs. It is of interest to realize that the shapes range from Pigalle's steeply pitched Maréchal de Saxe Mausoleum at St. Thomas' in Strasbourg to the wide-angled cenotaph design of Boullée. Thus neither the proportion nor the scale of the original Egyptian models were necessarily followed. A further deviation is to be found in Durand's example which contains a domed hemicycle in its interior, a decidedly non-Egyptian feature.[14] The fact remains, however, that the Egyptian funerary tradition is paramount in the conception of these monuments. Egyptian forms are used to symbolically evoke past meanings.

Another reason for the revival of a former mode is for unity with existing older architecture. A past style may be used in a building, or part of a building, in order to be consistent with the surroundings. Thus, Erwin Panofsky explains designs in the Gothic manner submitted for the completion of the San Petronio facade in Bologna.[15] The concept is that, as the church had been commenced in the Mediaeval Gothic of the late fourteenth century, this style should be continued throughout its building history for the sake of unity.[16] Therefore, although the facade was to be erected during the Renaissance, the use of the current classical style would be illogical, and against the principle of *conformità*. Unity could, of course, be achieved by covering up an entire building, in the contemporary fashion which was done by Alberti at Rimini with the Tempio Malestestiano. Financial and technical considerations make this impractical in most cases.

This idea of *conformità*, consciously or not, undoubtedly explains the architectural setting for J.-M.-N. Bralle's (1785–1863) fountain in Paris of 1808 (plate 49).[17] One of several erected at Napoleon's orders as a result of the completion of the Canal d'Ourcq and the subsequent increase in the city's water supply,[18] the fountain is in the form of an Egyptian gate with battered walls, cavetto cornices, and a torus molding. By blocking what would be the entry, a shallow niche has been formed that contains a statue of a figure in Egyptian costume. The figure, by P.-N. Beauvallet (1750–1818), is one of the copies after the Antinoüs of the Capitoline which was included in the spoils Napoleon brought back from Rome. Given this statue, whose original was itself in a revival style, the architect chose to frame it in an appropriately Egyptian manner. The architectural form is probably based on plates from the unofficial account of Napoleon's Egyptian campaign by Vivant Denon.[19] The work had been published six years earlier. Bralle, although replacing the winged orb with the Imperial eagle, and using a disturbingly heavy and unsupported lintel, has produced a monument unified in its parts by the logic of a style appropriate to the statue.[20]

It might also be considered that the fountain with its Egyptian statue makes up part of a city-wide architectural museum with which the Emperor memorialized his various campaigns, past and projected, throughout the world. Thus, to a Greek Temple of Glory, a Roman memorial column, and two Italian triumphal arches, is added an Egyptian gateway.

Not a uniquely Napoleonic idea, the exploitation of eclecticism for the purpose of creating an architectural museum is the third of the pre-nineteenth-century principles of revivalism. This concept is most notably exemplified by Hadrian's vast complex at Tivoli.[21] Modern archeology has verified the ancient description (125 A.D.) of the Villa provided by Aurelius Victor in which he tells of various edifices reproduced there by the Emperor. Modelled upon examples which had particularly impressed him, they included the Lyceum and Academy of

Athens, as well as the seaport of Canopus on the Nile Delta, not far from Alexandria. Sculpture, as well as architecture, from a variety of periods and locations was exhibited. Some statues were original, others were copies, as the above mentioned Antinoüs. Thus in his declining years Hadrian created for himself a huge private museum. The architecture and sculpture were selected from past styles; the first true instance of a revival.

A later direct parallel to this concept of eclecticism is to be found in Luigi Canina's Egyptian gate for the Borghese Gardens in Rome of about 1825 (plates 47–48).[22] Apparently conceived of as a specific imitation of the Villa Hadriana, the gardens contained various Greek- and Etruscan-inspired temples as well as the pylon entrance. Canina gives the following description and explanation:

> The second structure erected in this new enlargement was that made to communicate with the remaining part of the Pincian gardens, passing in front of the first casino. Primarily, this consists of a solid bridge over the public road, called the street of the Three Madonnas, and is built entirely of Tivoli stone cut in wedges, in the manner of ancient constructions. This bridge gives room for carriages, even in double file, to cross from one part of the villa to the other. To hide the odiousness of this separation, and to conceal the view of the ugly street which passes below, it was decided, from among the many projects for this purpose, to erect an edifice similar to those of the ancient Egyptians, in order to vary the appearance of these new buildings. To those who do not know the magnificence of the building art of the Egyptians (of which grand remains have been represented with great excellence, especially by the commission of celebrated Frenchmen who were there for many years), the imitation made here was not pleasant, because it was not in keeping with the other buildings: but what vindicates artistically the manner adopted is the approval of those who know the proportions and the ornaments of Egyptian buildings. In regard, then, to this choice, made in preference to many that could have been picked, these reasons can be advanced in its defense: first of all, considering that the Villa Borghese is the one which for its magnifi-

13

cence and for the variety of its buildings more than any other villa approaches the celebrated Villa of Hadrian, and that, counting among its parts a fortress, a hippodrome, and various temples in the manner of the ancients, it appears appropriate that in imitation of the Canopus of Hadrian, it too should have some construction like that of the Egyptians; therefore, it seemed an opportunity to imitate, for this, one of those many entrances, styled propylaea by the ancients, which were in front of nearly all the great Egyptian buildings. Like those, this is composed of two great pylons in which are placed the stairs for ascending to the upper floors. The Egyptians, as we can judge by the remains, placed between these pylons an entrance, which in this case could not be used, because in order to adapt it to the proportions of the building, it would have been necessary to narrow the passage at this point, and would furthermore have hidden the vista from the street; here, therefore, it was judged more to the purpose to suppress it, just as it is discovered in some similar buildings, whose remains are situated in Upper Egypt. On one side of these pylons are attached, as on Egyptian buildings, two porticoes, here composed each of four columns, and these serve as shelter in intemperate weather. In front of these pylons are erected two obelisks, just as the Egyptians did in similar cases; these, in the manner of the ancients, rise from the ground without being on any pedestal, as is done in modern Rome when they place antique obelisks from Egypt. Then on the front sides of these obelisks some things are written, according to the mysterious hiero- glyphic manner of expressing the great deeds of the Egyptians, in honor of the magnanimous Prince Camillo, and these were composed at my instance, by the erudite Cav. Gell, whose name is celebrated for the interesting discoveries which he has brought back principally from his trips to European and Asiatic Greece, as can be proved by his Troiad, his Argolid, his description of the island of Ithaca, his Pompeiana, and other highly esteemed works. If, then, this new building, constructed in the manner of the Egyptians, does not compare in greatness with those im- mense monuments of Egypt, we can find some support in the imitation which Hadrian made of the Canopus of the Egyptians in his Villa Adriana at Tivoli: seeing that in Egypt Canopus was a city sacred to Serapis one hundred and twenty stadii in distance from Alexandria, according to Strabo, in which great feasts in honor of the mentioned deity were solemnly celebrated; and that in Hadrian's villa this was nothing else, so far as we can see from the ruins, than a little artificial valley in which were placed along the sides some porticoes with little cells, and in the center a great niche from which probably issued the waters which formed a canal in the middle of the valley. So it is that if this imitation of Canopus, made by a great emperor who held the known world of his time in his domain, was reduced to such a small size it is not strange that the Egyptian edifice built in the Villa Pinciana does not correspond in grandness to those monuments which were the works of great sovereigns of that country who kept an entire population busy on construction. It would also be strange to pretend that this building, constructed simply for decoration, should be formed entirely of hard oriental granite such as the Egyptians generally used but which now is rare with us: but here instead granite was imitated only in appearance so as not to go too far away from the Egyptian style; and this imitation could best be made with a fabric of brick covered with stucco, because travertine or peperino or any other stone common here would never resemble Egyptian granite, and also the frequent joinings necessary in working with this stone would have further destroyed the resemblance to Egyptian granite, which we find is always worked in great masses. Vitruvius, too, tells us in what esteem buildings constructed of bricks were held among the ancients and narrates that sovereigns themselves, among whom was Mausolus, king of Halicarnassus, did not disdain to have homes built of bricks covered with stucco; and in this matter, Herodotus tells us that Asychis [Shishak?] had built in Egypt a pyramid entirely of bricks to surpass that which had been built entirely of stone by the sovereigns who preceded him, and that he placed on it an inscription which recorded the manner in which this work was constructed. So, if Asychis, ruler of Egypt, held it such honor to have built a pyramid of bricks, we must not disdain too much the means used to build this structure, which shows in general the style used by the Egyptians; still more, if we consider that no expense was spared in using cut stone where solidity required it, as in the construction of the lower bridge. The union of this bridge and the edifice, not visible to those who pass above, does not produce any discord in this respect, and the character of the Egyptian construction hides very well the division of the Villa, which the public road below produces at this point.[23]

The parallel to the ancient example is particularly helpful for the understanding of the monument and the ensemble of its setting. The meaning is vitiated, however, by the realization that the analogy is, philosophically, a superficial one. For the contents of Hadrian's museum were based on personal souvenirs, while those of the Prince were based on symbolic associations. Thus Camillo could identify with the Emperor by imitating his villa in this highly picturesque manner. Besides documenting the link to Hadrian's architectural museum, it is interesting to note from the quotation that a mixture of styles in one complex is "not pleasant because it was not in keeping," and is thus a violation of *conformità*. This objection, however, is counteracted by the archeological verisimilitude of the "proportions and ornaments," and the fact that it is inspired from an antique prototype. Thus, even if the pylons offend contemporary aesthetic canons, the sacrosanct cloak of ancient precedents garbs them in respectability. A second point is the attitude that a strict replica is not necessary when it would mean inconvenience, e.g., the omission of the narrow Egyptian entry between the pylon towers. Related to this is the adaptation of motifs, as in the "hieroglyphics" on the obelisks, the latter conceived of in painstakingly "correct" terms without bases. Although they are understandable as inscriptions, the writing is made to look like ancient hieroglyphs. Finally, the size, proportions, materials, and characteristics of Egyptian architecture are carefully noted, and then reworked to fit the contemporary conditions. Especially interesting is the realization that the Egyptian style calls for masonry "worked in great masses." This is an important concept to bear in mind in relation to the New York "Tombs" which will be discussed later. In any case, the combination of meticulous archeological knowledge, and creative architectural imagination emerges as a formulative basis of the monument. This is a significant principle of nineteenth-century eclecticism.

In considering the study of the history of architecture, the necessity of completeness and scope of investigation may be urged. Not only is it essential to look backward, as well as forward, but also to the side. In this context, architectural revivals require an understanding of their new attitudes as well as their associations with former epochs. Questions of what elements of the old vocabularies are used to express what new purposes must be considered, as well as such problems as what the evocative affiliations and methods are. It should be realized that the reasons for the use of past styles are varied and based on specific principles. The Egyptian Revival is applicable to these conclusions. It appears as a consequential, if not major, example of nineteenth-century eclecticism. The next chapter will deal with the sources and stimuli of the movement.

Notes

1. For the best treatment of pre-Piranesi Egyptian Revivals, see Nikolaus Pevsner and S. Lang, "The Egyptian Revival," *Architectural Review,* CXIX (May, 1956), pp. 242–254, now published as chapter thirteen in Nikolaus Pevsner, *Studies in Art, Architecture and Design,* I (New York, 1968).
2. For a discussion of these developments, see chapters four, five and six.
3. Interior of St. Andrew's Church, Dublin, by Francis Johnston, 1800–1807. John Betjeman, "Francis Johnston," *The Pavilion* (London, 1946[?]), p. 30; Architectural Publications Society, *Dictionary of Architecture,* 8 vols. (London, 1853[?]–1892), vol. II (1859), article on "Dublin." Note also the Wellington Monument, Dublin, by Robert Smirke, 1817.
4. Synagogue, Hobart (1843), *Universal Jewish Encyclopaedia,* I (1939), pp. 618, 620, possibly by James Alexander Archer of the office of James Blackburn. There were also synagogues in the Egyptian style of about the same time at Launceston, Tasmania, and Sydney, Australia. The former was extant in 1960, a simple brick building; the latter was destroyed about sixty years ago. For this information I am indebted to Mr. Daniel Thomas of the Art Gallery of New South Wales, Sydney. For Australian architecture of the period see: John Skinner Prout, *Sydney Illustrated* (Sydney, 1848); Joseph Fowles, *Sydney in 1848* (Sydney, n.d.); Morton Herman, *Early Australian Architects and their Work* (Sydney, 1955); J. Freeland, *Architecture in Australia* (Melbourne, 1968).
5. Roughly eighty monuments by thirty architects; not including European examples.
6. For a discussion of this imitation-association polarity see Carroll L. V. Meeks, "Pantheon Paradigm," *Journal of the Society of Architectural Historians* (hereafter, *JSAH*), XIX, 4, pp. 135–144.
7. Heinrich Wölfflin, *The Sense of Form in Art* (New York, 1958), pp. 13 ff.
8. H. Gallagher, *Robert Mills* (New York, 1955), pp. 115, 117; Frank J. Roos, "The Egyptian Style," *Magazine of Art,* XXXIII (1940), p. 220; Clay Lancaster, "Oriental Forms in American Architecture, 1800–1870," *Art Bulletin,* XXIX, 3 (October, 1947), p. 184; C. W. Eckels, "The Egyptian Revival in America," *Archaeology,* III (1950), p. 165; *Gleason's Pictorial Drawing-Room Companion,* IV, 21 (1853), p. 333; *ibid.,* VI, 17 (1854), p. 272, *ibid.,* VII, 1 (1854), pp. 7, 13; *Ballou's Pictorial Drawing-Room Companion,* VIII, 7 (1855), p. 107; J. Zukowsky, "Monumental American Obelisks," *Art Bull.,* LVIII, 4 (1976), p. 576.
9. *Architectural Magazine,* I (1834), p. 46; *ibid.,* III (1836), pp. 325, 386, 544; Society for the Diffusion of Useful Knowledge, *The Penny Magazine,*

American Edition (hereafter, *Penny Magazine*), III, 120 (1834), pp. 61–62, 66–67; *ibid.*, VII, 380 (1838), pp. 81–82.

10. Emil Kaufmann, "Claude-Nicholas Ledoux, Inaugurator of a new Architectural System," *JSAH*, III, 3 (1943), pp. 15–17.

11. Minard Lafever's Washington Monument project for Murray Hill in New York City (1854) is a possible exception. Jacob Landy, *The Architecture of Minard Lafever* (New York, 1970), pp. 140–146.

12. Richard Krautheimer, "Introduction to an Iconography of Mediaeval Architecture," *Journal of the Warburg and Courtauld Institutes,* V (1942), pp. 1–33. See also the same author's article, "The Carolingian Revival of Early Christian Architecture," originally published in the *Art Bulletin*, XXIV (1942), now published as chapter thirteen in Richard Krautheimer's *Studies in Early Christian, Medieval, and Renaissance Art* (New York, 1969).

13. Earl Rosenthal, "A Renaissance 'Copy' of the Holy Sepulchre," *JSAH*, XVII (March, 1958), pp. 2–11, now published in Earl Rosenthal, *The Cathedral of Granada: A Study in the Spanish Renaissance* (Princeton, 1961).

14. J.-N.-L. Durand, *Précis des leçons d'architecture données à l'école polytechnique*, 2 vols. (Paris, 1802, 1805), vol. II, 3e partie, pl. 1. Benjamin Latrobe employed a similar design in his project for the Richmond (Virginia) Monumental Church. Talbot Hamlin, *Benjamin Henry Latrobe* (New York, 1955), p. 218; Coleman Homsey, "Four Unpublished Drawings of Benjamin Latrobe" (unpublished term paper, Department of History of Art, University of Pennsylvania, 1959); Latrobe Papers, Library of Congress. My thanks are due to Dr. Paul Norton for showing me a photograph of a design found in the Latrobe Papers at the Library of Congress (plate 25).

15. Erwin Panofsky, *Meaning in the Visual Arts* (New York, 1955), pp. 196–205.

16. For a more detailed consideration of San Petronio and the persistence of the original style see Richard Bernheimer, "Gothic Survival and Revival in Bologna," *Art Bulletin,* XXXVI, 4 (1954), pp. 263–284; also, David Coffin, "San Petronio," (unpublished term paper, archives of C. L. V. Meeks, Department of History of Art, Yale University). For the continuation of the problem, see R. Wittkower, *Classic vs. Gothic: Architectural Projects in Seventeenth Century Italy* (New York, 1974).

17. Louis Hautecoeur, *L'art sous la Révolution et l'Empire en France* (Paris, 1953), p. 26.

18. At the same period Bralle designed a larger fountain using Egyptian motifs for the Place du Châtelet. It consisted of a huge palm shaft with four sphinxes at the base spouting water. Rebuilt in 1858, it is to be seen today in much the same form. Louis Hautecoeur, *L'histoire de l'architecture classique en France,* 7 vols. (Paris, 1943–1957), vol. V, pp. 37,

213–214. Fittingly enough, it was also a monument to the Egyptian Campaign.

19. Dominique Vivant Denon, *Voyage dans la Basse et la Haute Egypte pendant les campagnes du Général Bonaparte,* 3 vols. (Paris, 1802), pl. 38 (fig. 4), pl. 43 (fig. 3) (hereafter, Denon, *Voyage . . .*). For Denon, especially as a literary figure, see Judith Nowinski, *Baron Dominique Vivant Denon* (Rutherford, Madison, Teaneck, 1970).

20. Another example of the principle of *conformità* in the Egyptian Revival is the use of the "hieroglyphics" which Lebas caused to be inscribed on the new base of the Luxor Obelisk explaining its reerection in the Place de la Concorde. See note 9 above. This was also done by Emperor Theodosius for an Egyptian obelisk reerected in Constantinople on the spina of the Hippodrome.

21. Aurelius Victor, XXVI; Rodolfo Lanciani, *Wanderings in the Roman Campagna* (Boston and New York, 1909), pp. 127–183; Roberto Paribeni, *The Villa of the Emperor Hadrian at Tivoli* (Milan, 1930[?]); Roberto Vighi, *Villa Hadriana* (Rome, 1959); Axel Boethius and J. B. Ward-Perkins, *Etruscan and Roman Architecture* (Baltimore, 1970); William MacDonald, *The Architecture of the Roman Empire* (New Haven and London, 1965).

22. Luigi Canina, *Le nuove fabbriche della Villa Borghese, denominata pinciana* (Rome, 1828), pp. 11–13. There seems to be no basis for Hautecoeur's attribution to the Asprucci (Louis Hautecoeur, *Rome et la renaissance de l'antiquité* [Paris, 1912], pp. 32, 70, 130–132) nor even that the pylon gate was based on Norden's *Voyage* (*ibid.*, p. 32).

23. Canina, *Le nuove fabbriche . . .* The author wishes to thank Mr. Harold Allen and Mr. Anselmo Carini for the translation.

Sources and Stimuli

In the preceding chapter it was noted that among the eclectic moments in the history of Western art, there was an important one in Hadrian and in his "museum" at Tivoli. N. Pevsner and S. Lang have admirably discussed the various manifestations of Egyptiana that occurred between Imperial Rome and the late eighteenth century.[1] Their work has provided a valuable skeleton to which in this chapter, other information and three organizational concepts or attitudes have been added. The basic interest of Pevsner and Lang is in the pre-Piranesi periods. Their article demonstrates that an important Isis cult was located in ancient Rome, and that during the Middle Ages, from the early Church Fathers to the Crusaders, there were numerous references to Egyptian art and architecture. With the advent of the Renaissance interest in Egypt was fostered as early as the fourteenth century through the early Humanists' reevaluation of, and awakened interest in Classical Antiquity. This resulted in the use of Nilotic motifs by painters, sculptors and architects, based on the findings of primitive archeology. Note Raphael's use of the atlantes figure in the Stanza dell'Incendio, the source apparently based on archeological investigations of the time. The impetus gathered force and spread to France and Northern Europe via the Italian Mannerists like Primaticcio who in 1540 used Egyptian atlantes at Fontainebleau. In the late sixteenth and seventeenth centuries the interest was increased by the appearance of travel books on Egypt, as G. Sandys' *Relation of a Journey,* published in London in 1615, and the reerection of ancient obelisks in Rome.[2] By the mid-seventeenth century there was already a growing literature on Egyptology to provide an archeological basis for the use of the style. Pevsner and Lang, after carefully documenting this history, conclude with an elaborate section pointing out that through the ages, the Egyptian style had no single meaning. If it was associated with a great funerary tradition, it also symbolized the Land of Wisdom and Mystery. By the latter half of the eighteenth century, as will be seen, the style was used to achieve imaginative variety, playful exoticism, and primeval severity. The nineteenth-century manifestations of the style, with a true eclectic bias, demonstrate all of these meanings and attitudes, as well as adding new ones. It is the purpose of this work to demonstrate this. In this chapter the eighteenth-century interest in Egypt is investigated from the point of view of the four major intellectual centers of the era: Italy, France, Germany, and England.

In Italy the foremost exponent of the Egyptian style was G. B. Piranesi (1720–1778) who published a large collection of fireplace designs in 1769, several of which were in that style (plates 1, 2).[3] As there were also some Etruscan projects, the work included an elaborate apologia for the Egyptian and Etruscan styles. It was the major salvo from Piranesi in his ardent battle against the artistic primacy of ancient Greece. His position in the Rome versus Greece question has been fully covered by H. Focillon, E. Bourgeois, and Hyatt Mayor.[4] Suffice it to say, against the background of publications by Leroy, and Stuart and Revett dealing with Greek antiquities, the arch-Roman, Piranesi, wished to establish his adopted city as the great inspirational source for classical art. His sumptuous edition of the Roman monuments (1748) was to place before the world "the grandeur that was Rome." When the partisans of Greece claimed that Roman art derived from the former, using the argument of chronological precedence, Piranesi retreated to a second line of defense, countering that the Romans learned, not from the Greeks, but from the proto-Romans, the Etruscans. They, in turn, owed their cultural traditions to the Egyptians. Thus Greece and Rome had been educated in the arts by Egypt, the latter via Etruria.[5]

Piranesi was not the first Italian to become fascinated by Etruscan and Egyptian antiquity. In the second half of the seventeenth century

Antonio Gori and Filippo Buonarotti had excavated Etruscan sites around Cortona. Somewhat later Egyptian artifacts were unearthed at Rome in the Gardens of Sallustus (1714) and during the building of the Library of Cardinal Cassanetta (1719), to say nothing of the excavations at Tivoli. Indeed, so numerous were Egyptian finds that Benedict XIV established an Egyptian Museum at the Capitoline in 1748. Piranesi used some of these early archeological finds as motifs in the *Cammini* (fireplace design book); *viz.* a pair of Egyptian atlantes excavated at Hadrian's Villa about 1460. Another source must have been from the Tabula Bembo (or Tabula Isiaca), a curious Ptolemaic relief known through an early cinquecento copy.[6] A third source came from the illustrations for the two most important pre-Napoleonic travel books on Egypt, those by Norden (1755), and Pococke (1743). The plates of the former are more numerous and elaborate.

In addition to using such material as ammunition for his historical propaganda, Piranesi exploited the Egyptian style for objective aesthetic reasons. By choosing the fireplace as his vehicle, a non-antique element, he was enabled to give expression to free, if not fantastic, invention in an old style. He himself praised the use of the mode for its originality, imagination and "anti-monotony." It is this sense of the "bizarre," or the novel, which reinforced by exotic associations, establishes the rococo phase of the Egyptian Revival.[7]

The close connections between Italian artistic and intellectual life, and that of France during the seventeenth and eighteenth centuries provided a pathway for Egyptian motifs to travel north. Poussin became intrigued with Egyptian archeology in Rome. In three paintings of the Moses story he used elements from a mosaic depicting scenes of Egypt originally at the Temple of Praeneste and reinstalled in the Barbarini Palace at Palestrina, as well as motifs from an Isis cult burial vault.[8]

Of special importance was Bernard de Montfaucon's *L'antiquité expliquée* published in Paris in ten volumes between 1719 and 1724.[9] It was the first comprehensive archeological work in Europe, and discussed Egyptian as well as Greek and Roman antiquities. Montfaucon, a Benedictine, travelled in Italy collecting his Egyptian material from travellers, books, and such artifacts as the Tabula Bembo which he included in his plates.

The most influential event in Egyptological studies, however, and one which marked a decisively serious attitude towards them in France, was the Comte de Caylus' *Recueil d'antiquités égyptiennes, étrusques, grèques et romaines.*[10] In it Caylus uses the same Piranesi argument that the arts, having been formed in Egypt, passed to Etruria, and from there to Greece and Rome. More significant, the author sees with new eyes specific aesthetic qualities in Egyptian architecture not heretofore contemplated. He writes of its quality of grandeur, and considers such attributes as primativity, massivity, solidity, and simplicity as desirable and pleasing. Thus the aesthetic groundwork was laid for the future appreciation of Egyptian forms and properties. The Romantic Classicists, Ledoux, Boullée, and their later followers were to build upon these foundations.

But before these ideas were to germinate, and appear in the works of the Revolutionary architects, the Egyptian style in France was to follow in the rococo tradition of Piranesi. The pseudo-classical artist of the Louis XVI period borrowed profusely such Egyptian motifs as sphinxes, lions, atlantes, caryatids, and canopic figures for furniture and interior decoration.[11] Indeed, this typically eighteenth-century attitude towards the mode was to continue into the nineteenth century, and remain a side current throughout the entire movement. The rococo aesthetic in this sense was never abandoned entirely, even in the American use of the style.

In France with the advent of the Revolution and Empire, artisans continued the exploitation of Egyptian motifs. Cabinetmakers of the Louis XVI era as Jacob, Migeon, Weisweiler, Bénéman and the Rousseau brothers were replaced by Percier and Fontaine[12] (plates 21, 23), J.C. Krafft (fireplace, bookcase),[13] P.-N. Beauvallet (interiors and furniture),[14] and L. Biennais (coin cabinet for Napoleon) working in the Empire-Egyptian mode.[15] There was also the monumental ceramic work by Alexandre Brongniart (1770–1847), son of the architect. This was Napoleon's 115 piece Sèvres Egyptian Service ordered by the Emperor in 1808 as a gift for Tsar Alexander of Russia.[16] Although examples in this second generation were more archeological than those of the earlier one, it can hardly be said that the use of the Egyptian vocabulary in Empire furnishings was for anything other than to give variety and novelty to the existing Napoleonic style.[17] The taste of the time was naturally sympathetic to the heavy solidity of Egyptian forms, and Bonaparte's Nile campaign provided clear associations, but the underlying principles in the decorative arts were not those of architecture.

That the design could be more archeological was due to the vitally important publications that appeared after the Egyptian campaign of 1798–1799, and the succeeding occupation which ended in 1802. The first of these was Vivant Denon's account of the French army's battles in Egypt liberally illustrated with engravings of the country and its ruins.[18] For Egyptian antiquity it was the first attempt at scientific archeology showing measured drawings, current state of the ruins, specific details, and scholarly reconstructions. Hastily done, it was a preview of the monumental work commissioned by the Emperor and produced by an army, this time, of scholars, artists, scientists, and historians. This was the twenty-one volume *Description d'Egypte . . .*[19] Appearing in three folio sizes, this staggering opus included sections dealing with the topography, geography, natural history, current state, and most important for the Revival, the antiquities of Egypt. More carefully measured and painstakingly rendered than Denon's illustrations, the engravings of the monuments of ancient Egypt established the highest quality and finest tradition of scholarly archeology. They included a vastly expanded reportage of the current state of the ruins, details, and reconstructions. Napoleon's military adventure was a catastrophe, but his army of *savants* won him an unassailable position in the histories of art and science. It is Bonaparte's campaign and these two works which mark the serious beginning of the Egyptian Revival by producing a powerful and popular wave of interest in the Land of the Nile, and providing archeological sources of unsurpassed exactitude. Denon and the *Description* were the Leroy, and Stuart and Revett of the Egyptian Revival.

By the early nineteenth century there were three attitudes towards the Egyptian style which were to find architectural expression. The first was the rococo, which in architecture was to provide a picturesque effect, and thus may be designated as the Rococo Picturesque phase. The second was the Romantic Classical attitude. And the third was the archeological phase.

The Egyptian Revival in its Rococo Picturesque aspect was employed to provide novelty, variety, and exotic "bizzarria" for the decorative forms of the *style Louis Seize*. It was thus the expression of picturesque qualities in a rococo manner. As architectural counterparts to the minor arts previously discussed, there is a series of garden pavilions and other accoutrements of the landscape "picture." The most extensive program of this kind of Egyptiana was designed at Etupes (Alsace) [Doubs] for the Prince de Montbélliard in 1787 by J.-B. Kléber (1753–1800).[20] In the nobleman's vast gardens was a veritable "Egyptian Isle" reached by a bridge and containing a swing, bench, and bath house (plates 3, 5) all in the Egyptian style. While the bridge, swing, and bench are charming fantasies with motifs probably taken from Montfaucon or Caylus, the bath house, with its bagnio and billiard room, is remarkably archeological in its exterior presentation. Except for the disposition of the stairs it could have been copied from any of several small Egyptian shrines, e.g., the so-called temples of the North and South at Elephantina, or Hatshepsut's original temple at Medynet Abou. None of them had been adequately published in 1787. The precise source must remain somewhat of a mystery, unless it can be proposed that Kléber fortuitously achieved this result upon reworking the somewhat unreliable plates from Norden and Pococke.[21] It is ironic that this talented young architect was to be better remembered as the Napoleonic general who, a decade later as Viceroy in Egypt, was the victim of an assassin. In any case, his work at Etupes was admired in its own day for being "in the true Egyptian style," and for exhibiting a "richness and harmony of decoration."[22] This is significant as it illustrates the rococo taste for the exotic and the decorative.

In very much the same tradition, P.-F.-L. Dubois' (fl. 1800) two ice houses and sphinx bridge for M. Davelouis' park at Soisy-sous-Etiole [Etiolles, Essonne] of about 1800 may be cited (plate 4).[23] The *gla-cières* are built into the side of a romantically wooded hill, one containing a ballroom above, but appearing to be "Egyptian" only through the motifs of the wall decorations and the label on the plate of Krafft's publication of it. The other is more obviously in the style, not only through the profusion of decorative hieroglyphics upon the temple front, but also because of the flanking obelisks. Although these buildings do not seem particularly archeological, they, like Kléber's, were praised as being made up of truly Egyptian motifs. At the same time, they were admired for exhibiting "novel and picturesque forms."[24]

A third architect working in this phase of the mode was J.-A. Renard (1744–1807) whose separately housed assembly room for the Prince de Bénévant (i.e. Talleyrand) at Valancé [Valençay, Indre] in 1805 (plate 6) was a small Egyptian temple lavishly decorated, but not based on any of Denon's plates. In spite of this, it, too, was praised for the "truth and purity" of its style, as well as for the "harmonious and tasteful" decorations.[25]

Thus, in the Rococo Picturesque manifestation of the style in France, the primary quality was that of providing the ornamental function of the architecture with a varied and correctly exotic framework. Questions of symbolic iconography and expressive form were not considered.

The Revolutionary architects, at approximately the same time, did concern themselves with such concepts as expressive form, as has been pointed out by E. Kaufmann,[26] H. Rosenau, and J.-M. Pérouse de Montclos.[27] Pevsner and Lang discuss this aspect, citing works by J.-L. Desprez (1743–1804), Mauro Tesi (1730–1766), as well as Boullée and Ledoux.[28] Although Desprez was later to use Egyptian motifs at Haga Castle in Sweden, and Ledoux employed pyramids at each of the four corners of his canon foundry project,[29] the usual handling of the style was funerary.[30] The point is that, not only was there an iconographical allusion involved, but there was also a distinct feeling for the expressive qualities of the formal aesthetic attributes of ancient Egyptian architecture. These had been initially noted by the Comte de Caylus, and, more grudgingly, by Quatremère de Quincy in his essay on Egyptian architecture. The style was thus not looked upon as clumsy, barbaric, and untrained. It had standards in its own right. Quatremère de Quincy, the Hellenophile, was ever ready to show how Greek art was superior to all others, and especially to the Egyptian. But even he was forced to admit that there were positive characteristics inherent in the latter, such as uniformity, simplicity, heavy and massive solidity, and indestructibility. These are ideas that he expressed as early as 1785. As an old man in his eighties he maintained the same principles, writing of Egyptian architecture in terms of "extraordinary simplicity," "grandeur and solidity," "[massiveness] and uniformity."[31] Thus, over the span of half a century, neo-classical ideas could be embodied in the Egyptian taste. The properties of solidity, bareness, simplicity, massiveness, and grandeur were bound to appeal to the Romantic Classicists.

The final form the style took was the archeological one ushered in by the Napoleonic publications mentioned above. Curiously enough, these were to have a considerably greater influence on architecture abroad than in France. Whereas they served as a treasure house of motifs for the decorative arts of the *Premier Empire*,[32] few nineteenth-century French architectural examples were dependent upon them. The rue de Sèvres fountain (1808) by the young J.-M.-N. Bralle (1785–1863) (already discussed in preceding chapter) might be cited as one (plate 49).[33] A second is Bataille's peristyle addition to the Hôtel de Beauharnais in Paris (1806) (plate 51).[34] Built on the orders of Napoleon as part of the remodelling program for Prince Eugène's newly acquired *hôtel*, its style reflects the current vogue for Egypt. The specific form of palm columns *distyle in antis* cannot be traced to any Denon plates; the *Description* had yet to appear. The possible inspiration may have been from Denon's view of the temple at Esne with six columns *in antis* (plate 69).[35] The architect could have applied this model to the more familiar Greek scheme of two columns *in antis* producing the Parisian result. Denon's illustration gives it a somewhat lofty elegance like that of the peristyle with its steeply battered walls and high columns. The latter serves as a stairhouse linking the *piano nobile* of the earlier building with the ground level of the court-yard. Although the cornice itself is imposing, the whole effect plays down Egyptian massiveness by the width of the front opening, the large side windows, and the elaborate relief decoration on the wall surface. But the simple form, cavetto cornice, torus molding, winged orb, and order of the columns are unmistakable hallmarks of the style, and could only have been designed after a publication like Denon's.

For France, therefore, there are three aspects to the Egyptian style. The first is the Piranesi "bizzarria" tradition combined with the cur-rent *style Louis Seize*. The result is the Rococo Picturesque phase in which a partially Egyptian vocabulary is used in a non-Egyptian manner. The second phase, stemming from the Comte de Caylus and Quatremère de Quincy, is the Romantic Classical in which Egyptian aesthetics are exploited. The third is the archeological in which a specifically Egyptian vocabulary is combined with identifiable Egyp-tian forms. It is ironical that even before the publication of the more scholarly of the works, the *Description*, the enthusiasm for the Egyp-tian style had all but died in France. Never a strongly entrenched movement there, the Gallic Egyptian Revival was principally literary and philosophical.

Before discussing the more material results of the interest in Egypt engendered by the Napoleonic publications in England, another Con-tinental locus of activity in the new fashion should be noted. In the Germanic states, especially Prussia and Bavaria, the pattern is simi-lar to that in France.[36] The Rococo Picturesque aspect produced such items as the Hercules Bridge at Monbijou (Prussia) of 1787–1791 by C. G. Langhans (1733–1808) and J. G. Schadow (1764–1850). The use of paired sphinxes here is repeated at the entrance to the nearby Steinhöfel Park by the latter architect.[37] The work of the second gen-eration of this phase is most notably represented by the splendid Egyptian Room of the Residenz-palais at Kassel of about 1830.[38] The somewhat retardataire Empire style has been enriched with Egyp-tian motifs consisting of sphinxes, atlantes and canopic figures.[39]

A more archeological, if eclectic use of Nilotic forms may be re-

marked in the work of Friedrich Weinbrenner (1766–1826) at Karlsruhe where he designed a pylon gate with Gothic openings for a
synagogue (1798),[40] and where he used a small memorial pyramid
as his focal point for the neo-classical Marktplatz (1823).[41] In that
same year, and not far away, G. H. Bandhauer (1790–1837) erected
a brick cemetery gate at Rosslau which consisted of two brick pylons
with an entrance between.[42] Among its features are battered walls
and doors, cavetto cornices and abstract torus moldings.

The pyramid as a vehicle for Romantic Classical principles has been
discussed. Weinbrenner's appears to be only one of several that were
projected. Usually memorials, they were popular in plans for monuments to military heroes. Examples include P. J. Krahe's (1758–1840)
design for the General Marceau Memorial at Coblenz (1799), and
Georg Opiz's projected tomb for Prince von Schwartzenberg at Leipzig
(1815).[43]

For Egyptian Revival architecture, however, the French influence
in Germany was strongly marked upon Friedrich Gilly (1771–1800),
and Carl Haller von Hallerstein (1774–1817). The former, the arche-
type of the romantic artist-hero, died before a significant body of his
work could be realized. He did, nevertheless, leave sketch books with
grandly conceived projects, several of them memorials. His most
noted is that for Frederick the Great (1797) which consists of a Parthe-
nonic Greek temple set above an enclosure that includes a Roman
triumphal arch, and several pairs of Egyptian obelisks (plate 28).[44]
He also designed pyramid monuments, and at least one pyramid with
Doric porticoes.[45]

Haller von Hallerstein was a student of both the Gillys, Friedrich
as well as his father David (1748–1808). He was Bavarian court architect, and is the most Egyptian-oriented of the German Romantic Classicists. His designs for Walhalla (1814–1815), and the Munich Glyptothek (1814) illustrate the point.[46] For the former he suggested a
group of entrance buildings at the foot of the great hill that was to be
crowned by a Greek temple.[47] It is this propylaea which is Egyptian.
Three pylon gates of which the center one is higher than the other two
provide a tripartite entrance not unlike Thomas U. Walter's Egyptian

project for the Laurel Hill Cemetery at Philadelphia twenty years later (plate 64). Behind, and at right angles were to be a pair of flanking mastabas to serve as porters' lodges, a motif Jacob Bigelow was to use at Mount Auburn Cemetery in Cambridge, Massachusetts, in 1831 (plates 57, 58). Luigi Canina also employed the motif in his gate to the Borghese Gardens in 1828, as has been described in the first chapter (plates 47, 48).

On an even more monumental scale, however, are the designs Haller proposed for the Glyptothek (plate 24). One of the specifications in the competition rules was that the peripheral walls were to be as blind as possible with most of the light coming from above and from windows in the courtyard walls. The Egyptian style is particularly logical for an unfenestrated building. Haller's project is interestingly eclectic with its principal facade in the Greek manner, while the wings and courtyard front are Egyptian. More than that, they are carefully archeological in both detail and form. The architect's model must have been the temple at Denderah, as has been suggested by H. Vogel, but it seems more likely that Haller used the Denon publication rather than the more expensive and yet uncompleted *Description*.[48]

Thus Germany also produced an Egyptian Revival with Rococo, Romantic Classical and archeological phases. And the same may be said of England.

Although Vanbrugh exploited the obelisk and pyramid, their specific association with Egypt was not emphasized.[49] As may be expected, the initial vehicle for Egyptian motifs was the decorative arts. The first Wedgwood catalogue (1773) listed such items as: sphinxes, lotus plants, hieroglyphics, Egyptian deities, canopic figures, and various Ptolemies including Cleopatra.[50] These continued, reaching a height of popularity as ornamental motifs in the decade from 1805 to 1815. Brian Reade has pointed out the profusion of Egyptian motifs in late eighteenth- and early nineteenth-century English furniture.[51] This was particularly true of the Sheraton style (Thomas Sheraton, 1751–1806).[52]

In 1807 this Egyptian-Rococo fashion was joined by a more archeological one of pieces based on Thomas Hope's *Household Furniture* (plate 12).[53] Hope states that his sources were Egyptian objects in his own collection, as well as those of the Vatican, the Capitoline Museum, and the Egyptian Institute of Bologna. He also credits Denon. There must have been an influence from Percier and Fontaine whom Hope admired and befriended, although Percier's designs were published after Hope's. The latter's Egyptian pieces included a clock (as did Percier's), a table, a complete ensemble for a sitting room, and two fireplace designs, simplified from Piranesi. The contacts which this Englishman maintained with the major cultural centers of the Continent provide an explanation of the migration of ideas and aesthetics in the early nineteenth century.[54]

A simplification and popularization of Hopian principles in Egyptian style furniture was produced through the published designs of a minor cabinetmaker, George Smith.[55] It is noteworthy that a third of the Egyptian items in the work are for library furnishings, thus calling attention to the association of the style with the great Library at Alexandria, and, in general, with Egypt as the Ancient Land of Learning and Wisdom.[56]

Also at this time, Thomas Chippendale the Younger (1749–1822) executed a set of eight chairs, table, and desk in the Egyptian manner for Sir Richard Hoare at Stourhead. These were based on motifs from Denon.[57]

Except for Hope's attempts at producing an architectonic use of the Egyptian style in his furniture designs, interior decoration in the fashion remained solidly within the realm of providing variety in ornamental motifs, and as such was a part of the rococo phase of the movement.[58] George Dance the Younger (1741–1825) used Egyptian elements in this way at Shelbourne House (1779), and, later, at Stratton Park (1803–1804).[59] His brother, Nathaniel, designed Egyptian caryatids for, significantly, the library of Landsdowne House (ca. 1794). Indeed, the popularity which Piranesi, the originator of the phase, enjoyed in Britain at this time[60] is reflected in the number of Egyptian fireplaces that were executed. Somewhat more restrained than the Italian prototypes, they include examples at Shelbourne House (see above); Crawley House, Bedfordshire, with matching wallpaper (1806); Bayfordbury, Hertshire (1812) in the Great Library, and repeated in the house of the romantic painter Thomas Barker of Bath (ca. 1812).[61]

Piranesi Egyptianisms seem to have appeared in John Soane's (1753–1837) decoration for the Rotunda of the Bank of England (1796), although the younger Dance may have had a hand in these. The most complete Piranesi scheme, however, was executed by James Playfair (d. 1794) for the Billiard Room at Cairness House, Aberdeenshire, in 1793.[62] While not a direct copy of any plate from the *Cammini,* the hieroglyphs, sphinxes, and chimney arrangement all form a clear Piranesi-esque statement.

In architecture, the Romantic Classical concept seems to have appeared earliest with John Carter's (1748–1817) dairy in the form of a pyramid (1777),[63] followed the next year by Soane's design for a garden pyramid which he called an "Egyptian Temple" (plate 9).[64] Some twenty-five years later Joseph Gandy was publishing Egyptian-style gate lodges, one set as a pair of inhabitable pyramids and another as a pair of equally habitable pylon towers (in miniature) flanked by obelisks. Both sets are remarkable for their planar simplicity.[65] Although lacking the primordial boldness of a Ledoux Maupertuis pyramid, or the sublime monumentality of a Boullée cenotaph, these examples are, at any rate, noteworthy as indications of the sensitivity of English architects to the trenchancy of such geometric forms.

A more Rococo Picturesque treatment is to be found in Robert Lugar's (ca. 1773–1853) pavilion "in the Egyptian or Turkish style" (plate 84). In point of fact there are few Egyptian features, and the building gives a more "Hindoo" effect than anything else. This is certainly due to confusion in the architect's mind as to what is Egyptian. For, although he combines minarets, bulbous domes, and a crescent motif with cavetto cornices, batter elements, and the winged orb, he writes, "mixing one style with the other, as is frequently seen, makes us think but little of the mind that thus invades every idea of common sense. . . ." His attitude towards the design is that it provides a "bold style" which is "picturesque [and] romantic."[66]

The following year, 1806, James Randall (fl. 1810) published a spectacular example of a country mansion in the Egyptian manner (plate 10). Apparently using motifs from Denon, he organizes the plan in a typical Regency arrangement and applies Egyptian decoration lavishly to the exterior. The use of hieroglyphic reliefs, Hathor columns, and batters at the corner towers emphasizes the exotic novelty of the building which Randall states is a "most desirable" quality.[67]

The major work in the Egyptian Revival in Britain was the famed Egyptian Hall in Piccadilly. Also known as the London Museum, it was built by P. F. Robinson (1776–1858) for William Bullock in 1812 (plate 11). In architecture this was the earliest consciously archeological attempt in England to revive the Egyptian style, for it was specifically modelled on Denon plates. A contemporary description by the master of John Haviland, the greatest of the American Egyptian Revival architects, states, "[it] was originally designed in 1812 by P. F. Robinson, Esq. for W. Bullock, Esq. of Liverpool as a receptacle for a Museum that went by his name. . . . The elevation is completely Egyptian, that is supposing the ancient Egyptians built their houses in storeys. The details are *correctly taken* from Denon's celebrated work, principally from the great temple at Tentyra [Denderah]. The two *colossal* figures that support the entablature of the centre window are *novel* in idea and application; *picturesque* in effect; and add *variety* to the composition; while the *robust* columns beneath them seem built exactly for pedestals to the sturdy Ethiopians above. . . . The large projection of the superior cornice rising from the *colossal* sculptured torus that bounds the entire design, is *grand* and *imposing*." (The author's italics.)[68]

Although descriptive adjectives, typical for Egyptian architecture, as colossal, robust, grand, and imposing are employed, the significant qualities seem to be those of novelty, picturesqueness, and variety. Even if it would be tempting to attribute to the builders a consciousness of the association of the Egyptian style with the Land of Wisdom, Mystery, and Ancient Learning, thus explaining its use for this class of edifice, it is probably more correct to consider that the building was erected in that style as an eye-catching advertisement to the public. The novelty and curiousness of the exterior symbolized the quality of the exhibits inside.[69] This concept of the Commercial Picturesque is one which remains, in various examples, throughout the movement.

Although the Egyptian Hall was demolished in 1905, an idea of what it must have looked like can be given by the "Egyptian House" (ca. 1830) in Penzance at No. 6 Chapel Street (plate 16). Not an exact copy, it is, however, closely related to the London Museum. The same features and forms may be noted: cavetto cornices, torus moldings, winged disc, and corbel-arched windows. Apparently having always served as a shop, it is a clear example of the continuation of the Commercial Picturesque tradition, as is the Heavitree Brewery at Exeter, Devon, of about 1833 by R. Ford.[70] This must also be the explanation for the use of the style at John Marshall's Flax Spinning Mill (1838–1841) (plates 17, 19) in Holbeck, Leeds, by Ignatius Bonomi.[71] It is a two-building complex, an office and a mill. Bonomi's brother, Joseph, had done archeological drawings in Egypt for Lord Hay, as had David Roberts who seems to have had a hand in the Leeds design. The ultimate source must have been the Typhonium at Denderah (*Description . . .*, A. Vol. IV, pl. xxxII) (plates 18, 20). The mill which in its day was a masterpiece of functional design—the roof was a field upon which cattle grazed; interior columns were hollow for drainage— also housed the most modern flax-spinning machines. (The connections between modern engineering and the ancient Egyptian style are discussed in chapter six.) The association of flax and linen with Egypt, which has been suggested as an explanation for the use of the style, would seem tenuous.[72] Basically the structures must have been meant to attract attention, to advertise.

A different concept of the picturesque underlies the Egyptian building at Devonport, Plymouth (plates 13–15). Built in 1823 by John Foulston (1772–1842) as part of a group of buildings on Ker Street, the entire project was published by the architect in 1838.[73] In his explanation, Foulston writes, after defending the use of Grecian, Egyptian and Oriental architecture in modern structures, "Notwithstanding the grandeur and exquisite proportions of the Grecian orders, the author has never been insensible to the distinguishing beauties of the other original styles; and it occurred to him that if a series of edifices, exhibiting the *various features of the architectural world* were erected in conjunction, and *skilfully grouped,* a happy result might be obtained. Under this impression, he was induced to try an *experiment* (never before attempted) for producing a *picturesque effect,* by combining, in one view, the Grecian, Egyptian, and a variety of the Oriental. . . ." (The author's italics.) He concludes by pointing out that a combination of styles in one building would be, of course, "an abomination." Thus, whereas in Romantic garden parks a variety of styles could be seen, they were seldom to be seen together, although often one was to be viewed from another. Here, on the other hand, was a concept of a variety of styles unified through similarity of scale and material.

Although the Egyptian structure was to house a library,[74] reason enough for the style in America,[75] and although Foulston's statement contains an intimation of the Hadrianic idea of an architectural museum ("exhibiting the various features of the architectural world"); the main purpose was to contribute towards a picturesque effect. With the Greek town hall, Roman memorial column, and non-Conformist "Oriental" chapel, the Egyptian library helped to provide diversity for the architectural ensemble. This formal, rather than symbolic, value is what the architect thought most important to explain. In any case, what should be remembered from Foulston is his concept of the Picturesque *coup d'oeil.*[76]

For England, then, the Egyptian style served the same purposes as it had on the Continent. First, it provided novel and exotic motifs for the decorative arts, as well as architecture, in a Piranesi-inspired Rococo Picturesque phase. With the publication of the Napoleonic works on Egypt, particularly Denon, a stricter adherence to archeological verisimilitude was practiced. This was applied, in the minor arts, to the continuing eighteenth-century rococo principle. In architecture the sense of archeology contributed to the cult of the picturesque, bereft of its more frivolous rococo aspects. Instead of garden pavilions, Egyptian Revival buildings now served public needs. Although a third phase, that of the severer mood of geometric Romantic Classicism, was not ignored, the basic contribution of the English Egyptian Revival was toward picturesqueness, either as a commercial showpiece or in an aesthetic *coup d'oeil*.

Notes:

1. N. Pevsner and S. Lang, "The Egyptian Revival," *Architectural Review,* CXIX (1956), pp. 242–254, now published as chapter thirteen in Nikolaus Pevsner, *Studies in Art, Architecture and Design,* I (New York, 1968); see also Erik Iversen, "Hieroglyphic Studies of the Renaissance," *Burlington Magazine,* C, 658 (1958), pp. 15–21; Karl H. Dannenfeldt, "Egyptian Antiquities in the Renaissance," *Studies in the Renaissance,* VI (1959), pp. 7–27; Erik Iversen, *The Myth of Egypt and its Hieroglyphs* (Copenhagen, 1961); J. Baltrusaitis, *La quête d'Isis* (Paris, 1967).

2. See also, William S. Heckscher, "Bernini's Elephant and Obelisk," *Art Bulletin,* XXIV, 3 (1947), pp. 154–182.

3. G. B. Piranesi, *Diverse maniere d'adornare i cammini* (Rome, 1769), plates V, X, XIV, XVIII, XXI, XXIV, XXVI, XXVIII, XXXII, XXXVI, L. Plates XLV and XLVI are designs for the interior walls of the Caffè Inglese (plate 2).

4. H. Focillon, *Giovanni-Battista Piranesi* (Paris, 1928); Emil Bourgeois, *Le style Empire* (Paris, 1930), pp. 32–58; A. Hyatt Mayor, *Giovanni Battista Piranesi* (New York, 1952).

5. For further information on the architectural ideas of Piranesi see R. Wittkower, "Piranesi's 'Parere su l' architettura'," *Journal of the Warburg and Courtauld Institutes,* II (1938–1939), pp. 147–158. For Piranesi's only complete architectural monument, Sta. Maria del Priorato, with its profusion of obelisks, see W. Körte, "Giovanni Battista Piranesi als praktischer Architekt," *Zeitschrift für Kunstgeschichte,* II (1932), pp. 16–33.

6. This tablet is mentioned by Pevsner and Lang, "The Egyptian Revival," pp. 243, 249, but its relationship to the Piranesi designs is not. For a complete contemporary (1767) treatment of this, see Comte de Caylus, *Recueil . . .* (note 10 below), VII, pp. 34–119, pl. XII.

7. The tradition continued in Italy in the early nineteenth century in furniture (plate 22), and interiors, e.g., at Padua the Egyptian Room at the Pedrocchino of the Caffè Pedrocchi (1836–1837) by Giuseppe Jappelli (1783–1852). N. Pevsner, "Pedrocchino and Some Allied Problems," *Architectural Review,* CXXII (1957), pp. 112–115. Somewhat more archeological is Jappelli's Egyptian gate of about 1830 at the Villa Gera, Conegliano. R. C. Matiglia, "Giuseppe Jappelli, Architetto," *L'architettura,* I (1955–1956), pp. 538–551, p. 542, fig. 20. This architect's taste for Egyptianism may have been engendered through his teacher Gianantonio Selva (see note 45 below) as well as his involvement in the de-

sign of the medal struck in honor of his fellow Paduan, the Egyptol-
ogist Giovanni Belzoni, in 1820. Stanley Mayes, *The Great Belzoni* (New
York, 1961), p. 254. (See note 69 below).

8. Charles G. Dempsey, "Representations of Egypt in the Paintings of
   Nicholas Poussin," *Art Bulletin,* XLV, 2 (1963), pp. 109–119, originally
   a paper read at the Frick-Institute of Fine Arts Symposium, April 8,
   1961.

    Although no allusion to Egypt is implied, one might note the Egyptian-
   type building at the right in Poussin's *Ordination* (Bridgewater House,
   1647). It is behind the curiously Ledoux-like structure with the pyramid
   roof.

9. Bernard de Montfaucon, *L'antiquité expliquée et representée en figures,*
   10 vols. (Paris, 1719–1724).

10. Anne-Claude-Philippe de Tubières, Comte de Caylus, *Recueil d'antiquités*
    égyptiennes, étrusques, grèques, et romaines, 7 vols. (Paris, 1752–1767).
    Also of interest, *Correspondance inédit du Comte de Caylus avec le P.*
    Paciaudi, Théatin (1757–1765), suivi de celles de l'Abbé Barthelemy et
    du P. Mariette avec le Même, 2 vols. (Paris, 1877).

11. "Le retour d'Egypte," *Connaissance des Arts,* no. 33 (1954), pp. 62–67.
    Or one might even note the quasi-Egyptian decorative elements added
    to the Sainte Chapelle in Paris after 1793. François Geblin, *La Sainte*
    Chapelle et la Concièrgerie (Paris, 1931), p. 15. These were of course
    expunged by Viollet-le-Duc in his restoration.

12. Charles Percier and P.-F. Fontaine, *Recueil de décorations interieurs*
    (Paris, 1801), pp. 11, 22–23, 29, pl. VIII, XXVIII.

13. J. C. Krafft and N. Ransonette, *Plans, coupes, élévations des plus belles*
    maisons et des hôtels construit à Paris et dans les environs (Paris, n.d.
    [ca. 1802]), pl. LXXXIII, no. 4, CII.

14. P.-N. Beauvallet, *Fragmens d'architecture, sculpture, et peinture dans le*
    style antique (Paris, L'an XII [1804]), p. 7, pl. XII, XV, XVIII, XIX, XXVIII, XXX,
    XXXVII, XLI, XLIX, L, LII, LVIII, LXXI.

15. André Ferrier, "Le médaillier, object de curiosité," *Connaissance des*
    Arts, no. 86 (1959), pp. 60–65.

16. G. Mourey, "L'art decoratif," *Histoire générale de l'art français de la*
    Revolution à nos jours, III (1922), pp. 81–82; G. Lechevallier-Chevignard
    and M. Savreux, *Le biscuit de Sèvres* (Paris, 1923), p. 15, pl. XXII–XXVI;
    [Musée National de Céramique Sèvres] *Les grands services de Sèvres*
    (Paris, 1951), pp. 46–48; P. Verlet, S. Grandjean, and M. Brunet, *Sèvres,*
    3 vols. (Paris, 1953), vol. I, p. 226, pl. CVIII, CX, CXI.

    Napoleon ordered a duplicate set as a "consolation gift" to Josephine
    after their divorce in 1812. It was, understandably, refused by her. Even-
    tually it was presented to the Duke of Wellington by Louis XVIII in 1818.
    S. Grandjean, "The Wellington Napoleonic Relics," *Connoisseur,*

CXLIII, 578, pp. 228–230; Arts Council of Great Britain, *The Age of Neo-Classicism,* Exhibition Catalogue (London, 1972), item 1420, pp. 671–672.

These sources came basically from Denon although some motifs may be traced to Norden.

17. Besides the bibliographical items mentioned thus far, further literature on this may be found in J. Vacquier and P. Marmottan, *Le style Empire,* 5 vols. (Paris, 1920–1930), I, pl. XXXVII; III, pl. VI; V, pl. XX, XXXVII; N. McClellan, *Historic Wallpapers* (Philadelphia and London, 1924), pp. 306–307; J. Robinquet, *L'art et le gout sous la Restauration* (Paris, 1928), especially pp. 12–13; Joseph Billiet, *Malmaison* (Paris, 1953), p. 16; [Connaissance des Arts] *Le XIXe siècle français* (Paris, 1957), pp. 40, 43, 53, 76, 128, 132, 182, 206, 220; Robert C. Smith, "The Classical Style in France and England, 1800–1840," *Antiques,* LXXIV, 5 (1958), pp. 429–433; P. Tardy, *Le pendule français* (Paris, n.d.), pl. XXXIX; J. Stewart Johnson, "Egyptian Revival in the Decorative Arts," *Antiques,* XC, 10 (1966), pp. 489–494; Alvar Gonzalez-Palacios, *The French Empire Style* (London, New York, Sidney, Toronto, 1970), pl. 17, 18, 22, 41, 47, 54.

18. Dominique Vivant Denon, *Voyage dans la Basse et la Haute Egypte pendant les campagnes du général Bonaparte,* 3 vols. (Paris, 1802) (hereafter, Denon, *Voyage . . .*).

A three-volume English edition appeared the next year in London, and a two-volume one, with many fewer engravings, was published in New York also in 1803. By 1807 there were at least three English editions in America. See R. Alexander, "The Public Memorial and Godefroy's Battle Monument," *JSAH,* XVII, 1 (1958), p. 24. For recent accounts of the French campaign see J. Christopher Herald, *Bonaparte in Egypt* (New York, Evanston and London, 1962).

A condensed account and one vastly more objective may be found in Alan Moorehead, *The Blue Nile* (New York, 1962), pp. 55–112.

For the history of post-Napoleonic Egyptian archeology see the very readable work by Fred Gladstone Bratton, *A History of Egyptian Archaeology* (New York, 1968). There is also the anecdotal and sometimes unreliable pot-boiler by Brian M. Fagan, *The Rape of the Nile* (New York, 1975).

In the summer of 1976 there was a small but fascinating photography exhibit at the Grand Palais in Paris entitled *En Egypte au temps de Flaubert: les premiers photographes 1839–1860* (catalogue by Marie-Thérèse and André Jammes) in which were reproduced examples of the earliest photographs of Egyptian antiquities some by *amateurs,* some by professional archeologists (although certainly in that period the line between the two was a thin one to say the least).

19. [Commission des monuments d'Egypte] *Description de l'Egypte, ou, Recueil des observations et des recherches qui ont été faites en Egypte pendant l'expédition de l'armée française, publié par les ordres de Sa Majesté l'empereur Napoleon le Grand,* 21 vols. (Paris, 1809–1828). (hereafter, *Description . . .*).

It should be noted that bibliographers have been unable to agree on the total number of volumes, sometimes recording as many as twenty-five. The particular set used by the author was bound into twenty-one volumes. The material is the same, of course, the problem involves the number of bound groups. The volumes are not numbered one to twenty-one consecutively. Each section is separately counted. Thus the volumes on the antiquities are prefixed with "A.", e.g., "A. Vol. III."

20. J. C. Krafft, and P.-F.-L. Dubois, *Production de plusieurs architects français et étrangers* (Paris, 1809), pp. 17, 31–35, pl. LXIX, LI, LIV–LVI.

21. F. L. Norden, *Travels in Egypt and Nubia* (London, 1757) (a French edition appeared two years earlier); Richard Pococke, *Observations on Egypt* (London, 1743).

The more lavish illustrations are in Norden, but both these works were the standard Egyptological sources until the Napoleonic publications. Quatremère de Quincy in his essay on Egyptian architecture, written in 1785 but not published until 1803, used plates from both as his only illustrations. A.-C. Quatremère de Quincy, *De l'architecture égyptienne* (Paris, 1803).

22. Krafft and Dubois, *Production . . . ,* p. 33.

23. J. C. Krafft, *Recueil d'architecture civile* (Paris, 1812), pp. 1, 17, pl. LXXIII–LXXVII, CVII; E. Kaufmann, *Architecture in the Age of Reason* (Cambridge, 1955), p. 196. The Egyptian ice house in A. de Leborde, *Description des nouveaux jardins de la France* (Paris, 1808), p. 179, pl. 108, at Prulay, has very little Egyptian about it.

24. Krafft, *Recueil . . . ,* p. 1. "formes nouvelles, et pittoresques."

25. Krafft and Dubois, *Production . . . ,* p. 9, pl. IX–X. Also in this Rococo-exotic phase one might note J. B. Lepère's engraving of an Egyptian Temple and the pyramid at St. James, Neuilly. And there is that curiously prophetic example of the American predisposal to Egyptian forms in Hubert Robert's pyramid to the independence of the United States at Méréville for J.-J. de Laborde (1784). P. de Nolhac, *Hubert Robert* (Paris, 1910), pp. 58–59.

26. Emil Kaufmann: "Claude-Nicholas Ledoux, Inaugurator of a New Architectural System," *JSAH,* III, 3 (1943), pp. 12–20; "At an XVIII Century Crossroads: Algerotti vs. Lodoli," *Transactions of the American Philosophical Society,* new series, XLIII, pt. 3 (1952); *Architecture in the Age of Reason* (Cambridge, 1955).

27. H. Rosenau, *Boullée's Treatise on Architecture* (London, 1953); Jean-

Marie Pérouse de Montclos, *Etienne-Louis Boullée (1728–1799)* (Paris, 1968). Abridged English version published in New York, 1974.

28. See also M. Brion, *Romantic Art* (New York, Toronto, and London, 1960), pp. 30–35.

29. Ledoux also seems to have been the architect of the Maupertuis garden pyramid of ca. 1780.

30. For a fuller discussion of this, as well as the Egyptian funerary tradition in France prior to the late eighteenth century see chapter one.

   Another Swedish example might be cited in the 1782 design for a monument by Carl August Ehrensvärd on Gustaf Adolf Square in Stockholm. It was to be a pyramid with a Doric Temple interior. In point of fact, squat Doric buildings were called "Egyptian" in late eighteenth-century Nordic countries. Robert Rosenblum, *Transformations in Late Eighteenth-Century Art* (Princeton, 1967), p. 148, fig. 177.

31. Quatremère de Quincy, "On Order in Architecture," *Architectural Magazine,* III (1836), pp. 443–444.

32. The "Egyptian Service" (see note 16 above), for instance, was dependent almost entirely upon plates from Denon. This was true not only for the painted scenes, but for some of the shapes as well; e.g., sugar bowl in form of canopic jar, coffee cups modelled upon "vases." The originals for both are illustrated in Denon's plate CXV.

33. Of course, there is the topographical portrait of Napoleon at an Egyptian table, presumably during the Nile campaign, executed by Antoine Mouton in 1809 and now at Malmaison.

34. Bourgeois, *Le style . . . ,* p. 110; L. Hautecoeur, *L'art sous la Révolution et l'Empire en France* (Paris, 1953), p. 43; L. Hautecoeur, *Histoire de l'architecture classique en France,* 7 vols. (Paris, 1943–1957), V, pp. 286–287, fig. 178; "Le retour d'Egypte," pp. 62–67. The suggestion in this last article that the inspiration and forms are from the hypostyle hall at Karnac, is highly questionable when the heaviness as well as the specific forms of the columns of the prototype are compared with those of the nineteenth-century example. Also see Jacques Hillairet (Auguste Coussilan) *Dictionaire historique des rues de Paris,* 2 vols., 4th ed. (Paris, 1970), vol. II, p. 48. Perhaps one might consider the original plan for the "Pyramid of Austerlitz" erected by Marmont's troops in 1805 (in honor of the coronation of Napoleon), 10½ miles from Zeis and 21 miles from Utrecht, as a French Egyptian Revival monument, albeit in Holland, by what can only have been a folk artist. Actually as built, it is merely a large mound. Karl Baedeker, *Belgium and Holland* (Leipzig, 1905), p. 431. I am indebted to Dr. S. A. Callison for this reference.

   A far more elegant and sophisticated Egyptian Revival monument of Napoleonic inspiration appears not in France, but in England dedicated, significantly enough, to the Duke of Wellington. Erected in masonry near Taunton, Somersetshire, in 1817 by Thomas Lee, Jr. (completed after 1853 to a different design) it is an impressively lofty trylon (vis-à-vis obelisk) rising from a polygonal "mastaba" with such "correct" details as winged orb, cavetto cornices, torus moldings and battered walls. The author's thanks to John Zukowsky for sharing his information and photographs. Also see John Zukowsky, "Monumental American Obelisks: Centennial Vistas," *Art Bulletin,* LVIII, 4 (1976), p. 581.

35. Denon, *Voyage . . . ,* pl. LIV, fig. 3.

36. A somewhat fantastical view of Egypt had been provided in German by the generously illustrated (but short in text) *Entwürff einer historischen Architektur,* by J. B. Fischer von Erlach. It appeared in Vienna in 1721, and in Leipzig in 1725.

37. Hermann Schmitz, *Berliner Baumeister vom Ausgang des Achtzehnten Jahrhunderts* (Berlin, 1914), pp. 166, 181.

38. *Geschichte des Kunstgewerbes aller Zeiten und Völker,* 6 vols. (Berlin, 1935), VI, p. 256.

39. The fashion penetrated as far south and east as Vienna in furniture, at least; *viz.* "Empire fruitwood chair, Austrian, ca. 1815," F. L. Hinckley, *A Dictionary of Antique Furniture* (New York, 1953), p. 153. The sphinx heads under the arms are undoubtedly a reflection of Napoleonic influences following upon the marriage of Marie Louise.

    Also note the Empire piano ("Giraffenflugel") by Joseph Wachtl of Vienna (1820) at St. Annenmuseum in Lubeck with its pair of supporting atlantes.

40. R. Wischnitzer, "The Egyptian Revival in Synagogue Architecture," *Publications of the American Jewish Historical Society,* XLI, 1–4 (1951–1952), pp. 61–75; R. Wischnitzer, *Synagogue Architecture in the United States* (Philadelphia, 1955), p. 32.

41. H.-R. Hitchcock, *Architecture, XIX and XX Centuries* (Baltimore, 1958), p. 17. The use of black stone as the material is an added funereal note. The pyramid is the tomb of Prince Karl Wilhelm, the founder of Karlsruhe.

    Philip Otto Runge (1777–1810) the German Romantic painter, uses a similar pyramid as a background focal point in his *Rest on the Flight Into Egypt,* Hamburg, Kunsthalle, of 1805–1806.

42. Wilhelm van Kempen, "Die Baukunst des Klassizismus in Anhalt nach 1800," *Marburger Jahrbuch für Kunstwissenschaft,* IV (1928), pp. 1–88, especially pp. 48–49, 81–83.

43. Hans Vogel, "Aegyptisierende Baukunst des Klassizismus," *Zeitschrift für Bildende Kunst,* LXII (1928–1929), pp. 160–165.

44. Alfred Neumeyer, "Monuments to 'Genius' in German Classicism," *Journal of the Warburg and Courtauld Institutes,* II (1938, 1939), pp. 159–163; A. Rietdorf, *Gilly, Wiedergeburt der Architecktur* (Berlin, 1940), fig. 45 ff. For general background see E. Hempel, *Geschichte der Deutschen Baukunst* (Munich, 1949), especially p. 514 ff.

45. Rietdorf, *Gilly . . . ,* figs. 25, 26, 138, 139, 43, 44. This latter combination

deserves further investigation. It was employed by Ledoux and Durand (see preceding chapter), in France; Latrobe (preceding chapter, note 14) in America; Giantonio Selva (1751–1819) for his design of the Mont Cenis Monument to Napoleon of 1813 in Italy (E. Bassi, *Giantonio Selva* [Padua, 1936], p. 82, pl. XLIII); and Alferov (1780–1840) for his Kazan Monument to the Defeat of the Tartars (pl. XLIV B) in Russia in 1823–1830. (G. K. Lukomskii, *Monuments of Ancient Russian Architecture* [Petrograd, 1916], pp. 276, 278; T. T. Rice, *Russian Art* [West Drayton, 1949], p. 209).

46. Vogel, "Aegyptisierende . . ."; Hermann Beenken, *Schöpferische Bauideen der Deutschen Romantik* (Mainz, 1952), pp. 28, 62 ff.

47. This scheme, derived from F. Gilly's Frederick the Great Monument, was in part realized by Leo von Klenze (1784–1864) in 1831–1842 at Walhalla, near Ratisbonne.

   Also on the lower terrace there may be found a simplified Egyptian portal.

48. Vogel, "Aegyptisierende . . ."; Denon, *Voyage . . . ,* pl. XXXIX. Vogel's article contains an excellent description and analysis of this project.

49. H. Honour, "The Egyptian Taste," *Connoisseur,* CXXXV, 546 (1955), pp. 242–246.

50. E. Chellis, "From the Nile to the Trent," *Antiques,* LVI, 4 (1949), pp. 260–263. For the history of the Wedgwoods and their wares see E. Meteyard, *The Life of Josiah Wedgwood,* 2 vols. (London, 1866); M. H. Grant, *The Makers of Black Basalts* (Edinburgh and London, 1910); and particularly Harold Allen, "Egyptian Influences in Wedgwood Designs," *Seventh Wedgwood International Seminar* (Chicago, 1962).

51. Brian Reade, *Regency Antiques* (London, 1953), pp. 35, 52–53, 86, 88, 90–91, 94, 100, 110, 151, 162, 230, 232. See also J. Stewart Johnson, "Egyptian Revival in the Decorative Arts," *Antiques,* XC, 10 (1966) pp. 489–494.

52. Thomas Sheraton, *The Cabinet Maker's and Upholsterer's Encyclopaedia* (London, 1804–1806).

53. Thomas Hope, *Household Furniture and Interior Decoration* (London, 1807), pp. 26–27, 30, 32–33, pl. VIII, X, XIII, XLVI, XLIX.

54. For further information on Thomas Hope see M. Jourdain, *English Decoration and Furniture of the Later XVIII Century (1760–1820)* (London, 1922), p. 260 ff.; M. Jourdain, *Regency Furniture (1795–1820)* (London, 1934), pp. 11–13. (This work was enlarged and revised by Ralph Fastnedge in 1965.) Also note the excellent work by David Watkin, *Thomas Hope (1769–1831) and the Neo-Classical Idea* (London, 1968).

55. George Smith, *A Collection of Designs for Household Furniture and Interior Decoration* (London, 1808), pl. V, XLIX, LII, LIX, LXXXVIII, XCII, XCIV, XCV, CVI, CXXVIII, CXLV, CXLVII.

56. The earliest bookcase with Egyptian motifs in England seems to be one, basically Gothic in flavor, by Brockbank and Atkins, ca. 1795–1800. P. Macquoid and R. Edwards, *Dictionary of English Furniture,* 3 vols. (London, 1927), p. 125, fig. 27.

57. C. Hussey, *English Country Houses,* 3 vols. (London, 1955–1956), II, p. 238.

58. One of the latest examples is the entrance vestibule at Harewood House, Yorkshire, which had furniture as well as decoration in the Egyptian style according to a description of 1819. Hussey, *Houses,* p. 69; Jourdain, *Regency . . . ,* p. 18.

59. John Summerson, *Architecture in Britain 1530–1810* (Baltimore, 1953), pp. 277–278.

60. In this connection it might be significant to point out that the interior of the *English* Coffee House in Rome was designed by Piranesi in the Egyptian style (plate 2).

61. H. A. Tipping, *English Homes,* 9 vols. (New York, 1920–1937), VI, 1, pp. 375–392.

62. Hugh Honour, "The Egyptian Taste," *Connoisseur,* XXXV, 546 (1955), p. 243. The younger Playfair (W. H.) also included Nilotic elements in his work, e.g., the pair of sphinxes which flank the side-portal pediments in his Royal Institution (now Royal Scottish Academy) of 1823–1833 in Edinburgh. Further Edinbruggian Egyptianisms may be cited in two of Sir Francis Logatt Chantry's (1781–1841) works: the base of the statue of George IV at George and Hanover Streets of 1822 and the more archeological one in the monument to William Pitt the Younger at George and Frederick Streets of 1833.

63. *The Builder's Magazine* (London, 1774–1778), pl. CXXXVI, CXL.

64. John Soan(e), *Designs in Architecture* (London, 1778), pl. XXV. Note also an obelisk, plate VII, and a pyramid tomb, plates XXXVII–XXXVIII.

65. Joseph Gandy, *The Rural Architect* (London, 1805), plates XXXIX, XLII.

66. Robert Lugar, *Architectural Sketches for Cottages, Rural Dwellings, and Villas* (London, 1805), p. 26, pl. XXXVI.

67. James Randall, *Architectural Designs for Mansions, Villas, Lodges, and Cottages* (London, 1806), pl. XXII–XXIV.

68. James Elmes, *Metropolitan Improvements* (London, 1827), p. 157; H. Honour, "Curiosities of the Egyptian Hall," *Country Life,* CXV (1954), pp. 38–39. The "two colossal figures" were statues of Isis and Osiris by Sebastian Gahagan (fl. 1800–1835). Honour, "The Egyptian Taste," p. 245. That author rightly notes that the London Museum does *not* resemble Denderah.

69. The original interior by J. B. Papworth (1775–1847) was not Egyptian in style, but was replaced in 1821 by one that was. This was designed as a setting for Giovanni Belzoni's (1778–1823) exhibition of the sar-

cophagus of Seti I. It would seem logical that motifs from the publications of Thomas Hope or George Smith were used. See notes 53 and 55 above. (For Belzoni see M. W. Disher, *Pharaoh's Fool* [London, 1957], especially pp. 158–167; also Stanley Mayes, *Belzoni,* especially pp. 75–277.) At this time the building was owned by the painter, Robert Haydon, a cousin of John Haviland. The sarcophagus eventually ended in the collection of Sir John Soane. J. Soane, *Description of the House and Museum on the North Side of Lincoln's Inn-Fields,* 2nd ed. (London, 1835), p. 34. Haydon's Egyptian-style studio found an echo in the painter Edward Calvert's Egyptian Pavilion-cum-atelier of 1832. Raymond Lister, *Edward Calvert* (London, 1962), p. 40.

70. N. Pevsner, *South Devon* (Harmondsworth, 1952), p. 163. The similarity of the decorative details of all three of these buildings is noteworthy. Also the motif of the sun disc with drooping wings, a later Ptolemaic element found at Edfou, among others, is handled in an analogous manner in the Devonport Library and the Penzance Egyptian House.

71. K. J. Bonser, "Marshall's Mill, Holbeck, Leeds," *Architectural Review,* CXXVII, 758 (1960), pp. 280–282; G. B. Wood, "Egyptian Temple Architecture in Leeds," *Country Life,* CXXVIII, 3326 (1960), pp. 1363–1365.

72. Wood, "Egyptian Temple . . ."

73. John Foulston, *The Public Buildings Erected in the West of England* (London, 1838), pp. 1, 3, pl. LXXXVII–XCIII.

74. Today the building serves, in a happy irony, as an Odd Fellows Hall. (See chapter six.) A later example of a fraternal lodge, strikingly archeological in its details, may be noted at Boston, Lincolnshire, 1860–1863.

75. See chapter six.

76. For a somewhat different approach to the same complex, see C. L. V. Meeks, *The Railroad Station* (New Haven, 1956), p. 12. The Mount Zion Chapel was not, however, a synagogue.

Incidentally, there is an interesting Continental "Architectural Museum" at, of all places, the Antwerp Zoo, where in addition to a Moorish pavilion, a cottage ornée, and a Doric Reptile Hall, there is an Egyptian building modelled after the Temple at Philae by Charles Servais with wall paintings by M. Stalins and his son (1855–1856). The author is indebted to Robert H. Rosenblum for this item.

CHAPTER
3

Attitudes in America

The purpose of this chapter is to discuss Egyptian architecture as it was understood in the United States at the time of its Revival. The distant ancestry of this eclectic movement, as well as its immediate European sources, having been noted, the American climate of opinion must be investigated at this point. Later chapters are devoted to the specific meanings the use of the style evoked, and the formal patterns to which it was adapted.

For an American in the early nineteenth century, Egypt was not some vague land lost in the mists of time and geography. The fact that the culture and history of republican Greece and Rome were revered in the United States implied an awareness of that older civilization which the ancients themselves thought of as ancient. Although a citizen of the Federal period might feel more empathy with the Classical past, he nevertheless found in Egypt a part of the tradition he inherited from England and France (see preceding chapter). References to Egypt were common, and even prior to the high point during the 1830s and 1840s of Egyptian Revival architecture, numerous travel books about Egypt had been published or were available in the United States. In the years 1800–1810 at least four such books appeared; the next decade produced twelve; and during the 1820s there were seventeen.[1] Also works of Egyptian archeology were manifest, and frequently discussed in such publications as the *North American Review* where the scholarly writings of British and French authors such as Pritchard and Champollion were summarized and evaluated.[2]

But not only could Egypt be read about, it could be seen in the nascent museums of the country. Even if the earliest collections were oriented towards Greece and Rome, museums did include some representation from the Land of the Nile.[3] In the eighteenth century there was a mummy at the first-known American museum, that at Charleston, South Carolina. In 1823 the Massachusetts General Hospital owned and exhibited a Theban mummy with its coffin.[4] Three years later Charles Willson Peale exhibited two mummies at his museum. These latter were purchased by P. T. Barnum in 1842. But the first Egyptian collection of any size seems to have been that of Lieutenant T. Tanner which he bought from Giovanni Battista Belzoni (1775–1823), and presented to the Peabody Museum at Salem, Massachusetts in 1823.[5] The most extensive one was Col. Mendes Cohen's (d. 1847) of 680 items gathered in Egypt, and brought to this country in 1835.[6] Of equal importance was the collection formed by Dr. Henry Abbott (1812–1859) also in Egypt. After being catalogued in 1846, it was exhibited in America 1853–1854.[7]

In 1835 when the Egyptian Revival was already at flood tide, Joseph Smith, the Mormon prophet, purchased two mummies recently arrived in New York from Paris. In the chest of one was a papyrus which Smith claimed as a part of the *Book of the Dead*. One copy was printed in 1842, another with comments in 1844. It will be remembered that the Prophet had already translated the *Book of Mormon,* through the miraculous Spectacles, which had been written in "hieroglyphics" (1830).

Mormonism had two Egyptian Revival connections. The first was the hieroglyphic writings. It was claimed that the *Book of Mormon* had been written and buried by the Lost Tribes of Israel who had eventually wandered to America. Smith assumed their manner of writing to be that of the Egyptians, learned during the Bondage just as they had learned the art of architecture, a common nineteenth-century concept.[8]

The second point is the theory that ancient people had migrated to North America from Asia centuries before Columbus. This was a not unusual hypothesis in the early years of the Republic. With a newly won national identity, Americans sought to achieve an ancient past for their land. If vast territories to the West were to be explored and recorded in order to serve a Manifest Destiny, they were also to be investigated with an archeological eye for a past heritage. The following quotation is from a newspaper report in 1819 on the Stephen H. Long Expedition to explore the country between the Mississippi River and the Rocky Mountains:

> We anticipate much useful information from the result of this voyage; it appears to have been arranged by the government with a great conviction of its importance, and the design bears a strong resemblance to the French expedition into Egypt, in which the cause of science was not lost sight during their military operations. Although the Missouri is not embellished by such stupendous monuments of art as is the Nile, her Indian mounds afford matter for much interesting disquisition; and although no Thebes, nor mutilated statues of Memnon may be found, yet, some clue may yet be discovered to assist our historical researches into the ancient manners of the Aborigines. At all events, the field of science may be much extended by the party. To this object the government has been particular in its attention; and it is a matter of no little pride that such gentlemen as Drs. Baldwin and Say, and Messrs. Jessup, Peale [Titian R., the youngest son of Charles Willson], and Seymour, have embarked in the enterprise. Philosophy will undoubtedly be aided, and geology, botany, and mineralogy, will more than probably receive a powerful accession from the researches of some of these learned men; from the pencils of Messrs. Seymour and Peale we expect much pleasure: no important specimen will be lost, and no striking view omitted.[9]

It is noteworthy that the Napoleonic work, the *Description* . . . , had achieved popular fame and recognition, as had Denon's publication, which was apparently first used in America by the French emigré architect Maximilian Godefroy for the mastaba base of the Baltimore Battle Monument in 1815. Egyptian archeology was decidedly in the public mind even before 1820.

A second point is the reference to the Mississippi River as "the American Nile." Thus the oldest and newest lands had in common famous great river systems. This identification explains the naming of the Mississippi Valley cities as Cairo, Karnac, Thebes, and Memphis. By mid-century brashly confident Americans had reversed the process, referring to the Nile as "the Mississippi of Egypt."[10]

It was inevitable that in the wake of such sentiments theoretical archeology would seek connections between ancient Egypt and ancient America, the idea Joseph Smith had considered. In the eighteenth century it was a common belief in Europe that the Chinese were descended from a colony of Egyptians, e.g., the architects J.-G. Soufflot (1733–1780) and Sir William Chambers (1723–1796).[11] The passage across the Pacific seems to have been considered a minor obstacle by such home-grown archeologists as John Delafield who proposed in 1839 that the earliest inhabitants of the United States were Egyptians who had migrated through Asia to America.[12] This theory was accepted by Robert Cary Long, Jr. (1810–1849), the Baltimore architect who executed two major Egyptian designs: one for the Greenmount Cemetery Competition of 1845 (plate 65); the other, the 1836 project for his city's Records Office (plate 100). Long lectured and wrote on Mayan architecture which had become known to the American public through the publications of Frederick Catherwood (1799–1854) and John L. Stephens (1805–1852), two of the earliest excavators of Central American sites. Curiously enough, they had both travelled in and written about Egypt (1837, 1839).[13] Long considered that the aborigines of America had come from Egypt in the pre-Cheops period. In this way he explained the similarity of motifs such as pylons, pyramids, cavetto cornices and winged orbs.[14]

There were, however, more orthodox considerations of Egypt and its architecture available in the pre-Civil War period. Possibly the earliest scholarly description of ancient Egyptian structures to be written in America appeared in the March issue of the *American Quarterly Review* in 1829. Using Quatremère de Quincy's essay on Egyptian architecture, and, more fully, the first three volumes of the second edition of the *Description* . . . which had appeared the year immediately following the completion of the last volume of the first edition (1828), the correspondent devoted over forty pages to the history and description of Egyptian architecture admiring especially its simplicity, solidity, and grandeur.[15]

The first complete book on architectural history published in the United States, however, was Mrs. C. Tuthill's *History of Architecture* of 1844.[16] In it she writes not only of the strength and durability symbolized in Egyptian architectural massiveness, but also she presents the idea of the sublime, "What sublime emotions fill the mind [upon viewing Egyptian architecture]." Among the fifty pages she devotes to the style she speaks of its "size and magnificence" and its "grave and sublime [effect]." This is one of the key ideas behind the Egyptian Revival.

The roots of the concept of sublimity may be traced to Europe with Edmund Burke's formulation of the Sublime vis-à-vis the Beautiful.[17] The sublime aesthetic stated that emotional qualities like fear, astonishment, terror, dread and awe were produced by certain works of art. It was realized that Egyptian architecture could give the effect of awe and dread. Not only were its iconographic associations such, based as they were upon mystery and wisdom as well as the Cult of the Dead, but also visually these qualities were implied through the very characteristics of the style. These had been described by Sir John Soane as "immense grandeur [and] magnitude," "colossal . . . awful, and majestic."[18] These are all properties which help to evoke a sublime reaction in the viewer. Contemporary architectural criticism contains many similar characteristics in allusions to the style. Thomas Hope, who had travelled to the Nile, wrote in his history of architecture that the Egyptian style was "stupendous . . . of immense weight [in] an ingenious and solid manner."[19] John Flaxman in 1838 echoed these sentiments speaking of the Egyptians as "the wisest nation of antiquity," and their architecture as "stupendous."[20] In the *Architectural Magazine* during the 1830s J. C. Loudon published essays containing such comments as "What are called the wonders of Egypt (wonderful even in the fact that, though seen by so few, they should be familiar in description to so many) defy any parallel for magnitude."[21] There was in the "massiveness of proportion [and] feeling for the ponderous . . . a sense of gloom."[22] Thus as magnitude, grandeur, scale, massiveness of proportion are awe-inspiring, and ponderousness gives a sense of gloom, then the idea of solidity and durability may also produce a sublime effect, that of solemn reverence for timelessness.

There were more direct references to the sublime in relation to the Egyptian style,[23] but the clearest statement is in an essay by John Dowson in 1836 entitled "The Metaphysics of Architecture."[24] Greatly admired in America,[25] the article divides architecture into four categories: Grand, Magnificent, Sublime, and Beautiful. While it takes second place to the Roman in Grandeur, and to the Greek in Magnificence, in the third classification "The Egyptian style, from the largeness of its parts, is capable of the highest degree of sublimity." This is also true because Egyptian structures are vast and awesome. The idea is not, of course, original with Dowson—both John Martin and William Beckford found the Egyptian style to be one of exceptional sublimity.[26] But his expression of it is significant in view of the popularity in America of the *Architectural Magazine,* in which the essay appeared.

But even prior to 1800 the sublime capabilities of Egyptian monuments had been indicated through the paintings of Hubert Robert (1733–1803) who showed the Pyramids as awesomely massive and stupendous in relation to the microscopic human figures at their base.[27] Sometimes he portrayed this idea with views of the same subject in a casual setting of disorganized *ruine sentiment,* thus combining both the sublime and the picturesque. An even more emphatic representation was provided by Denon's friend, L.-F. Cassas (1756–1827)[28] who published in 1799, at the time of Bonaparte's Nile campaign, a set of engravings of ruins from sketches he had made during a trip to Lower Egypt fifteen years before.[29] Among the plates are four projected restorations for Egyptian temples and pyramid complexes (plates 7-8). These fantastic views of what he thought Egyptian architecture should have looked like are replete with ritual processions of Lilliputians obscured by huge clouds of incense and dwarfed by enormous Boullée-proportioned pyramids and temples.

The correspondences between the sublime effect of the Cassas illustrations, and a patently Romantic Classical project such as Boullée's pyramid (plate 26) indicates the principles common to both concepts. Thus the attributes accorded the Egyptian style by Caylus and Quatremère de Quincy, which in the last chapter were pointed out as being Romantic Classical values, i.e., primitivity, bareness, massiveness, may also be invoked to produce the sublime effect. This is not to say, of course, that all features of Romantic Classicism are calculated to call forth sublime emotions, but when austere geometry of form, sharp precision of delineation and severe simplicity of surface are combined with overwhelming scale, massive bulk and primordial composition, sublimity is achieved. The late-eighteenth-century German philosophers seem to have understood this. J. G. Herder (1744–1803) wrote in 1774 of the sense of primeval geometry in Egyptian forms and Immanuel Kant (1724–1804) cited the Great Pyramids as examples of the mathematically sublime.[30] And, of course, Denon himself spoke of the "order and simplicity . . . which raised [e.g., architecture] to the sublime."[31]

In America this concept of sublime Romantic Classicism in the Egyptian manner was perhaps most successfully realized in projects by A. J. Davis (1803–1892) (plates 36, 68, 115, 124). The overpowering scale of his Cemetery Gate design of 1828 (plate 68) shows this. Basing it in part upon a gate in Thebes given in Denon (plate 66),[32] and upon a Durand pylon illustration,[33] Davis, by including landscape elements such as trees, and architectural touchstones such as steps, imparts a feeling of vastness which is emphasized by the bare wall surfaces. In a design for a Gateway of about the same time (plate 115) similar effects of overwhelming size and unrelieved simplicity are indicated through the inclusion of a minute figure of a soldier on guard, and a restricted use of ornament. Davis was aware of the sublime properties of his Egyptian style. He writes of a large monument he designed in the mode (ca. 1840) (plate 36), "Not for an individual. It ought to be *simple* in its form, and *sublime by its magnitude and solidity*. It should be constructed so that even in ruins it would serve to *testify to posterity* the sense which the age had of the event it commemorated."[34] (Author's italics.)

Only a few years earlier in 1837 James Gallier, Sr., writing on the current state of architecture in America speaks of the Egyptian Revival style in much the same way, referring to it as "solid, stupendous, and time-defying . . . [whose] solemn and heavy . . . stern and severe proportions seem to speak of eternal duration. . . ."[35] Thus Mrs. Tuthill writing towards the end of the movement was only expressing earlier concepts of the Egyptian style when she spoke of its evocation of sublime timelessness through great size and massive solidity. Aspects of this are discussed in the next three chapters.

The second key idea of the Egyptian Revival is that expressed by Herder, that of proto-historic geometry which is a Romantic Classical tenet even when not combined with the sublime. The feeling for clear and precise geometry is the mainstay of the Ledolcian and Boullée-esque tradition. The Egyptian Revival crystallized this aspect of Romantic Classicism by simplifying further the vocabulary of geometric forms. In suppressing the triangular pedimental shape of Greek architecture, and the curves of Roman domes and arches, Egyptian Revival architecture limits the morphological choices to trapezoids and stepped corbels.[36] The block-like result with overhanging cornices to counter the battered walls presents architectonic forms of, curiously enough, a decisively rectilinear, rather than a trapezoidal, effect (see plate 36 for mastaba column-base with architect's guide lines).

In the discussion of the "Tombs" (Appendix III) it will be noted that the architect's specifications call for a solid-block impression for each part of the complex, deemphasizing the individuality of the stones in the masonry. The result, ideally, should make each architectonic section of the complex resemble a huge monolith, as if giants had been doing an exercise in solid geometry. Whether this does, or does not imply a sense of the sublime is not the purpose at this point. It is simply to show the Romantic Classical feeling for mathematically precise forms and the organic unity of each subdivision. The author of the *American Quarterly* article on Egyptian architecture was aware of this sensibility when he wrote of the masonry practices of the Egyptians, "It is impossible to find any buildings' surfaces better dressed, . . .

54

angles more sharp. . . . The joints are in all cases admirably dressed and so close as to be hardly perceptible."[37] It is the precision of geometry which delineates the various forms through "sharp angles," or what Mrs. Tuthill characterizes as "straight lines and angles." For nineteenth-century architecture, therefore, the Egyptian Revival, coming to its maturity later than the other antique revivals, and offering a reduced formal vocabulary, provided a final expression for Romantic Classicism.

The Egyptian Revival also provided a third aesthetic possibility, as a vehicle for Picturesque attitudes. Piranesi and Caylus' argument that Egyptian architecture was of an antiquity more ancient than the Antique was an appealing one for Americans, as has been indicated. But along with this exotic romanticism was a principle which was more formal than iconographic, the quality of variety. As in Europe, Egyptian interiors helped to give interest, or variety, to romantically picturesque houses. An early example from Philadelphia is a Gothic mansion by John Dorsey with an Egyptian boudoir[38] of 1810.[39] One of the latest, also presumably in a Gothic house, is an Egyptian Room at "Waverly" in Columbus, Mississippi, of 1858.[40] In between these dates in the 1840s, two row houses in Troy, New York (plate 92) were built with porches in the Egyptian style each having two wooden palm capitals and cavetto cornices—one of the few cases of the Egyptian Revival in domestic architecture. The forms must have been used to give interest and an air of novelty to otherwise undistinguished structures. The palm capitals, cavetto cornices and torus molding of the house at 58 Hillhouse Avenue, New Haven, is a similar example from the same period. Among others one might cite the "lotus" capitals in such churches as the First Church of Bennington, Vermont, of 1806. It was surely for the sake of variety that the unknown renovator of St. Mark's-in-the-Bouwerie, New York, installed fluted columns with lotus capitals (ca. 1850).

Even the most advanced concept of the Picturesque, the idea of an eclectic ensemble of separate buildings unified through similarity of materials and scale, and to be viewed all together, existed as early as 1829, seven years before the publication of Foulston's book which expounded the theory of the picturesque *coup d'oeil*. In Cooperstown, New York, a "gentleman architect," Eben B. Morehouse designed his own mansion, Woodside Hall. Its portico is in a vaguely Pompeian Ionic order preceded by "an Egyptian gate tower" (plate 37).[41] This pylon has a Gothic window—a pastiche Foulston would have abhorred— with battered walls and cavetto cornices. Built of red brick and trimmed with white-painted wood, as is the main building, it serves for a stairhouse between the street level and the terraces which lead past a "Renaissance" fountain up to the Ionic portico. It is, of course, doubtful that Morehouse had anything in mind more "advanced" than to create a somewhat novel picturesque effect. The analogy to Devonport must be fortuitous.

The idea of the Commercial Picturesque was, on the other hand, much more popular in America.[42] In point of fact, its beginning can be traced directly to England, and specifically to the first of these structures there, the Egyptian Hall in Piccadilly (plate 11). It will be recalled that that building had been erected by P. F. Robinson for William Bullock to exhibit the latter's collection of curiosities. Bullock sold the museum in 1820, travelled to Mexico publishing a book on this in France in 1824.[43] Somewhat after this, in 1827, he became interested in a scheme for building an ideal city in America. It was to be called Hygeia, and had been planned by J. B. Papworth, the designer of the original non-Egyptian interior for the London Museum.[44] Bullock's ideal city, like so many, was never realized, but he had interested Mrs. (Frances) Trollope (1780–1863) in the scheme. She settled for a time across the Ohio River from Hygeia in Cincinnati where she commissioned Seneca Palmer to build her a shop with tea room above.[45] It was to be a reproduction or modification of Bullock's London Museum, but actually when it was built in 1829 (demolished in 1881) it was more Oriental than Nilotic, although the exterior columns were of the Egyptian papyrus order. But the purpose of the exotic style cannot have been for any more profound reason than to attract attention to Mrs. Trollope's Bazaar. She may have hoped to civilize the uncouth Americans of the raw West, but her fancy store must have seemed only alien rather than curious. It was a dismal failure, and would, perhaps, have served better as a museum in the first place.

But the Egyptian style continued to be used for commercial architecture at least until the middle of the century. An iron firm, Isaac P. Morris and Company(?), 138 South Front Street, Philadelphia, by C. B. Cooper in 1847 (destroyed ca. 1959) (plates 43, 46); J. Haviland's Pennsylvania Fire Insurance office in the same city, 1838 (plates 42, 44, 45); and both the New Bedford (demolished 1889–1890) and Pittsfield (burned 1854), Massachusetts, railroad stations in 1840 (plates 39–41); all were in the Egyptian style. Although there may have been other contributing reasons, primarily the purpose must have been to attract public attention. The New Bedford depot by Russell Warren was described in a contemporary newspaper account as being "singularly odd and appropriate."[46] In chapter six the hypothesis that "appropriateness" in this case meant reassuring the timid traveller is discussed. "Singularly odd," however, is probably a heritage from the Egyptian Hall.

In America, too, the Egyptian Revival was built upon a foundation of knowledge and understanding of ancient Egypt as sympathetic as any in Europe. Conceptually it fits into two basic patterns. On one hand the style exemplified the ideals of Romantic Classicism. On the other, it served the purposes of the Picturesque. For the former it expressed sublime sentiments in a geometrically simple manner, while for the latter it provided variety of form. These principles, known in Europe, were more completely expressed in the United States. The next three chapters present a fuller discussion of the various manifestations of the Egyptian style and the more serious meanings it implied.

Notes:

CHAPTER 3

1. W. R. Dawson, *Who Was Who in Egyptology* (London, 1951). For a listing of Americans who traveled in Egypt and wrote about it see the *Philadelphia North American* for February 10, 1847.

2. *North American Review,* XVII, 41 (1823), pp. 233–242; XXIX, 65 (1829), pp. 361–389; XXXII, 70 (1831), pp. 95–126; LXI, 128 (1845), p. 267.

3. For early Egyptian collections in America see C. R. Williams, "The Place of the New-York Historical Society in the Growth of American Interest in Egyptology," *Bulletin of the New-York Historical Society,* IV, 1 (1920), pp. 3–20; W. B. Dinsmoor, "Early American Studies of Mediterranean Archeology," *Proceedings of the American Philosophical Society,* LXXXVII, 1 (1943), pp. 94–96; Lynn Poole, "Cohen, First out of Egypt," *Art News,* XLVII, 9 (1949), pp. 38–39; John D. Cooney, "The Acquisition of the Abbott Collection," *Bulletin of the Brooklyn Museum,* X, 3 (1949), pp. 17–23.

4. For the connection of Ancient Egypt and medicine see chapter six.

5. For Belzoni, see note 69 in preceding chapter.

6. This collection was eventually given to Johns Hopkins University, in 1884.

7. Cooney, "Abbott Collection," p. 17; *Gleason's . . . ,* VI, 17 (1854), pp. 260–261. This collection passed to the New-York Historical Society in 1860, and thence to the Brooklyn Museum (1948) where it formed the nucleus for that fine Egyptian Department.

   Also note William H. Gerdts, "Egyptian Motifs in Nineteenth-Century American Painting and Sculpture," *Antiques,* XC, 10 (1966), pp. 495–501.

8. For another Mormon hieroglyphic translation, that of fragments reputedly written by Moses and Abraham, see Joseph Smith, *Pearl of Great Price* (Liverpool, 1851).

9. *Washington Daily National Intelligencer,* May 10, 1819. The author is indebted to Prof. J. Poesche of Tulane University for this item.

10. F. W. Holland, "Letters upon Egypt," *Gleason's . . . ,* V, 26 (1853), p. 414.

11. Also see entries in Dawson, under J. J. Amiot, J. B. Biot, F. P. Gourdin, J. de Guignes, P. Lacour, and J. T. Needham.

12. John Delafield, Jr., *An Inquiry into the Origins of the Antiquities of America* (Cincinnati, 1839).

13. J. L. Stephens, *Incidents of Travel* (New York, 1837); F. Catherwood, *Descriptions of a View of the Great Temple of Karnak, and the Surrounding City of Thebes* (London, 1839). See also V. W. von Hagen, *Frederick Catherwood, Architect* (New York, 1950).

14. Robert Cary Long, Jr., *The Ancient Art of America* (New York, 1849), pp. 11, 13, 21.
15. "Egyptian Architecture," *American Quarterly Review,* V (1829), pp. 1–41.
16. C. Tuthill, *History of Architecture* (New York, 1844).
17. Edmund Burke, *A Philosophical Inquiry into the Origin of Our Ideas of the Sublime and the Beautiful* (London, 1757). See also W. J. Hipple, *The Beautiful, the Sublime, and the Picturesque in XVIII Century British Aesthetic Theory* (Carbondale, 1957).
18. John Soane, *Lectures on Architecture* (London, 1929), pp. 20–21.
19. Thomas Hope, *An Historical Essay on Architecture* (London, 1835), pp. 10–13.
20. John Flaxman, *Lectures on Sculpture* (London, 1838), pp. 54, 59.
21. "S. H.", "On Architectural Parallels," *Architectural Magazine,* II (1838), p. 50.
22. "M.", "On the Effect which should result to Architecture in regard to Design and Arrangement, from the general Introduction of Iron in the Construction of Buildings," *Architectural Magazine,* IV (1837), p. 278.
23. Charles Reed, "A Few Remarks on ancient Foundations and Modern Concrete," *Architectural Magazine,* III (1836), p. 80.
24. J. Dowson, "Essay on the Metaphysics of Architecture," *Architectural Magazine,* III (1836), pp. 245–249.
25. *North American Review,* LVIII, 123 (1844), p. 464.
26. Donald Pilcher, *The Regency Style* (London, 1947), p. 68. For John Martin and Egypt see also (*re* his series of the Plagues of Egypt): Dunham, "A Footnote to the History of Egyptology," *American Research Center in Egypt, Inc. Newsletter,* 42 (July, 1961). See also Thomas Balston, *John Martin* (London, 1947), pp. 77–79, 295.
27. *Vide, The Pyramids,* Hubert Robert (1760), Smith College Museum of Art. In the Rhode Island School of Design drawing of the same subject note the atlantes at the entrance to the pyramid. Although similar to the ones at Fontainebleau of 1540 (see beginning of chapter two) they are more probably directly taken from the two found at Hadrian's Villa.
28. Henri Boucher, "Louis-François Cassas," *Gazette des Beaux-Arts,* 5ᵉ periode, XIV (1926), pp. 27–53, 209–230.
29. L.-F. Cassas, *Voyage pittoresque de la Syrie, de la Phenicie, de la Palestine, et de la Basse Egypte* (Paris, 1799).
30. Immanuel Kant, *Critique of Judgement,* trans. by J. H. Bernard, 2nd edition (London, 1931), II, A, 26.
31. J. Christopher Herald, *Bonaparte in Egypt* (London, 1962), p. 250.
32. Denon, *Voyage . . . ,* pl. XLI, fig. 3.
33. J.-N.-L. Durand, *Recueil et parallèle . . .* (Paris, 1800), pl. I.
34. Metropolitan Museum of Art, acc. no. 24.66.1605.
35. James Gallier, "On the Rise, Progress and present State of Architecture in North America," *Architectural Magazine,* IV (1837), pp. 16–17. This

article originally appeared in the *North American Review,* XLIII, 93 (1836), pp. 356–384.

36. By mid-century architectural critics were attributing the absence of arches in Egyptian architecture not to the lack of technical knowledge, but to "the desire to preserve a uniformity in the structure." William Brown, *The Carpenter's Assistant* (Worcester, 1857), p. 18.

37. "Egyptian Architecture," *American Quarterly Review,* V (1829), p. 13.

38. Cf. Boudoir of the Queen in the Petits Appartements at Fontainebleau by Richard Mique (?) (1728–1794) in the Turkish style.

39. The author is indebted to Prof. Matthew Baigell of Rutgers University, the State University of New Jersey, for this information.

40. Clay Lancaster, "Oriental Forms in American Architecture, 1800–1870," *Art Bulletin,* XXIX, 3 (1947), p. 185.

41. Ralph Birdsall, *The Story of Cooperstown* (Cooperstown, 1948), pp. 225–228.

42. For examples of the Commercial Picturesque see plates 17, 19, 38–46.

43. William Beulloch [Bullock], *Le Mexique en 1823* (Paris, 1824). Plate IV of the atlas shows what at first appears to be an Egyptian pylon gate over a canal. It is, in fact, an Aztec one.

44. S. Giedion, *Space, Time and Architecture* (Cambridge, 1941), pp. 505, 510.

45. Clay Lancaster, "The Egyptian Hall and Mrs. Trollope's Bazaar," *Magazine of Art,* XLIII (1950), p. 94.

46. Robert L. Alexander, "Russell Warren" (unpublished M.A. thesis, Institute of Fine Arts, New York University, 1952), p. 151. The report was published in the *Boston Atlas* of July 3, 1840.

    Warren also designed Egyptianizing Corinthian columns for: the Foster House, Providence (1840); the Parker House Hotel, New Bedford (1840); and (less so) the Joseph Durfee House, Fall River (1842) (*ibid.,* figs. 37–38, 39, 42). This is not unusual as an aspect of the Corinthian order in the Classical Revival, but Warren probably picked up a taste for Egyptianisms from A. J. Davis whose partner he was in 1835–1836 (*ibid.,* pp. 104–149).

4

Formal Development

There are three formal aspects of the Egyptian Revival style, plus two further categories not strictly formal but based on stylistic criteria. Although a basic development may be observed from one of these phases to the next, it should be remarked that at the point of maturity of the movement all five existed concurrently. These divisions are: pseudo-Egyptian in which motifs are applied to a common classical core; the horizontal phase in which the entire form is specifically Egyptian; the vertical phase in which there is a merging of the Egyptian vocabulary with Gothic proportions. The two parenthetical aspects are: provincial work in which there is a stiffness and crudeness with extreme simplification; and, finally, "Egyptianizing" examples in which specific details are not archeologically pure Egyptian, but whose total effect echoes an Egyptian feeling or aesthetic.

The pseudo-Egyptian phase might be likened in terms of architecture, to the pseudo-classical paintings of such late eighteenth-century artists as Angelica Kauffmann, J.-M. Vien, A. Raphael Mengs, and, perhaps, Benjamin West. The subject matter and rather flat and simplified planarity of these artists who basically stand within a soft rococo tradition, may be contrasted to the austere hardness of such "true" neo-classical painters as David and Ingres. In the former group the superficial trappings of neo-classicism are evident, but the underlying eighteenth-century construction, elegance, and sentiment bespeak the dominant character of the works. In architecture the same classifications might be made in relation to the "pseudo-classical" architects A.-J. Gabriel and Richard Mique, as opposed to C.-N. Ledoux and E.-L. Boullée; the former popularized a more strictly classical *fashion* within the existing tradition, whereas the latter were indeed revolutionary in that they created a new *style* through their inventive reworking of geometric shapes, interrelated proportions, and a restricted use of decoration.

In like manner there appears an analogous division in Egyptian Revival architecture. Whereas the "pseudo" phases in the above examples, however, seem quietly to fade away; the two divisions in this case do not so happily fit into a Protean chronology. Although the first stirrings of the movement are indeed of the earlier type, this aspect continues into the mature period and alongside examples of the more archeological Egyptian manifestations.

The fact emerges that, on the one hand, the pseudo-Egyptian phase is one which is inextricably involved with a picturesque-rococo aesthetic; thus the purpose of the style in these examples is one that becomes related to ideas of novelty, variety, and the bizarre. On the other hand, the style (or fashion) in this guise is involved with certain specific historical associations such as the funerary tradition, or that of the Land of Wisdom and Mystery. It must be realized, of course, that the latter viewpoint would account for the use of the style in other phases of the Egyptian Revival, as well. In any case, these points will be discussed later. It also should be remembered from chapter two, "Sources and Stimuli," that picturesque-rococo examples are to be noted in Europe with such works as Piranesi's interiors for the Caffè Inglese in Rome (plate 2); the *style Louis Seize* garden pavilions at Etupes by J.-B. Kléber (plates 3, 5), Soisy-sous-Etiole by P.-F.-L. Dubois (plate 4), and Valencé by J. A. Renard (plate 6); Thomas Hope's furniture designs (plate 12); and P. F. Robinson's London Museum (plate 11).

In America it is not surprising that the young nation, lacking a genuine aristocratic tradition, would approach architecture from a more pragmatic, if mundane, viewpoint than the nations of the Old World. In the United States there was neither the wealth, nor the psychology conducive to elaborately decorated coffee houses, frivolous garden pavilions, or exotic exhibition halls. There was, however, a certain residue of this tradition in interest in the bizarre to create variety, as may be noted in Thomas U. Walter's Crown Street (Beth Israel) Synagogue in Philadelphia of 1849 (plate 91)[1] in which he supplied papyrus columns with open papyrus capitals for the shallow central entrance porch. The building has had applied to it cavetto cornices on both floors. And as a final Egyptian garbing, there is a simulated battered wall in raised relief upon the brownstone facade. Placed a few steps above the street level it remains, however, a three-bay, two-story town house typical of the 1840s. The obvious Egyptian features, the columns, lend a heavy decorative richness to the otherwise commonplace form.

Rather similar, although with porches at the left bay, a feature more typical of domestic urban architecture, are the two brick houses mentioned earlier, in Troy, New York, 166 and 168 Congress Street (plate 92).[2] Also of three bays and two stories, these rather ordinary row houses have been enriched by a single cavetto cornice of the reeded variety on the housefront, a Ptolemaic feature; and a porch with columns strikingly similar to Walter's. These must be dated in the later 1840s.

That these examples are indicative of the persistence of this "applied" Egyptian may be seen upon regressing in time to earlier manifestations of the same sort of handling. Almost thirty years before Walter's Synagogue, also in Philadelphia, his teacher, William Strickland, erected the Cherry Street (Mikveh Israel) Synagogue, 1822–1825 (plate 90).[3] This was a two-story stone building of the usual three bays with a raised first floor, and a lower second story under a slanting roof which, in turn, was crowned by a small cupola. It is described as having been in the Egyptian style both on the front and interior. But here again, and even more markedly, it is obvious that the structure is a house of the early Republic with a few semi-Egyptian motifs included in its design. There appears to be a cavetto cornice above the door with a winged disc. The frames of the door and each of the side windows are battered, but these could be as Greek as they are Egyptian. According to an 1824 guidebook, the interior columns supporting the dome were "copied from Tentyra" [Denderah]. This, however, does not seem to be borne out in the plans reconstructed in 1953 under the auspices of the American Philosophical Society. On the other hand, the winged disc is not shown on these drawings either.

In any case, both Strickland and Walter at other times showed a more archeological awareness of the Egyptian style than in their synagogues. In 1836 the former executed a fine, "pure" Egyptian Revival design for the Laurel Hill Cemetery Gate competition (plate 63), and in 1848 planned the Nashville Downtown Presbyterian Church (plate 93) which is certainly more Egyptian than the Mikveh Israel Temple.[4] The case of Walter is especially telling, for his other, more archeological, Egyptian designs are earlier than his synagogue; a design for the Laurel Hill Cemetery Gate, 1836 (plate 64)[5] and the Debtors' Prison at Moyamensing of 1835 (plate 105).[6]

Although it might seem from the above discussion that the pseudo-Egyptian style was employed at will and not a result of lack of archeological knowledge or taste, it should be kept in mind that very early examples may have been the result of a certain degree of understandable faint-heartedness in thrusting upon an unfamiliar public a specifically Egyptian monument. In spite of the references to Denderah in Strickland's synagogue, this may have been the case there. It is even more probably the case in his teacher, Benjamin Latrobe's (1764–1820) plan for a Library of Congress in 1808 (plate 97).[7] If the latter introduced the former to the style, he himself must already have been exposed to the possibilities of exotic revivals through his own master in England, S. P. Cockerell (1754–1827), the architect of the "Hindoo" Sezincote (1803) (executed, of course, after Latrobe's departure for America). But Latrobe chose to use the style only as an interior articulation for one room in an otherwise classical Capitol building. Although this particular project was never executed, it remains the first example of the style in America, and one of the earliest in the world, having been designed four years before P. F. Robinson's London Museum.

The hall is a long rectangle, roughly seventy by thirty-five feet, terminating in an apsidal form. It is approximately thirty feet high with the middle of three zones being the tallest and containing a gallery. The uppermost zone also contains a gallery. These galleries are, of course, the obvious solution to the problem of access to the shelves. The specifically Egyptian features include the twenty-eight open papyrus columns around three sides of the upper gallery, the eight papyrus bundle columns with open capitals in the "apse" of the lower gallery, plus the battered frames for the windows and bookcases of the middle zone. One of the latter is topped by a cavetto cornice. Other Nilotic elements are the battered fireplaces with cavetto cornices in the lowest zone. Although there can be no doubt as to the "Egyptianness" of these elements, they are combined in a most non-Egyptian manner. With the large windows and the equally large spaces cut into the walls for the bookshelves, as well as the chopping up of the elevation into distinct zones with galleries and the screening effect of the rows of columns, there remains neither a feeling of sublime vastness, nor a sense of solid, uniformly massive wall areas. In point of fact, there is a certain lightness engendered by the slenderness of the columns which in their decoration and form are archeologically correct, but which employ completely non-Egyptian proportions. The church-like plan of the room can hardly be considered Egyptian; not even in the sense of the Palladian-Vitruvian misunderstood "Egyptian" Hall of Lord Burlington's York Assembly Room of 1730. It would be tempting, indeed, to ally it with William Kent's (1685–1748) entrance hall at Holkham (1734) which appears to be a combination of a Roman basilica and an "Egyptian" Hall, but the uses of the two rooms are so entirely different, while the apse dispositions, the elevations, and the general proportions are so unrelated, that it would seem a forced, if not fanciful, parallel.[8]

The fact remains, therefore, that these and other examples of this phase do not project an actual sense or feeling of being Egyptian. They are recognized as Egyptian because of their use of various details. Often there are associative reasons for the use of such motifs, as, in the above case, the tradition, known since Roman times, and reemphasized in the Napoleonic campaign, of the great library at Alexandria.[9] Or these details are used to vary the architects' repertoire. But, as to formal architectural style, pseudo-Egyptian features must be considered only as decorative applications.

The actual emergence of the Egyptian mode as an independent style of its own occurs in the work of John Haviland (1792–1852) who is the Egyptian Revival architect par excellence. He designed and built its major monuments; not pseudo-Egyptian houses, nor merely Egyptian memorials and gateways, but habitable structures. Whereas many architects drew plans for edifices which were never executed, Haviland erected a series of fine examples of Egyptian architecture. It is also in his work that we encounter the classic phase of the movement, and the one that produces its most Egyptian aspect in which the horizontalizing elements are emphasized. In the 1830s this was not unusual. Furthermore, not illogically, Egyptian buildings of the 1840s, when Haviland had already abandoned the style, partake of a more pronounced verticality, also a general feature of architecture of that decade.

This mature phase of the movement is ushered in by Haviland's design for the New Jersey State Penitentiary (plates 106–110).[10] This half-radial structure was erected from 1832–1836. A long high battered wall with cavetto cornices and torus moldings is relieved otherwise only by battered niches recalling the flag-pole holders in temple pylons such as Edfou. The wall is broken in the center by the front building which houses the various receiving rooms and administrative offices. This block is made up of two pylons projecting in profile and joined by a low, one-story colonnade. There is a breaking up of the block with certain accents, such as the narrow battered windows, and the subdivisions of the profiled pylon walls into two narrower pylons tends to give the structure vertical notes. The heavy cavetto cornices of uniform height, the colonnaded portico with its squat papyrus bud columns, and the corbelled window above, combine, however, to press the structure earthwards. The great expanses of unrelieved masonry serve to emphasize this heavy weightiness and gravitational solidity. The sense of space-displacing mass is certainly stronger here than in Haviland's earlier (1828) Gothic Eastern State Penitentiary, in Pennsylvania.

But Haviland had not finished the building before he had designed another even more monumental and complex; and the most horizon-talizing of all Egyptian Revival buildings. In 1835 he had won the competition for the "Tombs," i.e., the New York Halls of Justice and House of Detention (plates 111–128).[11] The general effect of the main facade is, if anything, lower and less vertical than the one at Trenton. Instead of a recessed portico between two pylons in profile, the archi-tect has designed a massive portico projecting from the uniform plane of a thirteen-bay facade; hence there is a minimum of movement which might otherwise have been engendered by manipulating the geometric blocks of various architectonic units. Even more important than this flat plane is the heavy, unrelieved roof-line which runs straight across the entire structure with only the step of the attic above the central bay projecting for emphasis. The ponderous cornice with this attic is higher than the podium upon which the building sits, and there is half again as much masonry above the window frames as below. The ten windows are exactly alike, which produces a reiter-ated cadence extending across either side of the portico, whose three openings are meticulously the same as the fenestration. Thus, even when there are actual vertical elements, they are organized in a manner not attracting attention as individual features, but so as to become part of a group which in its total effect is horizontal.

Although the masonry is not intended to be viewed as individual blocks of stone with mortar, but rather, as one unified plane or sheath to give the effect of a solid geometrical entity, there is to be noted a faint indication of regular ashlar work with the delineation of joints. The stones in themselves are laid horizontally and arranged in a series of alternate bands of higher and lower measurements. As opposed to the vertical joints the horizontal ones are continuous as well as parallel, thus emphasizing again the flatness of the concept.

The projecting portico masks most of the great flight of steps which leads up to the *piano nobile*. In any case, the stairs are across all three bays of the central section, rather than, for example, only up to the middle portal as in the case with the plan by A. J. Davis (plate 124). Outside the portico, the steps are disposed around all three sides rather than being funnelled up through the front between the stair walls of an extended lateral podium.

By enclosing a system of courts, the building has been pushed out to the extreme edges of the entire city block in which it is placed. In this manner, by the sheer weight of measurements, it has a distinctly horizontal accent being two hundred feet wide by forty-four feet high.

In Haviland's later work, the Essex County Courthouse (plates 129–131)[12] in Newark, New Jersey, of 1836–1838, he compresses his building into the center of its plot, vis-à-vis the above, in an obvious gesture to economy. This building, however, is less complicated than the "Tombs," and considerably smaller. The general proportions of the structure are still wider than they are high, although the effect is somewhat more vertical than with the Halls of Justice, for the length of the facade has been diminished by six bays leaving three windows at each side of the single entrance portico. The proportions of the windows have not been noticeably changed, although, in point of fact, they are somewhat narrower, if the same height. The hipped roof and cupola above the slightly projecting recessed portico with its single bay preceded by a frontal flight of steps between stair walls, all combine to balance such distinct horizontal forces as the heavy cornices of uniform height, the stepped attic above the portico, and a masonry system identical to that of the "Tombs." Presenting less of a controlled sprawling effect than the Trenton prison, and more of a compact accenting one than the Halls of Justice, the Essex County Courthouse effects a more correctly Egyptian set of proportions than either; proportions which are impressive because they are of a vaster scale than the human one.

By 1838, in his final executed Egyptian work, the Pennsylvania Fire Insurance Company in Philadelphia (plate 42),[13] Haviland had passed into the vertical phase of the movement due, on the one hand, to the practical necessities of the age, i.e., the crowding of American cities and the search for more commercial space; and, on the other hand, due to the growing taste for Gothic proportions. Here, finally, the architect designed a building in the Egyptian style which is higher than it is wide, being of four stories and three bays.

It is this final phase in the 1840s that is exemplified most clearly by the projects of A. J. Davis. In his earliest work in the style, a gateway to a military establishment, executed about 1828 (plate 115),[14] he designed a massive entrance with a three-bay projecting portico heralding the effect of Haviland's "Tombs" facade, albeit somewhat higher in proportions, but distinctly horizontal with its huge entablature of considerably greater height than its base. The roof-line, however, remains flat, and uniformly without projections. This cannot be claimed for his later works beginning with his designs for the "Tombs" in 1835 (plate 124). The roof-line in these is not uniform, for there are projections not only forward, but also upward in the side and center units. The long, unrelieved flight of stairs up through the relatively narrow portico, as well as the extremely steep batter of the walls all contribute to provide a more vertical effect than is to be seen in Haviland's design. The differences in the two architects' attitudes towards this problem of proportional accent is perhaps best shown in Davis' project for adding two or three stories to the older architect's "Tombs" facade (plate 125).[15] With its steeper batter, taller, less heavily-corniced windows, and three-part roof-line projection flanked by domes, the Davis plan looks like a separate building, quite unrelated, that has been perched on top of Haviland's. In any case, in this comparison, Haviland emerges as the more successful, if more conservative, architect.

In the same year, Davis designed a project in the Egyptian style for the New York Athenaeum of Natural History (plate 99).[16] It has three bays in five stories, the two lower floors forming one unit while the three upper ones form a second, recalling the same architect's Colonnade Row of 1832 also in New York. The bi-partite division of the facade seems to be his most effective solution to the problem of achieving the lofty sense. Even so, the upper two open papyrus columns are exceptionally slender indeed for the Egyptian Revival at this point. These, with the Davisean windows in their long, vertical, slit-like appearance, and the complete absence of batter motifs set up the most vertically oriented project for the style to this date.

In two plans which must date from the 1840s, Davis proposes buildings in the Egyptian style with towers. A handsome design for a church (plate 96)[17] is probably the earlier, but in any case it is not as monumental as his former projects, for there is much attention to detail, and precise, refined workmanship which leads to a deemphasis of the masonry. Only in the ponderous composite papyrus columns, taken from late Ptolemaic models at Philae, is there a sense of awesome heaviness. The curtain walls are lightened by a capping row of cobra heads, rather than a strong terminating cavetto. There is profuse attention to symbolical detail in such motifs as the winged hourglass, the winged heart, and the metope sections with their royal cartouches containing the sign for gold. All these serve to dematerialize the walls, while the major vertical accent is achieved not only through the steep batter, but also by the tower itself which, with its narrow openings, pierces the pylon facade.

Much less Egyptian, and surely later, is the plan for a village chapel and school house (plate 98).[18] Designed to be in wood on an octagonal plan, a large tower rises from the front section. The Egyptian features include the torus moldings, batter motifs, a modified cavetto cornice on the tower, and a large royal cartouche over the door. It is the dominating aspect of this tower with its narrow openings, and steep batter, aided by the vertical arrangement of the clapboards which underline the direction of the structure's orientation.

Davis' final Egyptian project comes quite late; 1878 being the date of his plan for the Long Island Historical Society Library.[19] In this he has six stories in two parts with five bays of slightly battered windows. As opposed to his Athenaeum, the higher of the two parts of the elevation is the bottom one, thus giving the building an even loftier air. The entrance portico has a steep pitch to its batter, as do the windows, while the walls themselves have none at all. The pointed domes with the central pediment contribute to the feeling of verticality, but it cannot be said that the building is emphatically more so than his work of the later 1830s and 1840s.

Among the non-Davis examples falling into this subdivision the Odd Fellows' Hall at Third and Brown Streets in Philadelphia should be mentioned (plate 77).[20] Built in 1846 its unaccented, steeply battered block is punctuated by slender, three-story battered windows, and raised upon a ground floor which serves as a podium. Actually the fenestration is arranged to move from ground level to frieze with almost no interruption. The simple abstract pilaster forms in the base aid in this feeling as does the fluting of the cornice. The three-stepped corbelled arches above the cavetto-corniced windows stretch these accents even higher, and lighten the weight of the uppermost areas. Built on the corner of equally wide streets, the principal face is on the three-bay side which underlines a more vertical feeling than if it had been on the longer seven-bay side. It is perhaps because of the effectiveness of this combination of features that the vertical torus moldings have been omitted.

In the case of T. S. Stewart's Medical College of Virginia in Richmond of 1844 (plates 102, 103),[21] basically the same features produce a similar effect. At each of the four corners of the three-by-six-bay rectangle is a sharply battered "cube" pylon. The walls between are perpendicular. The side bays are three-floors high, and united by tall, steeply battered frames. The reeded cavetto cornice along the top seems especially high, but its slow, elegant curve gives more of a feeling of loftiness than weight, while the bundled palm columns, of the Edfou type, in the entrance, again on the narrow side of the building, are particularly tall in a feeling abetted by their long, uninterrupted reeded motifs.

Possibly the final statement in this phase is one of Strickland's last works, the Downtown Presbyterian Church of Nashville, designed in 1848 (plate 93).[22] The former church had been destroyed by fire on September 14 of that year.[23] Two days later a committee was authorized to procure plans. On its December 15 meeting the congregation considered two projects "by Mr. Briscoe Vannoy [the architect of the former church], and one in perspective with a front view and ground plot by Capt. Strickland, the architect of the State Capitol. The last, having been briefly explained by the chairman, was submitted to the meeting as the one selected. . . ." The church was built by 1851. The two palm columns of the portico were not erected until 1880 when the present interior decoration was executed, but they were made "in careful conformity to the original design."[24] Besides the extremely slender columns, the other Egyptian features consist of cavetto cornices, a winged disc over the portico, and battered window and door frames which are perhaps as Greek in form as they are Egyptian. Thus the fenestration is not as elongated as other examples, but the building is a tall one set on a high podium, and entered by a flight of frontal steps between the tower bases. The cornices are not particularly heavy, while the solid balustrades above them are deemphasized by flat panel inserts. The facade across the structure is considerably broken up by its recessed portico, and projecting tower bases. At this end above the balustrade is a pediment, a motif repeated on each of the eight sides of the uppermost tower stories. It is this double-tower facade with the lighter, smaller, and more pointed elements of the terminations that provides a strongly vertical emphasis. In a sense it would seem that the architect in this final aspect of the style had achieved a very personal solution to the problem of the use of Egyptian forms for specific aesthetic tastes, while at the same time stripping away a maximum of the exotic and the bizarre which the style so often was unable to avoid. Nevertheless, the Nashville church maintains the essential trappings of this style which in themselves are integrated rather than applied, vis-à-vis the pseudo-Egyptian group.

There is a further category of buildings which may be mentioned, parenthetically, in relation to the movement in general. It has been noted that there was a group of structures in Europe denominated as "Egyptianizing."[25] Presumably for the same reasons, there is a like classification for architecture in this country, i.e., buildings which do not use a specifically Egyptian vocabulary, but which in their general arrangement and use of abstracted Egyptian motifs give a decidedly Egyptian feeling. One of the most striking examples is the First Baptist Church of Essex, Connecticut with its Bulfinchian tower termination (ca. 1845) (plate 94).[26] There is no specific evocation of Egyptian detail, but the general arrangement of a pylon front with battered walls and a central tower acts as a frontal slab facade for the simple rectangular nave, and is strongly reminiscent of Davis' church design (plate 96), or even more closely of the Whalers' Church at Sag Harbor of 1843 attributed to Minard Lafever (plate 95.)[27] Whereas both the Essex Church and Lafever's are similar in plan, although the tower of the latter is thicker; the specific detailing is entirely different; the former's is Classical Revival, while the latter's is an abstracted Egyptian. The difficulties of working with wood seem to have persuaded Lafever to design an angular "cavetto" cornice with a conventionalized cobra frieze. Curiously enough, the fenestration of the two is strikingly similar to the Egyptian Revival motif of providing one or more stories of windows within a single framing device. This arrangement is particularly telling when employed on the pylon forms, and calls forth, once more, the flag-pole niches of Egyptian temples, providing an example of the adaptation of an ancient motif for modern use.

Nevertheless, the Essex church and others of its type represent a closing of a cycle that starts with pseudo-Egyptian monuments in which Egyptian details are applied to an otherwise non-Egyptian Revival structure; and ends with the Egyptianizing group that applies non-Egyptian detail to an otherwise Egyptian core. The paramount formal qualities of the ancient style, space displacing mass and geometric simplicity conceived of in terms of unbroken size, have been distilled out and synthesized into the reservoir of mid-nineteenth-century architectural forms. If the pseudo-Egyptian phase evokes Egypt in a "literary," or associative manner, then the Egyptianizing evokes Egypt in a "conceptual," or formal-aesthetic sense.[28]

As the history of no style would be complete without mentioning "provincial" examples, it remains only to mention a few of these. Suffice it to say that provincial works in Egyptian Revival exhibit two basic qualities: extreme simplicification in a style which already is founded on simplicity, and a crude stiffness in a style which is also based on rigidity. It might seem, therefore, that the differences between a provincial and sophisticated use of the style are excessively subtle ones. Comparison of the material will show, however, that this is not the case, for this super simplification is due to low budgeting, and the stiffness may be traced to lack of knowledge, or even faulty knowledge.

One thirty-eight South Front Street in Philadelphia (plates 43, 46) (destroyed ca. 1959) was originally built by Charles B. Cooper, "a master builder," in 1847 for the Isaac P. Morris Company(?), "an iron establishment."[29] It was described in its day as "imposing" and "curious"; thus it is a building designed to attract attention, and thereby advertise its occupant. At the same time it uses the oldest of styles to evoke the enduring qualities of the new material. The facade is of brick with cast iron decorative and framing elements. As it was no more than a modest four-story, three-bay commercial building, the services of a trained architect were dispensed with. All that was needed was a recognizable enough use of the style. Hence the Egyptian features are simplified in that they are restricted to the first floor, except in the cavetto cornice with its sparsely decorated torus molding ending abruptly within a foot of its downward course on either side. The *distyle in antis* arrangement of the street level uses a slightly more elaborate molding, but the two cast iron columns are utterly bare, save for two series of four horizontal incised lines giving a hint of bundling motifs. The result of this harshly unrelieved treatment is not only an excessive simplicity, but also an awkward stiffness.

The same might be said of the Farmington, Connecticut, Cemetery Gate of about 1850 (plate 73). It was modelled on Henry Austin's Grove Street gate of 1844–1848 (plate 71).[30] The thinness and smallness of the former, very non-Egyptian qualities indeed, are permitted by the material which is wood. The geometric abstraction of the decoration along with the somewhat astringent passage from the necking to the hardly recognizable papyrus bud capitals, which have been given horizontal rather than vertical incisions, betrays the work of an independently minded, if untrained, architect in a style whose essence demands at least a gesture towards ponderously moving bulges and slowly heaving undulations.

It would seem, then, that the Egyptian Revival was one which went through a series of developmental phases that lasted half a century until the end of the popularity of the style. Often two or more of these phases were concurrent. But, in any case, the movement started cautiously, and, in its earlier manifestations, without a particularly profound feeling for the essential aesthetic inherent in the style. Later, with the diffusion of archeological knowledge, free interpretations were essayed which then did achieve a sense of true understanding, and proficiency in expression. Following the general movement of architecture of the period, this phase may be subdivided into its horizontal mode in the 1830s, and the vertical in the 1840s. Whereas provincial works achieved a peculiarly austere simplification which, however, betrayed little feeling for the inherent qualities of the style's formal characteristics; a compromising force produced, over a period of time, a solid, practical kind of architecture in which the lessons of ancient Egyptian structures and their severe values were maintained. In some periods, e.g., the High Victorian, the Egyptianizing influence was to be in retreat and hibernation. But down to the present day the echoes reverberate.[31]

Notes:

CHAPTER 4

1. Rachel Wischnitzer, *Synagogue Architecture in the United States* (Philadelphia, 1955), p. 46. For descriptions see, *A Stranger's Guide to Philadelphia* (Philadelphia, 1854), p. 209; *Ballou's Pictorial Drawing-Room Companion,* vol. x, no. 2 (January 12, 1856), p. 25; George B. Tatum, *Penn's Great Town* (Philadelphia, 1961), p. 86.

2. Frank J. Roos, "The Egyptian Style," *Magazine of Art,* vol. xxxiii (1940), p. 255. By 1958 no. 166 had lost its Egyptian porch, but its tattered neighbor remained.

3. Wischnitzer, *Synagogue . . . ,* pp. 28–31; Agnes Addison Gilchrist, *William Strickland* (Philadelphia, 1950), pp. 62–63. For descriptions see *A Stranger's Guide . . . ,* p. 208; Thompson Scott, *Official Guidebook to Philadelphia* (Philadelphia, 1876), p. 266; Tatum, *Penn's . . . ,* p. 86.

4. Gilchrist, *Strickland . . . ,* pp. 91, 37 (respectively).

5. Robert C. Smith, "Two Centuries of Philadelphia Architecture," *Transactions of the American Philosophical Society,* vol. 43, pt. 1 (1953), fig. 25.

6. Roos, "The Egyptian Style . . . ," pp. 220–222; Claire W. Eckels, "The Egyptian Revival in America," *Archaeology,* iii (1950), p. 168; *First Annual Report of the Board of Inspectors of the Philadelphia County Prison* (Harrisburg, 1848); "The Philadelphia County Prison," *Pennsylvania Journal of Prison Discipline and Philanthropy,* iv (1849), pp. 138–142; *A Stranger's Guide . . . ,* pp. 243–244; Scott, *Official Guidebook . . . ,* p. 113; J. Thomas Scharf and Thompson Wescott, *History of Philadelphia* (Philadelphia, 1884), pp. 1836–1837; Tatum, *Penn's . . . ,* p. 179.

7. Glenn Brown, *The History of the United States Capitol* (Washington, 1900), p. 44; Talbot Hamlin, *Benjamin Henry Latrobe* (New York, 1955), p. 288.

8. Latrobe's other Egyptian work was his series of plans for the Monumental Church project of Richmond in 1812, in which he appears to have made several designs for a pyramid on a high base with various porticoes, some using the Doric order, and at least one employing columns very like those of the upper gallery in his Library plan. Although mentioned in Hamlin (*Latrobe,* p. 218), this problem has been discussed more thoroughly in an unpublished paper submitted to the Department of the History of Art at the University of Pennsylvania by Coleman Homsey, dated June 5, 1959. It brings to light four unpublished drawings owned by Mrs. Gamble Latrobe of Wilmington, Delaware. These are compared to two sketches for possibly the same project in the Ferdinand C. Latrobe Collection of the Maryland Historical Society in Balti-

more. Incidentally, another sketch of the same type among the Latrobe papers in the Library of Congress is of interest (plate 25).

Latrobe's son, Benjamin H., designed the Egyptian covered bridge at Harper's Ferry (plates 79–80). See Charles W. Snell, *Report on the History of the National Park Site of Harper's Ferry* (Harper's Ferry, n.d.), p. 40.

9. On page xvii of the "preface" to the *Description* . . . is a considerable discussion of this library and its importance.

10. [State of New Jersey] *Votes and Proceedings of the 57th General Assembly* (Woodbury, 1833), p. 151.

11. See Appendix III.

12. Roos, "The Egyptian Style," p. 222; Eckels, "The Egyptian Revival . . . ," p. 168; Joseph L. Munn, "Description of the Old Courthouse," *Essex County Courthouse* (Newark, 1908), unpaginated; *A History of the City of Newark,* 3 vols. (New York and Chicago, 1913), vol. II, pp. 619–621; *Newark Daily Advertiser,* v, 108 (1836); *ibid.,* v, 110 (1836); *ibid.,* VI, 252 (1838); *Ballou's . . . ,* VIII, 15 (1855), p. 232.

13. Richard G. Carrott, "The Architect of the Pennsylvania Fire Insurance Building," *JSAH,* xx, 3 (October, 1961), pp. 138–139. Facade doubled, 1900.

14. Metropolitan Museum of Art, Print Room, acc. no. 24.66.439.

15. *Ibid.,* acc. no. 24.66.1131.

16. *Ibid.,* acc. no. 24.66.438.

17. *Ibid.,* acc. no. 24.66.443. See Jacob Landy, *The Architecture of Minard Lafever* (New York, 1970), pp. 226, 285–286 for an intelligent clarification of much foolish speculation about this project.

18. Metropolitan Museum of Art, Print Room. acc. no. 24.66.799. A similar plan without the tower or the Egyptianisms was published as a Town and Davis project for a school in Henry Barnard, *School Architecture* (New York, 1848), p. 73.

19. *Ibid.,* acc. no. 24.66.1411.

20. *Philadelphia Public Ledger,* xxiv, 36 (1847), p. 2.

21. Roos, "The Egyptian Style," p. 221; Lancaster, "Oriental Forms . . . ," p. 184; Eckels, "The Egyptian Revival . . . ," p. 169; *Virginia Cavalcade,* II, 3 (1962).

22. Gilchrist, *Strickland,* pp. 37, 114. The somewhat severe aspect of this church is certainly "apt" for its Calvinist congregation. One has only to notice how close in feeling to it are certain slightly earlier Scottish churches such as the former Presbyterian edifice (now Arts Centre) at the crossing of King and Queen Streets, Aberdeen, built in 1831.

23. Records of the First Presbyterian Church of Nashville, Microfilm R-32, Joint University Library, Nashville, p. 5. The author is indebted to Dr. John Hoag for this material.

24. Joint University Library, Nashville, Microfilm R-46, pp. 7, 12.

25. See above chapter two, note 43. Vogel, in 1928, could only call the Egyptian Revival buildings he discussed, "Egyptianizing." It will be seen that this name has a somewhat different meaning in this essay. There are several Egyptianizing churches to be found significantly enough in Presbyterian Scotland from this period, e.g., John Steven's (1807–1850) St. Jude's Free Presbyterian Church in Glasgow of 1839.

26. See unpublished Historic American Buildings Survey report in the Carroll L. V. Meeks archives, Yale University.

27. Roos, "The Egyptian Style," p. 223; Jacob Landy, *Lafever,* pp. 225–235. There is no documentary proof of this attribution, but the tradition has been a long and strong one, and there is nothing in the style of the building which speaks out against this assertion. Prof. Landy feels the basic design was Lafever's, with some of the final details done by local builders. Originally the tower was topped by a copy of the Choragic Monument to Lysicrates which in turn ended in a high pagoda-like spire. In successive wind storms these latter two elements have been removed, leaving, successfully enough, a more "Egyptian" building.

28. This kind of Egyptianizing style is seen most notably in Europe in Gottlieb Bindesbøll's (1800–1856) Thorwaldsen Museum at Copenhagen (1839–1847) (plate 135). For the "Egyptian" impression it radiates, and for the place of the style in the primeval element of Romantic Classicism (note chapter two) see H. Bramsen, *Gottlieb Bindesbøll* (Copenhagen, 1959), pp. 158–159. Also Robert H. Rosenblum, *Transformations in Late Eighteenth Century Art* (Princeton, 1967), p. 148.

    A later form of Egyptianizing style would be the works of the Scotsman, Alexander "Greek" Thompson (1817–1875) whose extremely severe classicism imparts an almost Egyptian quality to such buildings as St. Vincent Street Church (1859) and Caledonia Road Free Church (1856–7, burned 1965), both in Glasgow. Curiously enough, among his Glaswegian commercial buildings, the "Grecian Building" (ca. 1865) is more "Egyptianizing" than his "Egyptian Halls" (1871–1873). He also built an atypically symmetrical villa with Egyptian columns at 200 Nithsdale Road in 1871. See Andrew McLaren Young and A. M. Deak, *Glasgow at a Glance* (Glasgow, 1965), items 53, 63, 64, 67, 68, and 70.

    Among American minor examples of this Egyptianizing aspect note 295 Washington Street, Store, Boston (ca. 1850) and T. U. Walter's bath house of 1846. More significant examples, however, are to be found throughout the United States in the second quarter of the century. One might cite, for instance, several designs by James H. Dakin (1808–1852) particularly his Bank of Louisville (1834) (frequently misattributed to Shryock), a drawing probably for the Planters and Merchants Bank of Mobile (1837), the reredos of the Government Street Presbyterian Church of Mobile (1836–1837), and a design for a prison (ca. 1845). All have some degree of batter and a feeling for massive but precise simplicity. See Arthur Scully, Jr., *James Dakin, Architect: His Career in New York and the South* (Baton Rouge, 1973).

29. *Philadelphia Public Ledger,* vol. XXIII, no. 66 (June 10, 1847).
30. A. L. Brandegee and E. H. Smith, *Farmington, the Village of Beautiful Homes* (Farmington, 1906); Julius Gay, "The Old Cemetery," *The Farmington Magazine,* I, 3 (1901), pp. 5–7.
31. For example, Philip Johnson's Nuclear Reactor at, ironically, Rehovot, Israel, of 1961. Even the ground plan seems like the Ptolemaic Temple of Horus at Edfou.

Iconography:
"L'Egypte Moralisée"

Undoubtedly a major reason for the use of the Egyptian style was iconographic. In the newly formed United States this Revival became a literal and specific *architecture parlante* in that it was employed in works which invited a symbolic treatment of their style. Whereas in Europe the Egyptian mode was seldom able to develop beyond its Rococo Picturesque phase of garden pavilions (as in the work of Soane, Kléber, Renard, and Dubois) and attention-attracting buildings (as P. F. Robinson's London Museum and Foulston's Devonport Library), American architects often conceived of the style in terms more far-reaching than those of variety and novelty. It is almost as if they carried the homilies of J. C. Loudon (which were mentioned throughout his *Architectural Magazine,* but best summed up in his *Encyclopaedia*[1]) on "fitness" and "expression" in architecture to their logical conclusion, i.e., their *in*clusion of symbolism. Indeed, an article in the *Architectural Magazine* speaking of the Egyptian style states, "Now this . . . should leave us to consider that the massive grandeur and beauty of Egyptian architecture do not claim our admiration on the mere grounds of solidity, scale, and elegance of individual parts; but on the *reasons* which legitimise these several distinctive features as *appropriate to the uses* of the building. . . ."[2] (The italics are the author's.)

In America A. J. Downing writing in 1842 was more explicit, "Whatever tends to heighten *expression of purpose* must grow out of some quality which connects itself *in the mind* with the use for which it is designed, and a genuine mode of increasing our admiration of any building is to render it *expressive of the purpose for which it is built.*"[3]

John Haviland, an architect particularly important for the Egyptian Revival, appears to have been especially aware of this attitude towards the meaning and fitness of a style. In 1822, writing of his Gothic designs for the Eastern State Penitentiary, he says, "The working drawings . . . will be furnished . . . to effect the desired convenience, strength, economy, and beauty of the design to its full intent and meaning." Somewhat later in this same journal he writes about the facade of the prison as follows, "On viewing the principal front, it will be seen with what success the designer has attempted to unite a simplicity of style with the *character the nature of the building required.*" He expresses the same feeling about an 1842 Classical Revival Lunatic Asylum he had planned, "[The architect has] condensed the most approved properties required in a building of this class—in compiling these requisites he has simply clothed it with that correct architectural *Expression* that the nature of the building . . . suggests, consistent with good taste and its Public Character."[4]

And it is also Haviland, the English-trained architect, who seems acutely aware of the uniqueness and difference of American architectural problems. It is as if he realized the possibilities implied in free and imaginative solutions to them. Such was the attitude which was to impart a new and deeper meaning to the Egyptian style. Writing in his journal in 1830 he expresses the idea that current English and European architectural publications are unsatisfactory for solutions to the very special building problems of America. He proposes to publish a magazine with "designs for Town and Country Villas, Churches, Court Houses, Jails, Banks, Monuments, with details, estimates, specifications, etc. . . . Several beautiful examples of Egyptian columns, and Entablatures will be given, taken from Napoleon's Egypt . . . for the use of the practical mechanic."[5] It is interesting to note that no other style or publication is mentioned.

Although there is a wide range of building types in the United States which employs the Egyptian style—domestic architecture being the notable exception—the most popular categories are cemetery gates and prisons. In both the roots appear to be iconographic. With the former the age-old funerary tradition of the pharaonic civilization comes to mind; and with the latter, the image of the land of eternal wisdom. The idea of the appropriateness of the Egyptian style for sepulchral monuments and gloomy tomb-like prison buildings seems obvious enough today. For the early nineteenth century, however, the rationalization was more complex, and, in a sense, different. In this chapter and the next the iconography of the style will be investigated.

In the case of cemetery gates and tombs, the idea of using the Egyptian style was, curiously enough, a radical one. It has been noted in chapter two, "Sources and Stimuli," that from the Renaissance on, obelisks and pyramids had been common currency in Western Europe as memorials and tombs. Actually these two forms were the most popular architectural motifs of the first Egyptian Revival which centered at Rome from the time of Hadrian until the triumph of Christianity. Certainly Hellenistic examples of the style should be considered as part of a Ptolemaic coda to, or survival of, the original inspiration. The Pyramid of Cestius and the Antinoüs obelisk[6] established prototypes for the Imperial era, to be revived again at the very outset of the Cinquecento: the obelisk appearing in the *Hypnerotomachia Polifili* of 1499, and the pyramid in Raphael's memorial chapel of the Chigi family in Santa Maria del Popolo. The strongest impetus for the use of both forms was subsequently supplied by Bernini. The continued exploitation of these motifs down until the nineteenth century held an echo of ancient Egypt, but they had become so familiar outside of the Nilotic ambiance that it can hardly be claimed they were solely the property of a pure Egyptian tradition. In any case, by 1800, the obelisk as a memorial,[7] and the pyramid as a tomb[8] had become accepted coin of the realm. Indeed, the former was so well entrenched even in the United States, that by 1833 when Mills designed his Washington National Monument (plates 33, 136) there were over a dozen obelisk memorials (vis-à-vis grave monuments) extant in this country.[9] Curiously enough, the Mills project, even with its Greek Doric peristyle, is, archeologically, the most "Egyptian" of them all with its huge shaft (Godefroy in 1815 had set a Roman column atop an Egyptian mastaba base in his Baltimore

Battle Monument) (plate 34) and its "correct" Egyptian door with cavetto cornice, batter motif, and winged orb. The doorway was "shaved off" and lowered in the 1884 completion campaign (plate 33). What is curious is that at this period a battle raged as to the appropriateness of the Egyptian style for cemeteries, a class certainly germane to memorials.

In spite of the funerary tradition of Egyptian forms, such as the obelisk and the pyramid, the more specific expressions of the style in cemeteries drew forth growls of disapproval. Thus, although there were at least fifteen Egyptian cemetery entrances built or designed between 1830 and 1850,[10] there was always an undercurrent of criticism as to the fitness of such pagan forms to Christian shrines.

James Gallier, Sr., the Irish-born architect who eventually settled in New Orleans, discussed the problem in 1836 in the *North American Review*. After speaking of the "aptness" of Grecian banking houses and Gothic prisons, he has the following to say about the Egyptian style at Mount Auburn Cemetery (1831) (plates 57, 58):

> The only remarkable display of this architecture is at the Mount Auburn Cemetery near Boston. Too much praise cannot be given to those who originated this design, and selected the place. . . . Its natural beauty is not equalled by that of the famous Campo Santo of Pisa . . . nor even Pere La Chaise [sic.]. . . . The most remarkable specimen of architecture, and that which seems to have diffused its character over the whole place, is the gateway. This is of Egyptian architecture; and, in imitation, the principal portion of the monuments are in the same style. We have, accordingly, a great number of pyramids and obelisks, and tombs supported by Egyptian columns, and fashioned in the heavy proportions of that style.
>
> It is very doubtful whether the Egyptian style is most appropriate to a Christian burial-place. It certainly has no connection with our religion. . . . Egyptian architecture reminds us of . . . paganism . . . solid, stupendous, and time-defying, we allow. . . . Now there is certainly no place . . . where it is more desirable that our religion should be present to the mind than

the cemetery which might be regarded as either the end of all things, or, on the other hand, as the gateway to a glorious immortality. . . .

We shall be told, perhaps, that very few persons have the same disagreeable associations with the Egyptian architecture that we have expressed; that its solid and heavy proportions become the tomb; and that it has the great merit of combining cheapness and durability. . . .

We are far from wishing that the architecture of Mount Auburn should be exclusively Gothic . . . nor would we exclude the obelisk, by far the most beautiful form of Egyptian architecture, whose stern and severe proportions seem to speak of eternal duration. . . ."[11]

Thus the pagan associations of the Egyptian style are suggested as an obstacle to its use.

In an illustrated book, part of a series of six on various rural cemeteries in America, Nehemiah Cleaveland wrote about Brooklyn's Green-Wood Cemetery with its simple portal in 1847. His text describes several obelisks, but for religious reasons the author is not sure of the propriety of using obelisks and pyramids as grave monuments. After quoting from the Gallier article, the author reproduces the consecration sermon of September 18th, 1845 in which the Rev. M. Farley condemns "heathen emblems," and then states "I do not so much object to the obelisk, Egyptian though it may be, and savouring, as some think, of an idolatrous homage of the sun; because its tall shaft with its pyramidal apex, losing itself in the air, and pointing to the sky, may seem to speak to the living of the heavenly home to which their departed friends have entered. But I prefer the cross, the symbol of Christ's victory over death and the grave. . . ."[12]

All this is the more interesting, because in a similar book from the same series entitled *Mount Auburn* there is a strong defense of the Egyptian style for funereal art:

As regards monuments or designs of the Egyptian style, for places of Christian interment, we are aware that an objection to them has been made, that they mark a period anterior to Christian civilization—a period of relative degradation and paganism; but it has ever been a pleasure with the thoughtful, to look beyond the actual *appearance* of a figure, to the right development of its original idea. The now mythologized doctrines of Egypt, seem to have been the original source of others more ennobling; and hieroglyphic discoveries have traced, and are tracing them far beyond the era of the pyramids, to an unknown limit, but to a pure, sacred, and divine source. When the art of writing was unknown, the primeval Egyptians resorted to symbols and emblems to express their faith; and these, as correctly interpreted, certainly present many sublime ideas in connection with those great truths which in an after age constituted the doctrines of "Christianity." Some of their sculptures and paintings were undoubtedly symbolical of the resurrection of the soul, a dread of the final judgment, and a belief in Omnipotent justice. The very *pyramidal shape,* of which the Egyptians were so fond, is believed to indicate an idea not disgraceful to a wholly Christian era. The reason why this form was chosen for their tombs, is declared by the learned Rosellini to have been, because it represented *the mountain,* the holy hill, the divine sanctuary cut in the mountain, i.e. *the tomb.* The *mountain* was sacred among the Egyptians as the abode of the dead, and was identical with the *sepulchre,* the nether world, and their *Amenti,* the future state. The image or figure of a hill became an emblem of *death,* and the pyramidal form, which initiated it, was a funereal symbol—an object consecrated to the abode of the departed. The "winged globe," which is carved on the gateway of Mount Auburn, is a most beautiful emblem of benign protection. In the form of a sun, with outstretched wings, it covers the facades of most Egyptian buildings, and was the primitive type of the divine wisdom—the universal Protector. We do not know of a more fitting emblem than this for the abode of the dead, which we may well suppose to be overshadowed with the protecting wings of Him who is the great author of our being—the "giver of life and death."[13]

Thus the defenders of the style evolved a kind of *Ovid Moralisé* for the appropriateness of its use. Indeed, the above quotation is certainly a more positive apologia than even the originators of the scheme saw fit to make; although the review of the publication of the Mount Auburn Dedication Address of 1831 by Joseph Story, the first president of the Mount Auburn Corporation, is not without interest. In part it says,

> The style is wanting, indeed, in those religious associations, which peculiarly recommend the Gothic for monumental purposes; but still it is remarkable for its originality of conception, massiveness, simplicity, and boldness of outline; and derived, as it is, from a land which is emphatically a monumental one, and one that may be regarded . . . as . . . one vast cemetery, it cannot be considered as out of keeping with associations of a place of burial. In regard to the design before us, it is in itself so beautiful, and has met with such general approval, that we conceive there can no longer be any reason for delaying to perpetuate it in the proper material. [The gateway was originally built of wood.][14]

In spite of the rumble of disapproval which eventually was to triumph by the 1850s, the respectability of the mode was certainly established through its use in the first rural cemetery of the land. This was the Mount Auburn Cemetery outside of Boston, in Cambridge, an important cultural center even in that day (plates 57, 58).

The rural cemetery movement was one more example of a new architectural problem which appeared in the early nineteenth century. Possibly *because* it was an innovation without the tyranny of specific traditional prototypes, it invited a "new style." Just as the show place for experimental and prophetic architecture in the later nineteenth century was to be at the various international expositions, so the new kinds of building types served as settings for unconventional and "progressive" architectural manifestations in the first half of the century. With the iconography of the Classical and Gothic firmly established, it would seem that the adventurous and inventive architect in seeking an original solution for such a new category would turn to a relatively unfamiliar style. Revivalism being the language of the time, the innovating dialect appears as Egyptian—

that fashion known, but not exploited heretofore. On the other hand, there would have to be, of course, some sort of rationale for it; some logical excuse. Thus, in this case, the Egyptian Revival answered ambivalent needs: those for originality, and connections with tradition.

In the first half of the century considerable increases in population resulted in the exhaustion of the customary burial spaces underneath church floors, and in small nearby graveyards. The solution was the rural cemetery. Large tracts of land at the outskirts were purchased by the cities themselves, as in the case of Rochester, New York, or by independent associations, as in the case of Mount Auburn; to be set aside as necropoleis. These were to serve a secondary purpose; that of providing pleasant wooded parks in which the citizens could stroll and enjoy the scenery.[15] This is a concept well-beloved by late eighteenth-century Romantics, and traceable to Rousseau's tomb on the Island of Poplars in the park at Ermenonville. In the case of the Mount Auburn Cemetery the Massachusetts Horticultural Society was the co-sponsor of the venture.

It is interesting to note that in 1825 the plan for the first rural cemetery was conceived and designed not by a professional architect, but by a medical doctor, Jacob Bigelow (1786–1879), who appears as concerned with the unhealthiness of burials under churches as he was with the growing crisis of finding enough space. He was Rumford Professor of Medicine at Harvard, and published *An American Medical Botany*, 2 vols. (Boston, 1818–1819), and *The Useful Arts Considered in Connection with the Applications of Science* (Boston, 1840). It was he who produced the plan for the gateway and lodges in the Egyptian style in 1831. The gate was of wood, as has been noted, painted in imitation of granite, to be replaced, when finances permitted, with a replica in stone. This was, in point of fact, accomplished in 1842. The archeological sources for his design, Bigelow stated, were "mostly taken from some of the best examples in Denderah and Karnac, in which the piers are vertical [vis-à-vis battered] and the curve of the cornice vertical in its lower half."[16] The relationship, by colonnades, of the lodges to the gate recalls Canina's Borghese Gardens entrance of 1824, discussed earlier (plates 47, 48).

Here, then, is another example of a revival architect's not slavishly copying any one monument, but reorganizing his material albeit rendering careful note of detail, so that the result is archeologically convincing. He must have studied the aforementioned models (plates 59, 60) in the Harvard copy of the *Description* . . . which had been presented by W. H. Eliot in 1822.[17] John Lowell who established the Lowell Lectures while sojourning at Thebes[18] was a member of the original Mount Auburn Corporation, a fact that may have provided an influence on Bigelow in his choice of the Egyptian style. In any case, the doctor-architect seems to have been cognizant of the enduring qualities of the mode, for he deems it important that the "size of the stones [the cap of the gateway was to be a monolith] and the solidity of the structure entitle it to a stability of a thousand years." It was to this monument, "the Pere La Chaise" of America, that other communities looked as a model, not only for a new type of burial ground, but also, often, for an architectural style.[19]

In 1836 the competition for the Laurel Hill Cemetery Gate in Philadelphia was held. This newly formed burying-ground-park was eventually to be given a Doric entry, but both William Strickland (1788–1854) and his former pupil, Thomas U. Walter (1804–1887) who between them have a prison, church, and two synagogues to their credit in the Egyptian style, proposed Egyptian gateways. Neither chose Bigelow's models, but, instead, used an even freer interpretation of the style, convincingly archeological, but untraceable to any specific ancient monument. Both are organized as wide, but shallow, tripartite forms, with Walter's (plate 64) rather chunky, broken elevation distinguished by the Piranesi-Egyptian corbel motif applied inside the main arch, while Strickland's (plate 63) lofty, but simpler arrangement of a single cornice over *distyle in antis* flanked by obelisks presents a particularly elegant effect.[20] (Small chambers were tucked in behind the facade of Walter's plan.)

In the same year the City of Rochester purchased land for an extensive rural cemetery to be called Mount Hope (plate 75).[21] By 1838, two years later, the plan had been laid out with an Egyptian gateway designed by John McConnell, a local architect.[22] This presented a third, and even freer, interpretation of the style. Whereas the three earlier examples might be called two-dimensional in that a sense of depth to the actual entrances is not apparent, the Mount Hope gateway takes on a triumphal "arch" aspect with its comparatively deep entry higher and longer than the flanking members which serve as porters' lodges. Torus moldings, cavetto cornices, and battered walls identify the style, as does the high lotus column which is placed on the roof over the entrance. This column was to support a sculptural group, never executed, of three angels. These would, presumably, help Christianize the effect of this pagan style.[23] Although the centralized accent of the entrance portico is balanced by heavy cornices, the whole effect is extremely plastic with the blockiness of the individual roof features emphasized. The sloping side roofs may serve as possible compliments to the cavetto and batter motifs. In any case, they have the unfortunate effect of further complicating the geometric forms of the entire propylaea. Especially confusing and peculiar is the column. An early description of Mount Hope states, "The necropolis is noted for its wild and picturesque scenery. . . . In natural beauty it vies with Mount Auburn or Greenwood, though, as yet, it contains but few monuments. . . . The gateway is of the Egyptian order, although the column which surmounts it, though pretty in itself, strikes us as being rather incongruous."[24] (To say the least.)

The next example appears to have been erected outside New Orleans by the Firemen's Charitable Association. Typically, the arboraeum aspect of the project was evoked by its name, Cypress Grove (plate 67). The Association was established in 1835,[25] and the first burial took place in 1837.[26] A description and engraving of it, as finished, was published in 1845.[27] It was apparently based on the Mount Auburn model with its single gate of vertical walls, a heavy reeded cornice, and porters' lodges at right angles to it in back. The architect was Frederick Wilkinson, who designed the gate in 1840.[28] In its unhappy current state without the imposing lintel, and decked out with garish signs, neon lights, and blinding white stucco, it presents a sorry survival, far removed from the impressive splendors of Denderah and Karnac.

Iconography

Not a rural cemetery, but certainly a manifestation of the same movement, was the rehabilitation of the Old Granary Burying Ground in Boston itself in 1840.[29] Isaiah Rogers (1800–1869), taking a cue from the nearby Cambridge example, designed a simple, single-entrance gate of dignity and finesse (plate 61). To such Egyptian motifs as the cavetto cornice, slightly battered sides, and winged orb, he added a symbolic winged hour-glass, and inverted torches (this last a Renaissance element from Desiderio by way of Algardi, Bernini, Pigalle, and Canova). So successful was this monument that it was duplicated with an iron fence divided by obelisks, by Rogers[30] for the Touro Cemetery in Newport, Rhode Island, in 1843 (plate 62).[31]

Although Rogers freely worked in his personal details, a greater independence of form is shown in Robert Cary Long, Jr.'s (1810–1849) Egyptian project of 1845 for Greenmount Cemetery in Baltimore (plate 65).[32] As in the case of Laurel Hill, another design was preferred. And likewise the portico is a tripartite arrangement. A central gate is flanked by obelisks which, in turn, are contained by lower, smaller entrances. Long's design is more inventive and compact in form than those of Strickland and Walter; its vocabulary includes battered walls, cavetto cornices, and a winged orb.

Hardly less famous or important to the movement than the Mount Auburn Cemetery, is the one in New Haven on Grove Street (plate 71). In point of fact, it was conceived of earlier than the former, the need being recognized by 1796 when James Hillhouse and thirty-one others purchased the first sector of the "New Burial Ground."[33] The area was divided into family plots which, in turn, were sold. This seems to have been the first such arrangement in the country.[34] The last burial in the old graveyard on the Green was in 1812,[35] and in 1821 that entire cemetery was removed and reburied in the Grove Street enclosure.[36] For over a decade it served merely as a utilitarian adjunct to the municipal services, but with the establishment of Mount Auburn, efforts at improving the graveyard began. In an 1833 essay appears the first intimation that it could be a park as a picturesque setting for contemplative recreation, "an ancient rural place of tombs possesses its attractions so long as we retain a particle of sentimental or antiquarian curiosity in our souls."[37] By 1840 a committee had been formed to raise money for the improvement of the burying ground, "to give to the place a becoming air of seclusion and solemnity."[38] In the committee report of 1839 not only had Mount Auburn been mentioned as an admirable model, but also the Egyptian style for the gate and wall had been decided upon with preliminary drawings of them on view. Although there is no indication in the records of the drawings or their architect, they may have been Henry Austin's (1804–1891) work, for on June 14, 1840 he was paid $50 for services rendered to the committee.[39] Besides Austin, however, the committee included the architect, Ithiel Town (1784–1844) and the sculptor, Hezekiah Augur (1791–1858). It appears that the latter is responsible for the design of the present surrounding wall and its corner piers executed in the Egyptian manner with batter and cavetto cornices.[40] Indeed, upon inspection, these betray a different masonry style than the gate itself; the former, also random ashlar brownstone being made with individual stones of greater irregularity and variety of size. The following year Augur resigned from the committee.[41]

With the surrounding wall practically completed except along Grove Street, a subcommittee was formed in 1844 to procure final plans for a gateway. Three were submitted by midsummer, the only architect identified being Henry Austin.[42] It was his plan that was accepted. The cornerstone ceremony took place July 18, 1845, and the entire work finished in 1848.[43] The only alteration the committee suggested to Austin's plan was the addition of the inscription, "The Dead Shall Be Raised." This was taken from the text of the funeral address delivered in 1821 upon the reburial of the transposed remains from the "ancient" burial ground on the Green. It is from 1 Corinthians 15:52, "In a moment, in the twinkling of an eye / At the last trump, the dead shall be raised." Thus, as at Mount Auburn with its scriptural message on the lintel ("Then Shall The Dust Return / To Earth As It Was, / And The Spirit Shall Return / Unto God Who Gave It."), and at Mount Hope with its three angels, here is another example of the Christianization of the pagan monument. And here, too, was a monument repeatedly admired in the committee reports and dedication speeches for its massive and enduring qualities which were to guard the dead for all time.

Indeed, the sense of the actual masonry, more pronounced here than in previous examples through the random ashlar with raised joints, is what especially evokes a sense of time-defying solidity and mass. Although Strickland employed the *distyle in antis* scheme in his Laurel Hill project, this is the first executed example for a cemetery gate. It is more "Egyptian" in its heaviness and massiveness, as well as its archeological "correctness" than the Strickland design. The pylon form, battered walls, papyrus-bud order, torus moldings, cavetto cornice, and winged orb are all Egyptian features readily accessible to Austin through Ithiel Town's copy of the *Description . . . ,* or one of the editions of Denon. The general model seems to stem from a reduced version of the portico of the temple at Esne (Denon, pl. 54, fig. 3; *Description . . . ,* A. vol. I, pl. 73), or that at Hermopolis Magna, especially the columns (*Description . . . ,* A. vol. IV, pl. 52) (plates 69, 70).

The progeny of the Grove Street gate includes two other New England examples. In 1848, the year of the completion of the New Haven prototype, Gen. H. A. S. Dearborn (1783–1851) designed and erected the gate for the Forest Hills Cemetery at Roxbury, Massachusetts (plate 72).[44] Although unhappily replaced by a Gothic structure in 1865, it apparently was built of wood, painted and sanded in imitation of brownstone, with the understanding that it, like Mount Auburn, should be replaced later in more durable stone. If the "ashlars" are regular, the general effect is that of a contracted Henry Austin gate with its heavy cavetto cornice, torus moldings, battered walls, and *distyle in antis.* In this case, however, the columns are of the open-papyrus order. But the familiar motif of the winged orb surmounting a Biblical inscription is there. ("Though I Walk Through The Valley of The Shadow of Death I Will Fear No Evil," and, verso, "I Am The Resurrection And The Life.") Although not having as wide a front, it is markedly similar to the New Haven entrance.

The earliest official guidebook for Forest Hills is noteworthy on two accounts. Written in 1855 at the end of the Revival, the author repeats the appropriateness theme,

There is a difference of opinion as to the propriety of using, as is much the custom, the Egyptian architecture about our burial places. A relic of paganism, it is by some estimated out of place in a Christian cemetery. But it is essentially the architecture of the grave. Its original examples are the monuments of remote ages, of buried cities, and of peoples. Imposing and somber in form, and mysterious in its remote origin, it seems peculiarly adapted to the abode of the dead, and its enduring character contrasts strongly and strangely with the brief life of mortals. Nor is it without the symbols of immortality, which the purer faith of the Christian can well appropriate and associate with the more sacred and divine promises of the gospel.

It is interesting to realize that the style evoked not only a whole funerary tradition, but also a sense of the enduring and the timeless, qualities deemed important for a Christian necropolis in its guardian role. Thus, not only are the connotations and characteristics of the mode presented, but the original argument against it and the answering rationalization are also reported. The tenacity of the objection must be one of the explanations for the abandonment of the style in the 1865 rebuilding.

The second point to be noted is that the source of the work is given as, "an ancient portico at Garsery on the Upper Nile." This statement can be traced to a short description of Forest Hills in a Boston guidebook published four years earlier, in which "Garsery" is placed "above the First Cataract." Neither Denon nor the *Description* . . . deals with sites above the First Cataract. The author has been unable to find any monument resembling the Forest Hills gateway in any site above that initial cataract. Nor does there seem to be a locality called "Garsery." As the 1851 guidebook also speaks of the gate as being "in imitation, essentially, of some of the gateways at Thebes and Denderah," a phrase familiar for the nearby Mount Auburn, but not applicable here; the absolute reliability of the source may be questioned, to say the least.

The other gateway dependent upon the Grove Street example is the one for the Old Burying Ground at Farmington, Connecticut (plate 73), which was discussed in the previous chapter. Neither the architect nor the date can be completely ascertained, but local tradition places it ca. 1850 as a copy of the Austin work,[45] and the stiff provincialism of the excessively simplified style would point to a local carpenter's hand.

The two remaining cemetery gateways, at the end of the period, are of the propylaea type, as at Mount Hope. Both were in Philadelphia. The Mikveh Israel Burial Ground entrance of ca. 1845 was a simple rectangular building of stuccoed brick with wood and sheet metal trim (plate 76). It had slightly battered walls, angular cavetto cornices, diminutive torus moldings, a false door (a favorite Old Kingdom device for similarly shaped mastabas), and Egyptian pier fence posts with alternate open and closed lotus iron pickets between (a Ptolemaic motif found on chapel and curtain walls at Esne and Edfou). There were the familiar Revival motifs of corbelled arches, in this instance, blind, and a stepped roof line. There was not only economy of material, but also of style in the simplified mass of the building with its sparse ornamentation and severely smooth surfaces. The use of the stucco, the color scheme, and the special treatment of the blind corbel motifs point more closely than anything else to its being a somewhat less mature work in the mode, by the unidentified architect of another Philadelphia building, the Odd Fellows Hall of 1846 (plate 77) discussed in the preceding chapter.

It would seem that the cemetery entrance, for an old urban, rather than new rural graveyard, must have been part of a rehabilitation program similar to Rogers' contribution to the Old Granary Burying Ground in the early 1840s. As Strickland's 1822 Egyptian synagogue, not demolished until 1860,[46] was also for the Mikveh Israel congregation, a precedence for the style had been established over and above the usual funerary one. But the much more evolved cemetery entrance is certainly not in the same fashion as the Strickland house. Thus on the basis of circumstantial and stylistic evidence, a date of about 1845 would not seem out of order.

Curiously enough, when the Philadelphia Odd Fellows proposed to lay out their cemetery in 1849, they chose as architect for its gateway one whose style in the Egyptian vocabulary was quite removed from that of their recently-built Hall at Third and Brown Streets. The thirty-acre rural cemetery on Islington Lane was embellished by a massive brownstone propylaea from a design of Stephen Decatur Button (1803–1897) of the Philadelphia firm of Hoxie and Button (plate 74).[47] It was a particularly heavy and plastic example with the usual characteristics of torus molding, cavetto cornice, batter, and a winged orb. A tripartite arrangement, it had wings as entrances for carriages to the right, and pedestrians to the left. The center block is two stories high, and raised further upon a podium. A recessed portico, *distyle in antis,* leads to a chapel. Above this are the offices and gatekeeper's quarters. Most curious is the eighty-one foot high tower on top near the facade in the form of a great Egyptian pier. Thus the formal arrangement is that of a Christian church of the single-tower facade type, making unnecessary the usual urge to supply some sort of Christianizing detail. The complicated breaking up of the individual parts into various projections, recessions, depths, and levels combined with the heavy richness of the large winged orb and the open-papyrus order columns betrays the work of an architect far removed, in the originality of his synthesis, from the archeological inspirations, and their more Romantic Classical expressions of a decade earlier.[48]

Thus, over a twenty-year period three basic types of cemetery entrances were executed in the Egyptian style: the simple, single gate (as at Mount Auburn, Old Granary, Touro, and Cypress Grove) based on Ptolemaic works at Denderah and Karnac; the tripartite, "two-dimensional" arrangements, freely employing Egyptian forms and details in a new manner (as in the projects of Strickland, Walter, Long, and Austin); and finally, the propylaea type, handled in the most inventive manner of all, using non-Egyptian forms with applied archeological details (Mount Hope, Mikveh Israel and Odd Fellows).[49]

Throughout the period there was the dilemma of the appropriateness of the style. On the one hand, there was the ancient funerary tradition of Egypt, as well as the connotation of enduring timelessness; while, on the other, was the association of the style with the most pagan and idolatrous of the ancient civilizations. Therefore,

Iconography

the architects designing in the mode took extra precautions to indicate the Christian purpose of their work. In this case, in the newest of nations, building in new forms for new purposes, the oldest of styles was used as the initial inspiration.

Notes:

CHAPTER 5

1. J. C. Loudon, *Encyclopaedia of Cottage, Farm, and Villa Architecture* (London, 1846), pp. 1106, 1112–1113.
2. "M.", "On the Effect which should result to Architecture in regard to Design and Arrangement from the general Introduction of Iron in the Construction of Buildings," *Architectural Magazine,* IV (1837), p. 278.
3. A. J. Downing, *Cottage Residences* (New York, 1842), p. 11.
4. University of Pennsylvania, Haviland Papers, MS, vol. I, pp. 13, 53; vol. VI, p. 103 (respectively).
5. *Ibid,* vol. VI, p. 103.
6. William S. Heckscher, "Bernini's Elephant and Obelisk," *Art Bulletin,* XXXIX, 3 (1947), p. 156, n. 4.
7. Alfred Neumeyer, "Monuments to 'Genius' in German Classicism," *Journal of the Warburg and Courtauld Institutes,* II (1938–1939), pp. 159–163. Also Robert Alexander, "The Public Memorial and Godefroy's Battle Monument," *JSAH,* XVII, 1 (1958), pp. 19–24; abridged in Robert Alexander, *The Architecture of Maximilian Godefroy* (Baltimore, 1974), pp. 101–112.
8. Fritz Novotny, *Painting and Sculpture in Europe, 1780–1880* (Baltimore, 1960), p. 212.
9. See Appendix I. The most important of these was the Bunker('s) Hill Monument, although the earliest may well have been the memorial obelisk celebrating the 300th anniversary of the discovery of America by Columbus (i.e., 1792). It was built in Baltimore by the Chevalier d' Anmour, the French consul in that city. Claire W. Eckels, "The Egyptian Revival . . .," pp. 165–166. In any case, Mills had already written approvingly of the use of both the obelisk and pyramid in his "Essay on Architectural Monuments," *Analectic Magazine,* vol. XV, new series, vol. I (April, 1820), p. 320.
10. The first Egyptian Revival cemetery gate in this county appears to be Maximilian Godefroy's at the Westminster Cemetery, Fayette and Green Streets, Baltimore (ca. 1813–1815) (plate 56). It is also known as the First Presbyterian Churchyard. Alexander, *Godefroy . . . ,* p. 86. Paired pillars with cavetto cornices have engaged obelisks with winged hourglass motifs. The real impetus, however, was provided by Dr. Jacob Bigelow's Mount Auburn gate in Cambridge, Massachusetts, of 1831.
11. James Gallier, "American Architecture," *North American Review,* XLIII, 93 (1836), pp. 356–384. Condensed as, "On the Rise, Progress, and present State of Architecture in North America," *Architectural Magazine,* IV (1837), pp. 3–9.

12. Nehemiah Cleaveland, *Green-Wood* (New York, 1847), p. 71.

13. C. W. Walter, *Mount Auburn* (New York, 1850), pp. 17–20.

14. "Rural Cemeteries," *North American Review,* LIII, 113 (1842), pp. 385–412, especially pp. 391–392.

15. Walter, *Mount Auburn,* p. 10; Prof. Dennison Olmstead, "Dedication Speech for the Grove Street Burying Ground," *New Haven Palladium,* V, 169 (1845).

16. Jacob Bigelow, *A History of the Cemetery of Mount Auburn* (Boston and Cambridge, 1860), pp. 26, 141.

17. "The Zodiac of Denderah," *North American Review,* XVIII, 41 (1823), pp. 233–242, p. 236 n.

18. Edward Everett, *A Memoir of Mr. John Lowell, Jr.* (Boston, 1840).

19. Descriptions of the Mount Auburn Cemetery, of the period, besides those already mentioned: "Description of the Mount Auburn Cemetery," *North American Review,* XXXIII, 73 (1831), pp. 397–406; Gen. H. A. S. Dearborn, *Report to the Massachusetts Horticultural Society* (Boston, 1832); *The Picturesque Pocket Companion and Visiter's* [sic] *Guide through Mount Auburn* (Boston, 1843); also accounts in the *Boston Daily Advertiser* (September 9, 1851), and the *Boston Atlas* (September 16, 1851). Note also, Bainbridge Bunting and Robert H. Nylander, *Survey of Architectural History in Cambridge. Report Four: Old Cambridge* (Cambridge, 1973), pp. 69–72.

20. Agnes A. Gilchrist, *William Strickland* (Philadelphia, 1950), p. 91. Both original drawings at Library Company of Philadelphia.

21. William Mill Butter and George S. Crittenden, *The Semi-Centennial Souvenir of Rochester* (Rochester, 1884), p. 65.

22. J. M. Parker, *Rochester,* (Rochester, 1884), p. 227.

23. See engraving dated 1838 by Alexander Anderson, Metropolitan Museum of Art, acc. no. 24.66.1690.

24. *Ballou's . . . ,* IX, 24 (1855), pp. 376–377.

25. [B. M. Norman] *Norman's New Orleans and Environs* (New Orleans, 1845), p. 115.

26. *The Picayune's Guide to New Orleans* (New Orleans, 1904), p. 152.

27. [Norman], *Norman's New Orleans . . . ,* p. 105.

28. Samuel Wilson, Jr., *A Guide to the Architecture of New Orleans 1699–1959* (New York, 1959), p. 48.

29. Clay Lancaster, "Oriental Forms in American Architecture," *Art Bulletin,* XXIX, 3 (1947), p. 184. Although Solomon Willard may have been the stonecutter, he was not the architect as claimed by Eckels. C. W. Eckels, "The Egyptian Revival . . . ," p. 166.

30. *Newport Herald of the Times* (July 14, 1842), p. 3.

31. Inscription over the gateway: "Erected 5603 [1843] from a bequest made by Abraham Touro."

32. Richard H. Howland and E. P. Spencer, *The Architecture of Baltimore* (Baltimore, 1953), pp. 98, 132.

33. A. N. Skinner, *Report Relative to the New Haven Burial Ground* (New Haven, 1839), p. 42; also pp. 16, 18.

34. E. Strong Bartlett, *Historical Sketches of New Haven* (New Haven, 1897), p. 42.

35. Henry H. Townshend, *The Grove Street Cemetery* (New Haven, 1948), p. 15.

36. [City of New Haven] *Proceedings of the City of New Haven in the Removal of Monuments from its Ancient Burying-Ground, and in the Opening of a new Ground for Burial* (New Haven, 1822), pp. 12–13.

37. B. Edwards, *The Burial Ground at New Haven* (New Haven, 1833), p. 201.

38. New Haven Colony Historical Society, Records of the Joint Committee on the New Burying Ground in New Haven [hereafter: "NHCHS, Records . . ."], *Circular*, 1840.

39. NHCHS, Records . . . , p. 10.

40. *Ibid.,* p. 16. For Augur's sculptural work see George H. Hamilton, "Hezekiah Augur; An American Sculptor" (unpublished M.A. thesis, Yale University). For his design of wall and corner pylons, see Townshend, *The Grove Street . . . ,* p. 23.

41. Townshend, *ibid.,* p. 23. Hamilton ("Augur," p. 65) suggests this was for financial reasons.

42. NHCHS, Records . . . , pp. 53–55. Austin also executed a Gothic design. Both are in the architect's sketch book which is in the Rare Book Room of Yale University Library.

43. *New Haven Palladium,* v, 169 (July 19, 1845); Skinner, *Report . . . ,* p. 28.

44. *Forest Hills Cemetery* (Roxbury, 1855), pp. 78–80, 118–123; [I. S. Homans] *Sketches of Boston* (Boston, 1851), pp. 6, 8; Nathaniel B. Shurtleff, *Topographical and Historical Description of Boston* (Boston, 1871), p. 268. Gen. Dearborn (1783–1851) is not to be confused with another Dearborn closely associated with Mount Auburn, *viz.* Nathaniel Dearborn (1786–1852), author of *A Concise History of and Guide through Mount Auburn* (Boston, 1843) and a guidebook for Boston, *Boston Notions* (Boston, 1848). The General exhibited early interest in Egypt in his publication, *A Memoir on the Commerce and Navigation of the Black Sea, and the Trade and Maritime Geography of Turkey and Egypt* (Boston, 1819). He also wrote *Letters on the Internal Improvements and Commerce of the West* (Boston, 1839); and in 1847 he was nominated vice-presidential candidate on the Native American ticket with Zachary Taylor as running mate. (Taylor won the 1848 election, but on the Whig ticket with Millard Fillmore.)

45. Julius Gay, "The Old Cemetery," *The Farmington Magazine,* I, 3 (1901), pp. 507.

46. Thompson Scott, *Official Guidebook to Philadelphia* (Philadelphia, 1876), p. 266.

47. "Biographical Sketch of Stephen Decatur Button," *American Architect and Building News* (July 16, 1892), p. 37; *The Stranger's Guide to Philadelphia* (Philadelphia, 1854), pp. 228–229; *Ballou's . . . ,* X, 2 (1856), p. 25; Scott, *Official Guidebook . . . ,* p. 313; George B. Tatum, *Penn's . . . ,* p. 87.

48. It is on the basis of this ponderous decor that Rachel Wischnitzer had once attributed the Philadelphia Crown Street Synagogue, built in the same year, to Button. Later she found documentary evidence which placed it in the *oeuvre* of Thomas U. Walter. Rachel Wischnitzer, "Thomas U. Walter's Crown Street Synagogue," *JSAH,* XIII, 4 (1954), pp. 29–31.

49. As for European examples, two existed in Germany, neither for a rural cemetery, however: Friedrich Weinbrenner's pylon gate, with Gothic openings, at Karlsruhe of 1798. (See Rachel Wischnitzer, "The Egyptian Revival in Synagogue Architecture," *Publications of the American Jewish Historical Society,* XLI, 104 [1951–1952], pp. 61–75; and Bandhauer's Rosslau Cemetery portal of 1828. (*Marburger Jahrbuch für Kunstwissenschaft,* IV [1928], pp. 48–49).

   In England the rural cemetery movement took place shortly after that of the United States with the building of Kensal Green in 1833 (*The Penny Magazine,* III, 150 [1834], pp. 297–300), which by 1837 had an Egyptian monument in the mausoleum of General Ducraux by John Cusworth. N. Pevsner, *London, Except the Cities of London and Westminster* (Harmondsworth, 1952), p. 302; H. Honour, "The Egyptian Taste," *Connoisseur,* CXXXV, 546 (1955), p. 246. As for the use of the Egyptian style in such matters, the first occasion seems to be at Sheffield with S. Worth's Sharrow Vale of 1836 ("Domestic Notices," *Architectural Magazine,* IV [1837], pp. 81–82); followed by Stephen Geary's Highgate Catacomb of 1838 with Christianizing crosses inserted as metopes in the cavetto cornices (plates 53, 54). (He was also the architect of London's first gin palace: Nikolaus Pevsner, *London, Except the Cities of London and Westminster* [Harmondsworth, 1952], p. 363.) The cemetery was not consecrated until May, 1839, however. *The Penny Magazine,* VIII, 495 (1839), pp. 489–490. A year later, in 1840, saw the gateway which was to annoy Pugin, the Abney Park Cemetery at Stoke Newington by William Hosking (Pevsner, *London . . . ,* p. 429) (plate 52).

   For a discussion of the late-eighteenth-century background leading up to the creation of that Parisian "rural" cemetery so admired by Americans during this period, see Jacques de Caso, "'Venies ad tumulos.

Respice Sepulcra', Remarques sur Boullée et l'architecture funéraire à l'age des Lumières," *Revue de l'Art*, 32 (1976), pp. 15–22.

An Egyptian gate to a park, but not a cemetery-park, is to be found as far afield as Russia at Tsarskoe Selo (plate 55). Built 1827–1832 by the English architect Adam Menelaws (Menelas) (d. 1831), it is in the form of a double pylon with cast-iron bas-reliefs. (Cf. I. K. Brunel's plan for Clifton Suspension Bridge of 1831 discussed in next chapter [plate 78].) See G. H. Hamilton, *Art and Architecture of Russia* (Baltimore, 1954), pp. 222, 256, pl. 167A; also see E. S. Gladkova, L. V. Emina, V. V. Lemus, *Gorod Pushkin* (Leningrad, 1961), pp. 28–29, 144; date of 1828 given on p. 167. Originally the gate led to neo-Gothic ruins. (Catherine the Great's pyramid to three of her dogs built there in 1781 by Charles Cameron is discussed on p. 126 of the Leningrad publication.) Without the funerary association this gate must be considered purely as an example of the Picturesque. Of course Menelaws' English background can explain his being chosen as architect for this late picturesque garden concept, and the idea for it is certainly not out of keeping with what was already there, Cameron's pyramid and other "fabricks"; but perhaps the taste for Egyptianisms received further impetus from a newly erected structure in a recently accessioned Romanoff possession, i.e., the somewhat heavy-featured Egyptian temple and small bridge by Jacub Kubicki (1758–1833) near the Belvedere Palace in Łaziénski Park, Warsaw (Ujazdów) of ca. 1820. Menelaws was far more archeologically correct in his handling of the style than his Polish cohort. Jerzy Z. Lozinski and Adam Miłøbedz, *Guide to the Architecture of Poland* (Warsaw, 1967), p. 258. Yet another example of the mode in the area: the emphatically Egyptian cast-iron suspension bridge of 1826 in St. Petersburg by Kristianovich and Treter. See note 17, chapter 6.

Iconography Continued: "Science and Knowledge; Sublimity and Mysticism"

It has been noted in the last chapter that the Egyptian style was a popular one for the special kind of new funerary architecture of the nineteenth century. In this chapter the mode will be discussed in its non-sepulchral connotations.

In principle, therefore, this section will treat with meanings other than funereal that the style evoked—why it was appropriate, or fitting, for specific types of structures. It has already been noted that there was a strong feeling for the picturesque which continued from the eighteenth century, exemplified in some domestic architecture as well as in those buildings which were referred to as a "commercial picturesque" class. What should not be overlooked, however, is the fact that architects and critics of the period were well aware of such qualities of the Egyptian style and its civilization as durability, wisdom and mystery. Thus, as we have seen in chapter four, if a contemporary description of the Isaac P. Morris and Company(?) Building in Philadelphia of 1847 (plates 43, 46) underlines the picturesque property of its cast-iron front in the Egyptian style by citing it with approbation as being "curious and imposing," it must also be realized that the company sold iron, and that the purveyors of this "new" building material wished to call attention to its solidity and durability, attractive characteristics commonly associated with the Egyptian style.[1] Similarly, Haviland's discreet use of the fashion for an insurance company building (plates 42, 44–45), although lending a Foulstonian touch to Independence Square, and certainly executed in a more subtle manner than that at Devonport, must have implied, once more, a feeling of solid, enduring dependability as would be associated with the agelessness of still-extant Egyptian temples.[2] The persistence of such a public image for an insurance company continues to this day in the example of a familiar trademark using the Rock of Gibraltar.

As has been noted earlier, there was a distinct feeling for not simply the great *age* of Egyptian monuments, but, in addition, their strength, solidity and immortality in the face of the ravages of time. Thus there was the concept that, in order to be viewed today, the structures of this extreme antiquity must have been built in such a manner as to last for eternity. Applicable words and phrases of the architectural critics of the period are legion; among them, "But what a contrast do the frail memorials of our times present to those *immortal* structures . . ."; "the ingenious and *solid manner* [of the architecture]"; "grandeur and *solidity*"; "*solid*, stupendous, and *time-defying*"; "for the purpose of *durability*." (The italics are the author's.) America's first architectural historian speaks of "massiveness [in Egyptian architecture] . . . conveying ideas of *duration and strength*." And even if the poetry is bad, the sentiment is clearly expressed in an item from the American edition of the *Penny Magazine*, "And time has not begun to overthrow / Those temples, palaces, and piles stupendous / Of which the very ruins are tremendous. . . ."[3] Indeed, one wonders how many early nineteenth-century architectural critics knew the Arab proverb, "All things are afraid of Time, but Time is afraid of the Pyramids." The attitude, then was that great age did not imply fragility, but, rather, dependable and reassuring permanence. This is in contrast to the eighteenth-century idea that ruins showed time's, or nature's, inevitable conquest over the petty works of man.

With sentiments such as these it is possible to conceive of the style's being also appropriate to structures of the new technology, e.g., railroad stations (plate 38–41) and suspension bridges (plates 78, 82, 83). The iron horse had not yet proved itself as a safe mode of transportation with its infernal and terrifying steam, smoke, and speed. It is tempting to speculate on the idea of reassuring the timid traveller by garbing the architecture of the railroad in a "dependable" style, as in the project for Kennington [Kensington] Common in London (1836) (plate 38),[4] and in the stations at Pittsfield, Massachusetts (plate 41),[5] and New Bedford (plates 39–40)[6] (both in 1840, the latter by Russell Warren).[7] The fact remains, however, that for the public, at least, these buildings also evoked a sense of the commercial picturesque, the fashionable or stylish.[8]

Undoubtedly the same may be said of the use of the style for suspension bridges. There was, of course, a need for confidence in the safety of such convenience, as may be noted in a contemporary civil engineering text, "Doubts have been expressed as to the durability of [suspension bridges, but they are] unfounded."[9] In a letter to the *Architectural Magazine* in 1834 the suggestion is made, "Egyptian architecture is peculiarly applicable to engineering work, particularly for the piers, etc. of suspension bridges." As this was written in comment upon E. Trotman's extolling Egyptian architecture as being of "simple and sullen grandeur," well-fitted to the sites chosen for it, and visually effective from a distance, the appreciation of formal aesthetics should be remarked in this connection.[10] Isambard Kingdom Brunel's Clifton Bridge design of 1831, in England, is the first example of an "Egyptian" suspension bridge (plate 78).[11] It was for the second competition, and was the one finally accepted although unfortunately never carried out in its entirety.[12] It involved a "scheme having a span of 702 feet, and low pylons erected high up on the rocks in an Egyptian style, they were to be encased in metal, decorated with hieroglyphics showing the various stages in the building of the bridge, and topped by sphinxes."[13] Although Brunel wrote officially of the project in terms of the grandeur of the style's being appropriate to the grandeur of the site,[14] an idea presaging Trotman's (see above); privately, in a letter to his brother-in-law, he discussed it in terms of "taste": "Well, I have to say that of all the wonderful feats I have performed since I have been in this part of the world, I think yesterday I performed the most wonderful—I produced unanimity amongst fifteen men who were all quarrelling about the most ticklish subject—

taste—The Egyptian thing I brought down was quite extravagantly admired by *all*. . . ." (Brunel's italics.)[15]

But over and above this question of "taste" there were functional reasons for the use of the style, notably the adaptability of the pylon form and that of the Egyptian pier to suspension techniques. The combination of modern technology and ancient Egypt became an international motif for bridges with notable examples from Italy[16] to Russia.[17]

The most obvious instance of this in America was the railroad bridge over the Potomac at Harper's Ferry (plates 79, 80). A Civil War casualty, it was a complicated structure with a complicated history.[18] The original structure (1835–1837), planned by Benjamin H. Latrobe (the son of the Capitol architect who had designed the Egyptian Revival Library of Congress) and Louis Wernwag, proceeded in a straight line of seven wooden spans across the river to the village. It was a covered bridge built in the Egyptian style with its stepped attic over the entrance not unlike the later New Bedford depot. In 1841 the Harper's Ferry end was remodelled to provide an upstream entrance in addition to the original one. The new part of the resultant Y-shape was realized in a much more Egyptian manner than the earlier part, with markedly battered walls and heavy cavetto cornices not only at the entrances but along the sides as well. The straight section of the "Y" was rebuilt in 1851 by Wendel Bollman, an assistant of the younger Latrobe's, as an iron suspension bridge with Egyptian piers.

Among other North American examples of suspension bridges employing Egyptian forms (piers, obelisks, or pylons): Charles Ellet, Jr.'s Fairmount Bridge near Philadelphia of 1841; E. W. Serrell's Lewiston Suspension Bridge over the Niagara River of 1850–1851; the Covington-Newport Bridge over the Licking River in Kentucky, 1854; J. A. Roebling's double-level wonder at Niagara Falls, 1852–1854 (plate 83); a bridge over the St. John River in New Brunswick of ca. 1853, probably by E. W. Serrell (plate 82); and another Canadian example over the Desjardin Canal at Hamilton of about 1855.[19]

One more type under the classification of new technological construction is also related to bodies of water, i.e., reservoirs and pumping stations (plates 85–88). Significantly enough, while aqueducts inspire thoughts of Roman engineering, the control, storage and distribution of water somehow seem more related to the Nile with its yearly life-giving floods, and the land's irrigation-based economy. These aspects of the ancient Nilotic civilization were known since antiquity, and revived through the various hydraulic projects of Mohammed Ali who hired European engineers to deal with these problems in the 1830s.[20] With river god prototypes in sculpture and painting harking back to the famous Hellenistic example of the *Nile,* the evocation of Egypt in such matters would seem a familiar, if loose, relationship. But the use of the style is more closely due to the wish to avoid such rigid prototypes as those of Greece, Rome, or even the Middle Ages. Egyptian was particularly tempting in that its very stylistic features are ones, as in the case of suspension bridges, which are especially suited to the engineering demands of the projects themselves. The walls of a reservoir have to be thickest at the bottom and may gradually taper upwards. This is admirably expressed by the batter design of an Egyptian wall. With "few and bold details" the drab, utilitarian plan for such a structure becomes an object of "taste," grandeur, or even sublimity with a modicum of expense. The transformation is accomplished in this manner with the appeal to economy—a familiar reason for using the style.[21]

The first such example is surprisingly early: the Albany Reservoir, built in 1811, demolished in 1875 (plate 85).[22] It must be admitted that this structure, described in *Ballou's* as "peculiar," is basically within the picturesque tradition, combining, as it does, an Egyptian retaining wall, and a Moorish pump house. There are single gateways on each of the four sides of the former with heavy cavetto cornices and strongly accented batters. Matching Egyptian tower-piers with the same features mark the four corners. In the center is the mosque-like pumping building with its bulbous dome surmounted by a spire and the Muslim crescent. This picturesque eclectic arrangement, a dozen years earlier than Foulston's Devonport, is probably more in the tradition of such archeologically vague confections as

Robert Lugar's design of a few years before for "an Egyptian or Turk-ish pavilion" (plate 84).[23] In the latter, the English architect places such Egyptian motifs as battered doors and windows, cavetto cornices, and winged orbs among otherwise Muslim features as the minaret, bulbous dome, crescent, and cusped arch. But Lugar considered these all of the same vocabulary, believing "Egyptian" and "Turkish" to be one. Indeed, as we have seen, he states, "mixing one style with the other, as is frequently seen, makes us think but little of the mind that thus invades every idea of common sense." The Albany Reservoir may thus also be considered as a part of the commercial picturesque use of the style.

Much more archeological, however, is the distributing reservoir of New York City's Croton system supervised in its erection by the young James Renwick, Jr.[24] (plates 86, 87). It was completed in 1842. In plan and elevation it is markedly similar to the Egyptian portion of the Albany example, although considerably more monumentaliz-ing with massive corner towers, and imposing center pylons on three of the four sides. In extent and impressiveness it is on a scale, even, of ancient Egyptian monuments, covering two entire city blocks, rising to over fifty feet in height, and having a capacity of twenty-one million gallons. While J. B. Jervis, the probable designer, must surely have known of the prototype at Albany, his home state's cap-itol, and appears to have used it as his initial model, he has, besides vastly increasing its size, eliminated any non-Egyptian detail, and even within that vocabulary made his structure more severely sim-plified employing undecorated horizontal torus moldings and cavetto cornices along with a marked batter to the walls. Admired in its day for the solid durability and finish of its masonry, the reservoir was also referred to as an ancient temple, "an illustration of what art and science can accomplish."[25]

It must surely have been the influence of this important engineer-ing feat which provided the inspiration for the style of the engine house of the Northern Liberties and Spring Garden Water Works in Philadelphia two years later (1844–1845) (plate 88).[26] No actual res-ervoir is involved, only the pumping station; thus there is no demand for massive Egyptian walls. The building itself, a rather nondescript Georgian with dormers and a Villa-style ventilator, has applied to it a weirdly monumentalizing Egyptian doorway, battered and with a cavetto cornice. The necessity for a high chimney stack, an element decidedly foreign to the original inspiration for the house, has been solved strikingly by designing the stack as a huge water plant, a papyrus-bud column. Thus, while the New York reservoir is an example of understood and appreciated Egyptian Revival characteristics, the earlier and later water works are within the realm of picturesque eclecticism. Here again, in this category, the style was employed for a new building type which called for original and free solutions. The faint iconographic echoes as to the reason for the style were bolstered by practical and functional ones of greater import.[27]

But if "new" science called forth the use of Egyptian motifs as the "respectable" garb of stability, durability, and dependability; "old" science conjured up the style as the symbol of ancient secrets and knowledge. Egypt was indeed the Land of Wisdom and Mystery,[28] and had been considered so since the time of Herodotus. More recently the Comte de Caylus in his great reevaluative work, *Receuil d'antiquités . . . ,* had given an added impetus to the idea, referring to the Egyptians as "ce peuple sage et éclaire."[29] Thus the style was thought appropriate for synagogues, fraternal lodges, libraries, medical colleges, courthouses and prisons, all of which had connotations of mystery and/or wisdom in their backgrounds.

Two synagogues of Philadelphia (plates 90, 91), Strickland's Mikveh Israel (1822–1825) and Walter's Beth Israel (1849), already discussed in the earlier chapter on formal development, and the two Jewish cemetery gates discussed in the preceding chapter (plates 62, 76), were in the Egyptian style.[30] Certainly there was a quest for a Jewish Synagogue style. In the effort to establish the extreme antiquity of Judaism, the Egyptian Revival was more attractive and serviceable than Mediaeval or Classical revivals. And although eventually rejected because of the unhappy associations of the Children of Israel with the Land of Pharaoh, there may be something to be said for the initial logic of this choice. Indeed, as Mrs. Tuthill points out, the Jews learned architecture in Egypt, having worked at brick-making and labored to build for Pharaoh.[31] She further suggests that because of this, the Biblical descriptions of the Temple of Solomon recall, more than anything else, Egyptian architecture. Thus to the evocation of great age inherent in the style, is added the argument of plausibility.

Curiously enough, the three Egyptian Revival churches (plates 93–96), Lafever's First Presbyterian at Sag Harbor (1843), the Essex, Connecticut, First Baptist (ca. 1845), and Strickland's Downtown Presbyterian in Nashville (1848–1851), as well as A. J. Davis' Egyptian Revival church design, all may owe their style to a related idea.[32] As the sects involved were Calvinistic, the severe simplicity of the mode would certainly have been attractive. But it should also be noted that these cults wished to return to the primitive form of Christianity emphasizing the original teachings of Christ, rejecting later interpolations. Thus there was the emphasis on the Bible, both New *and* Old Testaments. Therefore, if the Jewish style of architecture could be conceived of as Egyptian, it would have a particular appeal for these "primitive" Christian sects.

A more definite connection with ancient Egypt, however, is to be found in that civilization's status as the Land of Mystery. Pevsner and Lang have ably demonstrated this as well as the background for Egypt's being the source of hermetic mysteries. The Free-Masonic movement owes its dependence upon Egyptian rites and emblems to Cagliostro and Carl Friedrich Köppen who introduced these embellishments in Paris and Berlin in the seventies and eighties of the eighteenth century. However fraudulent these ideas and rituals were, they became part of the standard operating procedure of Freemasonry, and by 1791 they were ennobled through the publication of Mozart's *Magic Flute*.[33] While stage sets of the period were usually generalized flats that could serve in a variety of productions, Karl F. von Schinkel designed, in 1815, an Egyptian-flavored group specifically for the Berlin production, which became the standard scenic interpretation of that opera.[34] Curiously enough, there were few Egyptian style Masonic lodges before the mid-nineteenth century.

Pevsner and Lang mention one at Boston, Lincolnshire, of 1860–1863 which they claim derives from Denon. In the United States there were none prior to the Civil War, although there was certainly an awareness of the movement's dependence upon ancient Egypt. In 1835 John Fellows, an American mason, published an elaborately detailed account of the sources of Freemasonry as originating in Egypt, and passing to eighteenth-century England by way of Pythagoras and his influence on the druids (!)[35] It was the milder, less politically insidious fraternal order known as the Odd Fellows which used the style for its hall in Philadelphia (plate 77) at Third and Brown Streets (dedicated 1846, completed 1847), and for its cemetery gate (plate 74) of 1849.[36] Considering themselves a collateral branch of Freemasonry, and therefore equally dependent from ancient Egypt, "the mistress of learning, land of mystery," the Odd Fellows emphasized the fraternal aspects of the order which combined occult secrets and ritual from the Land of the Nile with the benefit systems of Mediaeval guilds.[37] Thus their motto, "Friendship, Love, and Truth." It is interesting to note from the detailed contemporary newspaper account of the opening of the "splendid hall" that it was not only thoroughly Egyptian in its exterior, but also decorated on the inside with paintings of "Egyptian architecture, pillars and colonnades, the whole surmounted by the emblem of immortality—the winged globe." The artist, referred to as both "Hielge" and "Heilge," also executed views of Egyptian scenery. To make the effect even more complete, the furnishings and woodwork were in the Egyptian style as well.[38]

But if the inspiration of hermetic mysteries provided the most thorough example of Egyptian Revival, the evocation of the Land of Wisdom motivated the greater number of architectural works. One of the most important centers of learning in classical antiquity was at Alexandria with its famed library. The fact that this was a Hellenistic city seems not to have bothered those nineteenth-century architects who wished to allude to the library and its great scholarly heritage. From Greek, Roman and Mediaeval writers, down to the *savants* of the *Description . . . ,* there are frequent references to the famous library as a center of knowledge. Indeed the Greeks themselves looked to Egypt for learning.[39] This kind of association, then, becomes an explanation for Latrobe's plan for the Library of Congress (1808) (plate 97), the first American example of the mode, and Foulston's Devonport Library in England (1823) (plates 14, 15). A later example would be Thomas S. Stewart's plan for a Library and Conservatory (plate 101) which apparently was never executed but, because of its verticalizing proportions and its similarity in treatment to the same architect's Medical College of Virginia (see below) of 1844, must have been done in the mid 1840s.[40] By extension, the associational symbolism applies as well to such other repositories and settings of learning and knowledge as Robert Cary Long, Jr.'s initial plan for the Baltimore City and County Records Office (1836) (plate 100),[41] A. J. Davis' project for a school (plate 98) and for the New York City Lyceum (or Athenaeum) of Natural History (1835) (plate 99), as well as his much later Long Island Historical Society Library plan of 1878. European parallels of this sort include Carl Haller von Hallerstein's 1815 project for the Munich Glyptothek (plate 24),[42] and Michael Gottlieb Bindesbøll's Egyptianizing Thorwaldsen Museum in Copenhagen (1838–1847) (plate 135).[43] This kind of association can even be found exemplified as far afield as South Africa where the style was used for two educational institutions, South Africa College by James Adamson and G. G. Lewis in Cape Town (1839–1840) and the Gymnasium (in the Continental European sense of the term) at Paarl (1858); although the later case is less archeologically inspired.[44]

A singularly interesting example of this type of symbolic use of the style is found in a relatively late work, Thomas S. Stewart's Medical College of Virginia (1844–1845) (plates 102–103).[45] This was the original building for that institution, and is still used today having been restored in the 1930s (by H. Coleman Baskerville) when the interior was completely remodelled, although again in the Egyptian style. It is an example of the vertical phase of the movement. (Discussed in the earlier chapter on formal aspects.) As to the "meaning" of the style, however, the building takes on added interest in that not only is it a place of learning and knowledge—reason enough to evoke the Land of Wisdom—but it is a center of medical science. The ancient writers constantly referred not only to the great medical skill of the Egyptians, but also to the highly developed specialization of their physicians.[46] Indeed, from the Renaissance on in Western Europe there is a strong tradition of learning the power of healing from ancient Egypt.[47] Furthermore, that father of genealogy, Manetho, handed down in various fragments by Josephus, Africanus and Eusebius, mentions the son of Menes (the first pharaoh), Athothis, as being a learned physician who wrote anatomical works. In his account of the Third Dynasty, there is one of his rare references to a non-royal personage, the Egyptian Asclepios, Imuthes, who had great medical skill and "was the inventor of the art of building . . . and devoted attention to writing as well."[48] Thus, the first recorded architect of all time was a brilliant physician and wise scholar. Assuredly, with associations such as these, the Egyptian would seem appropriate as a style for a school of medicine.

The most significant group of buildings whose meaning relates to the idea of the Land of Wisdom and Mystery is that which comes under the heading of courthouses and prisons (plates 104–114, 116–134). At this juncture, it may be deemed sufficient to indicate the range of monuments, mentioning their sources, and to suggest the possible iconography for their style. It should be noted that in the earliest case in America the style was applied solely to a prison, later to a courthouse *and* prison complex, and eventually to a courthouse alone. Thus, the primary association is that of penal architecture.

To understand the complexities of penitentiary building in the early nineteenth century it is necessary to realize that this was an era of humanitarian reform. That attitude had produced a wave of countless societies devoted to public education, women's rights, abolition of slavery, temperance, improvement of working conditions, as well as penal reform. In the case of this last there were two opposing attitudes both predicated on regenerating the criminal rather than merely punishing him. One was known as the "silent system," in force at Sing-Sing and Auburn in New York. The Auburn system was based upon the prisoners' working together in shops, but having separate cells at night. The prime commandment was to maintain silence, for there was to be no contact between the convicts by word or signal at any time. The other method, known as the "separate system," was practiced with eminent success in Pennsylvania. Prisoners remained in separate cells the entire time, working, eating, and sleeping there. With both these regimes, each criminal was to contemplate his sins, and, it was hoped, repent and firmly resolve to amend his ways. Also the contagion of criminal ideas between inmates could be eliminated. The proponents of the Auburn system claimed that theirs was the more economical, while those of the Pennsylvania system maintained that theirs was the more efficient and practical in the regeneration of inmates.[49]

Although it has been demonstrated that prisons existed prior to the nineteenth century which were either radial, as in the case of the Maison de Force at Ghent (1773), or cellular, as in Clement XI's Silentium (1704); the fact remains that John Haviland's Eastern State Penitentiary (1823–1828) was the first prison built which was not only radial and cellular, but also, more important, it was the first one in which each of the cells could be observed from one central point.[50] In this manner control and inspection could be exercised in the most efficient way, while the principles of regeneration and reform could be served through maintenance of the separate and silent discipline.

The Eastern State Penitentiary was a Gothic pile whose style evoked the wish of the commissioners (1820), "The exterior of a solitary prison should exhibit as much as possible great strength and convey to the mind a cheerless blank indicative of the misery which awaits the unhappy being who enters within its walls."[51] In other words, at the outset of the prison reform movement, the architecture which was to house the various experiments was not new or different. The emotive image that was to be called forth was the traditional one of gloominess.

The success of the Philadelphia penitentiary and its progressive new system was so resounding that in 1832 a committee from the New Jersey Legislature which was "to procure plans for the new state prison in Trenton" chose the Pennsylvania jail as its model and Havi-

land was the architect.[52] The structure (plates 106, 107, 110), however, was to be more economically built than the earlier one. Haviland
proposed to achieve this in two ways. The first was that the prison
was to be half-radial in plan (plate 106), thus of fewer units and
smaller; and, secondly, its style was to be Egyptian, which would,
therefore, involve fewer and bolder decorative details than a Gothic
or Classical vocabulary.

As his focal point Haviland concentrates his ponderous Egyptian
decoration on the entrance block (plate 110), a colonnaded portico
between pairs of pylons seen in profile. The subdivisions may be read
as quoining. At first glance this seems a somewhat peculiar, if inventive, arrangement of Egyptian motifs. Usually Egyptian architecture
is thought of as a series of frontal pylons with doorways at their centers. Haviland's principle, however, is not without organizational
prototypes as may be seen from a side view of Medinet Abou (plate
108) reproduced in a plate in the *Description . . . ,*[53] a publication
which it is known Haviland owned.[54] A closer source, pointed out by
Frank Roos, is from Volume I of the *Antiquités* of the same publication from which the architect has used the squat papyrus-bud columns including their abacus hieroglyphics as shown in the so-called
Temple du Sud (plate 109). He has recreated the elevation of the
porch, adding two more columns, but retaining the hieroglyphic frieze
and the raised podium. In the second story he has placed battered
windows on each side of a corbelled arch. The latter motif, as we have
seen, is one which appears on and off throughout the revival, but
which does not seem to have antique Egyptian prototypes. It probably evolved from one of Piranesi's Egyptian fireplace designs of
1769 (plate 1).

Through these two examples, Haviland was to exert the first influence of American architecture abroad. Significantly enough, it was
the practicality and hygiene of these prisons which most attracted
the penal inspectors from France and England at first, and Prussia,
Russia, and Belgium later. As the New Jersey building was the more
recent, improved one, it served as a model for many European prisons
commencing with England's Pentonville in 1840. Ironically, these
Haviland buildings were more influential by far in Europe than in

America, where after a brief eclipse the Auburn plan was eventually to triumph. But whereas the Europeans were impressed by the central control point, running water, ventilation, water closets, and heating system of the architect's Trenton design, the Egyptian style was not adopted for export. The tradition of royal castles used as prisons remained too strongly imbedded in the minds of those reformers for them to deviate from mediaeval prototypes.[55]

It was a different story in this country. At the beginning, of course, as has been noted, there still remained a feeling for the aptness of the "gloomy" Gothic castellated style, as at Eastern State Penitentiary. But the momentum of reform seems to have swept before it these sentiments as to appropriateness. For if the Trenton building was Egyptian for economy's sake, it would also seem to evoke a new sense of enlightened justice and eternal wisdom. It was this eternal wisdom which Egyptian architecture may be said to recall. Writing to the New Jersey commissioners in 1832, Haviland stated *re* the economy and aptness of the style, "[I am] avoiding useless ornament, and employing only members best calculated to present the desired properties of the institution."[56] The "members" which were to impart "the desired properties" of the prison were the Egyptian details.

In 1835 when the City of New York held a competition for its proposed Halls of Justice and House of Detention, John Haviland's Egyptian design (plates 111–114, 116–123, 127, 128) was awarded first premium.[57] The reasons given were that it was the most apt, the most economical, and the most practical of all the submitted plans. The architectural committee of the city had been particularly impressed with the New Jersey State Penitentiary, having set down in its minutes detailed sketches and descriptions not only of the practical aspects, but also the style. In New York, as the jail unit was a House of Detention, the inspection and control were not as important as at the New Jersey prison. For this reason, and because of the limitations of space, Haviland abandoned his radial system. What is significant, however, is that he maintained the Egyptian style for this later complex. A contemporary newspaper account of the exhibition of the competing models remarks, after paying special tribute to Haviland's design, "we think it ought to enter as an essential principle into all

115

edifices of this description, that, considering the coercive purposes to which they are to be appropriated, their exterior aspect should be pleasing, and, at the same time, imposing to the eye—not gloomy and terrific as they too often are, as if intended to remind us ever of the depravity of our species and the degraded condition to which it may be reduced. If our own opinion only were to be consulted we should certainly prefer an admixture of the Gothic and Egyptian styles."

It is small wonder that the committee chose Haviland's project if the above sentiments reflected their own. Certainly these were more "progressive" and "American" feelings than were exhibited by the recently arrived (from England) William Ross who prefixed his design in the castellated style with a quotation from Scott's *Marmion,* "The battered towers, the Donjon Keep / The loop-hole grates where captives weep / The blanking walls that 'round it sweep."

The sublime nature of this reforming mission had been suggested in Haviland's master, James Elmes' characterization of Egyptian architecture as structures of "immortality," "sacred solemnity," and "awesome grandeur." This may explain his own design of a courthouse and jail unit in the Egyptian style in 1805 which Haviland must have known. It is also revealing to note Elmes' article on prisons in his *Dictionary of the Fine Arts,* in which he cites as the most significant contemporary example of penal architecture Ledoux's prison at Aix (ca. 1784) (plate 104), "in a style which savours somewhat of that of the Egyptians, but simple in its details."[58]

Actually, Haviland's first design for the Halls of Justice, the "Tombs," as the complex later came to be nicknamed, does not appear to have been overtly Egyptian, but rather, a classicizing one of a colonnade between pavilions with battered walls. The arrangement of these end pavilions recalls somewhat the Aix prison. Behind this unaccented long facade were to be the various municipal offices, while at the rear of the city block, in a separate courtyard, was to be the House of Detention.

In his final plan (plate 111), however, he changed the style to Egyptian, thickened the frontal block, and projected forward a heavy portico, placing to the rear three wings each with its separate function of: debtors' prison, court room, and police offices. Although this type

116

of projecting portico does not have an exact archeological prototype from ancient Egypt, Haviland may have been aware of A. J. Davis' similar arrangement for an Egyptian entrance gate exhibited in 1828 (plate 115). Behind the portico runs a great three-aisled hall bisecting the building and leading into the most important area of the complex, the courtroom. This particular arrangement echoes the not unsimilar function of the hypostyle hall in ancient Egyptian temples such as Denderah (plate 113) which led from a portico to the innermost sanctum sanctorum.

The E-shape of the plan recalls similar public buildings by James Gandon in Dublin, the Four Courts (1776–1796) and the Custom House (1781–1791)[59]; and earlier, J.-H. Mansart's south wing of Versailles of the 1680s, as well as Ferdinand Fuga's Palazzo Corsini in Rome (1729–1732). The interior sequence of raised projecting portico, hall and rotunda is similar to Robert Adam's Kedleston Hall (ca. 1761). This longitudinal section was published in the *Vitruvius Britannicus,* IV of 1767, surely known in Elmes' office. Actually the plan is a reworking of a traditional academic one reduced and adapted to practical limits. Its origin may be related to projects by Ledoux, Boullée and Durand, using a domed Greek cross within a hollow square. Von Schinkel's Altes Museum in Berlin (1824–1828) is an early example of a break from the rigid geometry of this formula. Haviland carries this further, incorporating such features as secondary entrances to the ends of the frontal block which had been used by Ledoux at the Governor's Palace at Aix (ca. 1784), and in Richard Elsam's plan for, significantly enough, a county courthouse and prison published in 1824.[60] A more striking comparison may be made between the "Tombs" and a Russian government building directly outside the Kremlin walls (plate 126). Now demolished, it was known through various early nineteenth-century engravings. The number of columns in the Moscow building is the more usual six, instead of four, while the order seems to be Doric. But the projecting portico appears raised, and topped by a stepped attic—one step more than the "Tombs," perhaps as a result of the proportional difference caused by the greater number of columns. The lateral entrances, while not Egyptian pylons, are inside of arches just as the

117

"Tombs" counterparts are likewise recessed. It should be kept in mind that Haviland came to America after a year's sojourn with his uncle in Russia. It is known that he owned a four-volume set of books entitled *Russia in Miniature,* as well as the volume of the *Penny Magazine* in which was republished a view of this building.[61]

A second strikingly similar arrangement in both plan and elevation can be found in William Stark's (d. 1813) Justiciary Courthouses of 1807–1814 in Glasgow. Significantly enough, the original plan called for municipal offices and a prison also to be housed in the building. The order is Doric but there are the raised projecting portico with both pediment and attic as well as the end pavilions with side entrances.[62]

Haviland's plan of the second component of the complex, the House of Detention, is the severely regimented cell block, in itself a hollow rectangle. After the radial system, this allows for maximum visual control, and is actually better adapted to the small area involved.

Haviland designed Newark's Essex County Courthouse (plates 129–131) later in 1836.[63] It is a law court building, and has no attached prison, but it is interesting to note that the style is here employed in a building which is purely judicial and governmental in purpose. Compared to the two earlier examples, this is a rectangular structure with a recessed portico. Its effect is thus less plastic in its elevation, and more vertical in its proportions. The elaborate open-papyrus order of the columns reflects an elegance and loftiness not so pronounced in the Trenton and New York examples which used squatter Egyptian prototypes.

The architect's last Egyptian prison design was done in 1842 for the Dauphin County Jail in Pennsylvania.[64] Both this and a Gothic design were rejected in favor of his Romanesque project.

There are other Egyptian prisons designed by architects of the time. In 1835, Thomas U. Walter completed his Moyamensing Prison (plate 105) in Philadelphia (whose main building was a more verticalizing Gothic than that of the Eastern State) by placing an Egyptian Debtors' Prison alongside it.[65] This was simply a small rectangular cell block and keeper's quarters with an Egyptian front consisting of three battered openings. The center one was interrupted in its lower half by a recessed portico of two papyrus columns *in antis* recalling in truncated form Haviland's Trenton entrance of a few years earlier. In any case, Walter used the same model for his order.[66] In this combination of Gothic and Egyptian he seems to have taken to heart the advice of the unnamed newspaper correspondent who had suggested this eclectic scheme in that same year when reporting on the "Tombs" competition (see above). The entire complex has, alas, been recently demolished.

But if Walter's pylon front seems impoverished in detail, and awkward in concept, there are other more effective examples in the style. Such is the former Sixth Precinct Police Station in New Orleans with its freely designed palm columns which cannot be traced to any archeological publication's plates or descriptions, and its weird frieze of simplified metopes and cavetto triglyphs. Perhaps there is an echo of the reeded cavetto cornices of Ptolemaic temples. The entrance motif of a gateway between stubby columns upon a high podium may owe something to the Trenton portal. But the more obvious model is the New York "Tombs" in the order of the columns, the attic arrangement, the rhythm of the frieze, and the precisely executed winged orb (plate 128).[67]

In 1857–1858 John Francis Rague built the last of these Egyptian prisons as the Dubuque City Jail.[68] Rague was not without talent or training. A student of Minard Lafever in New York City until 1831, he later designed the old state houses of Illinois and Iowa, as well as buildings at the University of Wisconsin. In 1857 he was given the commission to design the jail which he did in the Egyptian style. The building was described as being modelled on the New York "Tombs." In view of the visual evidence, this is surprising, for the two buildings seem hardly related at all. In point of fact, the "Egyptian-ness" of the Dubuque building is somewhat less than obvious. It is curious that Rague, an architect not without sophistication, would have executed such a work with Egyptian motifs so stiff and abstracted. But it should be remembered that in 1831, when he left New York, there were few Egyptian Revival buildings extant in this country, although

A. J. Davis appears to have held an exhibit of some of his Egyptian designs in 1828 at the National Academy of Design.[69] This was the year the monumental twenty-one-volume Napoleonic work on Egypt was completed, but perhaps no set of this publication had gotten to Iowa by 1857. The same may have been true of the Denon work of which the American edition contained few plates, in any case. There were, however, engravings of the "Tombs" which appeared from time to time in the various illustrated news magazines of the day. In February of 1857 a view of this New York building (plate 134) appeared in *Ballou's Pictorial Drawing-Room Companion*.[70] The generalized handling of the column capitals, the deemphasized winged orbs and the strongly accented lintels are characteristics both the engraving and the Dubuque building have in common. It is also interesting to note the strange and most unarcheological arrangement that Rague has used for the bottoms of the columns. In the engraving, an unconsciously Mannerist vision of an Egyptian pile in a blizzard, this section is covered with snow so that the "artichoke" form is not noticeable. The Iowa architect, therefore, has merely repeated the design on the upper part of the base, as a zig-zag motif below, rather than following the logic of botanical morphology (plates 132, 133).

The use of the Egyptian style in prisons may be equated with the ideas of the reforming humanitarians of the 1830s. In rejecting the traditional prison architecture of the mother country, Americans turned to that style which must have symbolized, for them, values beyond mere man-manipulated ones—those of the incorruptible righteousness of law and order. At the same time there was the implication of reform rather than degradation and depravity. While ancient Egyptian structures eternally guarded hope for men in the next world, Egyptian Revival buildings temporarily guarded men for hope in this world. This was indeed a sublime mission, for the style would seem to evoke a sense of severe and just law, as timeless and enduring as the most ancient of man-made structures; structures of a civilization more antique than the Antique; and a civilization which was that of the Land of Mystery and Wisdom. And it was this eternal wisdom which was symbolized by a style of architecture which, like the objective justice of law, was clear, orderly, awesome, and immortal.[71]

Thus, this group of Egyptian Revival prisons and courthouses may be considered not merely as a collection of isolated curiosities, but, rather, as part of a tradition extending from the time of Ledoux to the American Civil War. The sources of the style have been noted as being freely interpreted by the various architects. It might be said that they employed an archeologically correct vocabulary within a creatively inventive grammar. When applied to prison architecture, the Egyptian Revival style not only presented an imposing effect economically, but also became, for a time, the architecture symbolic of enlightened prison discipline—a discipline which was utilitarian as well as humanitarian.

In sum, therefore, the iconography of the Egyptian Revival, the symbological reasoning for its use, is not always clear-cut. But the fact remains that the architects and patrons, if not the general public, were of an educated and intellectual milieu which surely understood certain associative values implicit in the style. If added to these, the freedom from architectural rules of proportion, taste, and form are taken into consideration along with the concept that certain functional benefits might be exploited, the attractiveness of the mode may be understood. For the earlier nineteenth century, Egyptian motifs conjured up feelings of immortal durability and age-old hydro-technology, applicable for the "new" sciences of civil engineering; ancient knowledge and mysterious wisdom for the "old" sciences of learning and medicine; hermetic ritual and mystic drama for the occult sciences of secret orders; severe simplicity and primitive stoicism for fundamental religions; and timeless objectivity for sublime values,[72] both human and humane.

Notes:

CHAPTER 6

1. "Cast iron is one of the most valuable building materials, owing to its great strength, hardness and durability. . . ." D. H. Mahan, *Civil Engineering,* 5th edition (New York, 1851), p. 55.

2. Richard G. Carrott, "The Architect of the Pennsylvania Fire Insurance Building," *JSAH,* 20 (October, 1961), pp. 138–139.

3. James Elmes, *A General and Bibliographical Dictionary of the Fine Arts* (London, 1826), unpaginated, article on "Architecture"; Thomas Hope, *An Historical Essay on Architecture* (London, 1835), p. 11; Quatremère de Quincy, "On Order in Architecture," *Architectural Magazine,* III (1836), p. 443; James Gallier, "On the Rise, Progress and Present State of Architecture in North America," *Architectural Magazine,* IV (1837), p. 16; "M.", "On the Effect which should result to Architecture in regard to Design and Arrangement, from the general Introduction of Iron in the Construction of Buildings," *Architectural Magazine,* IV (1837), p. 278; C. Tuthill, *History of Architecture* (New York, 1844), p. 333; [The Society for the Diffusion of Useful Knowledge], *The Penny Magazine,* American Edition, III, 54 (1833), p. 48 (respectively).

4. W. J. Short, "Design for a termination to a Railway," *Architectural Magazine,* III (1836), pp. 219–224. Although the author speaks of the character of the style as being "expressive of strength" (p. 223), he seems more interested in its being "a pleasant object when viewed from the high turnpike [and the] immediate neighbourhood . . . possessing architectural beauty . . . [and] elegance and grandeur," (pp. 219–220). The most important reason for the style, however, seems to be the economy with which it can be built (p. 220).

5. George Bliss, *Memoir of the Western Railroad* (Springfield, 1863), pp. 59, 65, 88; J. E. A. Smith, *History of Pittsfield, 1800–1876* (Springfield, 1876), p. 543; *Sixth Annual Report of the Directors of the Western Railroad Corporation* (Boston, 1841), p. 8; *Ballou's Pictorial Drawing-Room Companion,* VIII (1855), p. 264. The building, it seems, sported among its Egyptian characteristics a winged orb (which does not appear in the *Ballou's . . .* engraving), *North American Review,* LIII, 113 (1842), p. 411.

   Along the same railroad line (the Worcester and Western Railroad) there were three smaller stations in the Egyptian style (all having undoubtedly been built 1840–1845); *viz.* Brighton, the first regular station out of Boston, a diminutive "Tombs" design with three battered windows flanking each side of a central recessed entrance porch *distyle in antis* topped by a stepped attic; Chester Factories, Massachusetts, consisting of two pylons connected by a colonnade with a large square pylon (upper story serving as a water tank) in the center; and State Line (near West Stockbridge) Massachusetts which also sported a large square pylon *cum* water tower. See William Guild, *A Chart and Description of the Boston and Worcester and Western Railroads* (Boston, 1847), pp. 13, 57, 67, 71. My thanks to Mr. James Massey for bringing this publication to my attention.

6. C. L. V. Meeks, *The Railroad Station* (New Haven, 1956), p. 54; *Boston Atlas* (July 3, 1840), "Shawmut"; *Ballou's* . . . x, 10 (1856), p. 153; Samuel Rodman, *Diary* (New Bedford, 1927), pp. 203–205; Robert Alexander, "Russell Warren" (unpublished M. A. thesis, Institute of Fine Arts, New York University, 1952), pp. 149–151.

7. In this same category one might even note the Egyptian style Beam Engine of 1845 at the York Railway Museum in England.

8. The diarist, Samuel Rodman, during a short stop-over, felt "a curiosity" about the Pittsfield building (so much so that he missed his train as it continued westward). This may have been, however, simply because the style was the same as that of his own town's depot, i.e., New Bedford. Rodman, *Diary,* p. 229.

9. Mahan, *Engineering,* p. 258.

10. *Architectural Magazine,* I (1834), p. 246; E. Trotman, "On the Extent to which the Elementary Forms of Classic Architecture are, from their Nature and Origin, Fixed or Arbitrary," *Architectural Magazine,* I (1834), p. 20.

11. Actually an earlier example of a suspension construction in the Egyptian style was the Brighton Chain Pier of 1823 by Captain (later Sir) Samuel Brown. *Penny Magazine,* II, 105 (1833), pp. 454, 456. It was a series of four iron pylons advanced into the sea. In 1896 it was washed away. (Plate 81)

12. Eric de Maré, *The Bridges of Britain* (London, 1954), pp. 173–174; Brunel submitted plans in other styles, e.g., castellated Gothic. Nikolaus Pevsner, *North Somerset and Bristol* (Harmondsworth, 1958), p. 423.

13. Cf. the hieroglyphics on the 1836 base to the Luxor obelisk in the Place de la Concorde.

14. "The Egyptian gateways [of the Clifton Bridge] will be on a scale equal to those of some of the largest of the ancient models." *Penny Magazine,* I, 10 (1832), pp. 84–85.

15. de Maré, *The Bridges . . . ,* p. 174. Of course, Robert Stephenson and Francis Thompson's Britannia Tubular Bridge over the Menai Strait (Wales) of 1846–1850 was considered Egyptian in its day, but this was perhaps due as much to its Egyptianizing forms (echoing Brunel's Clifton Bridge) as to its guardian Nubian lions.

16. There still exists near Anzio at Minturno a handsome example whose heavy masonry consists of four paired lotus columns with sphinxes in front of each. The marked Brunelesque effect and the date (1832) leads one to suspect an English engineer. See Karl Baedeker, *Southern Italy and Sicily* (Leipzig, 1896), p. 18. I am grateful to Dr. William MacDonald of Smith College for having pointed out this monument to me.

17. Egyptian suspension bridge entirely of iron with three [sic.] columns *in antis* near St. Petersburg, ca. 1830. H.-R. Hitchcock, *Architecture, XIX and XX Centuries* (Baltimore, 1958), p. 58. Also Andrei L. Punin, *Provest' O Leningradskikh Mostakh* (Leningrad, 1971), pp. 65–67.

18. Charles W. Snell, *Report on the History of the National Park Site of Harper's Ferry* (Harper's Ferry, n.d.), pp. 40–42; Edward Hungerford, *The Story of the Baltimore and Ohio Railroad,* 2 vols. (London and New York, 1928), vol. I, pp. 147–152; David B. Steinman and S. R. Watson, *Bridges and their Builders* (New York, 1941), p. 162.

19. *Gleason's . . . ,* I, 15 (1851), p. 232; George B. Tatum, *Penn's Great Town* (Philadelphia, 1961), pp. 63, 170; John F. Lewis, *The Redemption of the Lower Schuylkill* (Philadelphia, 1924), p. 43; Steinman and Watson, *Bridges . . . ,* pp. 209–210; *Ballou's . . . ,* IX, 18 (1855), p. 273; David B. Steinman, *The Builders of the Bridge* (New York, 1945), pp. 176, 189; *Ballou's . . . ,* VIII, 24 (1855), p. 369; Richard S. Kirby and P. G. Laurson, *The Early Years of Modern Civil Engineering* (New Haven, 1932), p. 155; Steinman and Watson, *Bridges . . . ,* p. 212; Steinman, *The Builders . . . ,* pp. 167–189; *Gleason's . . . ,* VII, 9 (1854), p. 136; *Ballou's . . . ,* XII, 17 (1857), p. 264 (respectively). The elder Roebling considered an emphatic Egyptian style for the Brooklyn Bridge (1857). See David McCullough, *The Great Bridge* (New York, 1972), p. 218.

20. John L. Stephens, *Incidents of Travel* (New York, 1837); Eliot Warburton, *The Cross and the Crescent* (New York, 1845). Actually Belzoni originally came to Egypt to interest Mohammed Ali in an irrigation pump he had invented; this in 1815 before his archeological career.

21. Mahan, *Engineering,* p. 146. Bralle's public fountain in Paris of 1808 (see chapter one) surely can*not* be considered a prototype for this idea.

22. *Ballou's . . . ,* X, 8 (1856), p. 120; Cuyler Reynolds, *Albany Chronicles* (Albany, 1906), pp. 392, 410.

23. Robert Lugar, *Architectural Sketches for Cottages, Rural Dwellings, and Villas* (London, 1805), pp. 25, 10, pl. XXXVI.

24. John B. Jervis, *Description of the Croton Aqueduct* (New York, 1843); F. B. Tower, *Illustrations of the Croton Aqueduct* (New York and London, 1843); Philip Hone, *Diary* (New York, 1927), pp. 570, 610, 624; *Gleason's . . . ,* VII, 25 (1854), p. 400; E. Peter Humphrey, "The Churches of James Renwick, Jr." (unpublished M.A. thesis, Institute of Fine Arts, New York University, 1942), p. 139; Metropolitan Museum of Art,

Renwick Sketchbook, acc. no. 35.23.23, pp. 6, 20, 27, 28, 30.

Actually, as Ms. Selma Rattner (who is currently working on Renwick) has pointed out to me, there is really no firm evidence that the design of the Distributing Reservoir on Murray Hill was conceived of by Renwick. His name is not mentioned by Tower or even Jervis who was the chief engineer of the entire project. It is probably the latter who *designed* the structure while Renwick *supervised* its erection, which would at least account for the latter's rather detailed drawings in the Metropolitan Museum Sketchbook. In point of fact, in B. J. Lossing, *History of New York City* (New York, 1884), p. 674, there is a brief biography of Renwick, presumably in consultation with him as he was still alive then, in which it is stated that as assistant engineer he "supervised" the building of the Distributing Reservoir. Of course, he could have assisted Jervis in the initial concept, but his authorship really would seem to stem only from tradition rather than demonstrable fact. All of which is rather too bad as it would have made a nice chronological beginning to the career of an architect most noted for his French High Gothic Cathedral some ten blocks away.

I am extremely grateful to Ms. Rattner for having saved me from some sloppy scholarship which I should have been more careful about initially.

25. Hone, *Diary,* p. 610; Tower, *Illustrations . . . ,* pp. 122, 123 (respectively).
26. *Stranger's Guide to Philadelphia* (Philadelphia, 1860), p. 37; Thompson Scott, *Official Guidebook to Philadelphia* (Philadelphia, 1876), p. 52. Tatum, *Penn's . . . ,* pp. 86, 182.
27. Another of these new building types related to civil engineering are turnpike lodges, proposed in the Egyptian style because of its "simple and bold details." "W", *Architectural Magazine,* II (1835), p. 475. For earlier Anglo-Egyptian lodges see note 64, chapter two.
28. Erik Iversen, "Hieroglyphic Studies of the Renaissance," *Burlington Magazine,* C, 658 (1958), pp. 15–21.
29. Comte de Caylus, *Recueil d'antiquités égyptiennes, étrusques, grèques, et romaines,* III (Paris, 1752), Avant-propos.
30. That these were not isolated examples may be seen from Friedrich Weinbrenner's Egyptian Synagogue in Karlsruhe of 1798, Rachel Wischnitzer, *Synagogue Architecture in the United States* (Philadelphia, 1955), p. 32; and the Egyptian Synagogue at Hobart, Tasmania, of 1843, *Universal Jewish Encyclopedia,* I (1939), p. 618, 620, (plate 89), plus those of Launceston, Tasmania, and Sydney, New South Wales, of about the same time (see chapter one, note 4). The Egyptian synagogue in Copenhagen is considerably later than the period here under discussion.
31. Tuthill, *History . . . ,* pp. 34, 60, 61. The author assumes, interestingly

enough, that, because of the quantity of mud brick at "Saccara," the pyramid there was built by the Israelites, and that, therefore, it is later in date than the Great Pyramids at Gizeh.

32. Indeed there is a tradition that the Sag Harbor church was intended to symbolize the Temple of Solomon. Jacob Landy, *The Architecture of Minard Lafever* (New York, 1970), pp. 230, 287. These monuments were discussed more thoroughly in the earlier chapter on formal aspects of the revival.

    One might also include in this group the Methodist Episcopal Church in New Orleans of James Dakin which had an Egyptian kiosk *distyle in antis* as a base for its spire. Built in 1836, it burned in 1851. Scully, *Dakin,* pp. 60–61.

    For other Egyptian flavored Calvinisms see chapter four, notes 22, 25, 28.

33. The claim that the title page derives from Piranesi is questionable.

34. George Freedly, *Theatrical Design from the Baroque through Neoclassicism,* 3 vols. (New York, 1940), vol. 1, col. 7; also Edward J. Dent, *Opera* (New York and Harmondsworth, 1945), plates 7 and 8. The date given is 1816. One might even think of the three temples of Nature, Reason and Wisdom (Act I, Scene 3) as properly being in the Gothic, Classical and Egyptian styles respectively.

35. John Fellows, *An Exposition of the Mysteries or Religious Dogmas and Customs of the Ancient Egyptians, Pythagoreans, and Druids, Also an Inquiry into the Origin, History, and Purport of Freemasonry* (New York, 1835); see also, George Godwin, "On the Institution of Free-Masonry," *Architectural Magazine,* III (1836), p. 194.

36. This building was discussed in the earlier chapter on formal aspects. See also, Henry L. Stillson, *The Official History of Odd Fellowship* (Boston, 1914), p. 292; Pascal Donaldson, *The Odd Fellows' Offering for 1849* (New York, 1849), title page and frontispiece; *Philadelphia Public Ledger,* XXIV, 36 (1847), p. 2.

37. Stillson, *Official History,* pp. 29–33, 707–708.

38. Two of the original Egyptian Revival chairs are owned by John Milner and James C. Massey.

39. Herodotus, II, 4; Plato, *Phaedrus,* 59.

40. James C. Massey, ed., *Two Centuries of Philadelphia Architectural Drawings* (Philadelphia, 1964), pp. 44–46, drawing 60.

41. Richard H. Howland and E. P. Spencer, *The Architecture of Baltimore* (Baltimore, 1953), pp. 126, 92.

42. Hans Vogel, "Aegyptisierende Baukunst des Klassizismus," *Zeitschrift für Bildende Kunst,* LXII (1928–1929), pp. 160–165.

43. Gustav Pauli, *Die Kunst des Klassizismus und Romantik* (Berlin, 1925), pp. 42, 221; Henrik Bramsen, *Gottlieb Bindesbøll* (Copenhagen, 1959), pp. 158–159.

44. Ronald B. Lewcock, *Early XIX Century Architecture in South Africa* (Cape Town, 1963), p. 138.

45. Roos, "The Egyptian Style," p. 220–221; Clay Lancaster, "Oriental Forms in American Architecture, 1800–1870," *Art Bulletin,* XXIX, 3, (1947), p. 184; C. W. Eckels, "The Egyptian Revival . . . ," p. 169; *Virginia Cavalcade,* II, 3 (1952). The author has been able to discover but scant information on this not unskilled architect who appears to have been trained in Philadelphia, possibly in Strickland's office. At least in 1835 he wrote from that city inquiring about the "Tombs" competition. See also note 40 above.

46. E.g., Herodotus, II, 84.

47. Karl H. Dannenfeldt, "Egypt and Egyptian Antiquities in the Renaissance," *Studies in the Renaissance,* VI (1959), pp. 7–27. Indeed, Dr. René-Nicholas Desgenettes of Napoleon's Institute of Egypt in Cairo asked, in a circular letter to French medical officers, to have sent to him reports of any traces of ancient medical lore which they might run across; he reminded them "that Egypt was the cradle of medicine." J. Christopher Herald, *Bonaparte in Egypt* (London, 1962), p. 175.

48. Manetho, Book I, Dynasty I, 2; Book I, Dynasty III, 2. (This was, of course, Zoser's architect Imhotep, the builder of the Step Pyramid at Saqqara.)

49. See more detailed discussion in Appendix III.

50. Thomas A. Marks, "Pattern of Law," *Architectural Review,* CXVI (1954), pp. 251–256; Norman Johnston, "Pioneers in Criminology, John Haviland," *Journal of Criminal Law and Criminology,* XLV, 5 (1955), pp. 509–519; *The Builder's Magazine* (London, 1774–1778), plates CLXXVI, CLXXVII, CLXXX; James Neild, *The State of Prisons* (London, 1812).

    For the progeny of Haviland's ideas on prison architecture in France, see Bruno Foucart, "Architecture carcérale et architectes fonctionistes en France au XIXe siècle," *Revue de l'Art,* 32 (1976), pp. 37–56. It should be noted, however, that Peter Speeth's building in Wurzburg was not originally a prison (it was a casern for the archibishop's guards); also, it still stands (as a youth hostel, in an interesting comment on the adaptability of *architecture parlante.*)

51. Philadelphia, Pennsylvania, Archives of the Eastern State Prison, Minutes of the Building Commissioners, MS. (ca. 1820), p. 115.

52. Roos, "The Egyptian Style," p. 222; Eckels, "The Egyptian Revival . . . ," p. 168; [State of New Jersey] *Votes and Proceedings of the 57th General Assembly of the State of New Jersey* (Woodbury, 1833), pp. 142–153, 281, 361; [State of New Jersey] *Journal of the Proceedings of the Legislative Council of the State of New Jersey* (Somerville, 1834), pp. 9, 11, 13–14; Henry E. Barnes, "A History of the Penal, Reformatory and Correctional Institutions of the State of New Jersey, Analytical and Documentary," *Report of the Prison Committee of the State of New Jersey,* II (Trenton, 1917), pp. 73, 84, 89–91; *New Jersey State Gazette,* VII,

349 (1836); *Ballou's* . . . , VIII, 21 (1855), pp. 328–329.

53. *Description* . . . , A., vol. II, pl. 15.

54. Haviland Papers, University of Pennsylvania, vol. VI, p. 122.

55. H.-R. Hitchcock, *Early Victorian Architecture in Britain*, 2 vols. (New Haven, 1954), vol. I, p. 194; also note paper read at the Frick-Institute of Fine Arts Symposium, April 8, 1961 by Matthew Baigell, "The Eastern State Penitentiary by John Haviland."

56. Haviland Papers, vol. II, p. 304.

57. Sources for all material relating to the New York "Tombs" credited fully in Appendix III.

58. Elmes, *Dictionary* . . . , "Architecture"; "Prisons"; *The Exhibition of the Royal Academy*, MDCCCV (London, 1805), p. 34.

59. Haviland owned a volume entitled *Views of Ireland*. Haviland Papers, vol. VI, pp. 122–123.

60. Published in M. A. Nicholson, *The Practical Builder* (London, 1825). Although it is not known whether Haviland owned this particular book, he did possess, according to a partial inventory of his library, seven other volumes of Nicholson's work. Haviland Papers, vol. VI, pp. 122–123.

61. *Penny Magazine*, IV, 235 (1835), p. 465.

62. Andrew Young and A. M. Doak, *Glasgow at a Glance* (Glasgow, 1965), item 23.

63. Roos, "The Egyptian Style," p. 222; Eckels, "The Egyptian Revival . . . ," p. 168; Joseph L. Munn, "Description of the Old Courthouse," *Essex County Courthouse* (Newark, 1908), unpaginated; *A History of the City of Newark*, 3 vols. (New York and Chicago, 1913), vol. II, pp. 619–621; *Newark Daily Advertiser*, V, 108 (1836); *ibid.*, V, 110 (1836); *ibid.*, VI, 252 (1838); *Ballou's* . . . , VIII, 15 (1855), p. 232.

64. Haviland Papers, vol. VI, p. 152. There seem to be no drawings of this plan extant.

65. Roos, "The Egyptian Style," pp. 220, 221–222; Eckels, "The Egyptian Revival . . . ," p. 168; *First Annual Report of the Board of Inspectors of the Philadelphia County Prison* (Harrisburg, 1848); "The Philadelphia County Prison," *Pennsylvania Journal of Prison Discipline and Philanthropy*, IV (1849), pp. 138–142; *Stranger's Guide* . . . , pp. 243–244; Scott, *Official Guidebook*, p. 113; J. Thomas Scharf and Thompson Westcott, *History of Philadelphia* (Philadelphia, 1884), pp. 1836–1837; Tatum, *Penn's* . . . , p. 179.

66. *Pennsylvania Journal of Prison Discipline*, p. 244.

67. The author used to think that this building might have been the work of the elder Gallier whose familiarity with the Egyptian style was noted in an earlier chapter. Possibly an even stronger candidate was James Dakin who came to New Orleans to join his brother in the architectural

firm of Dakin and Dakin, in 1835; this move was not made, however, until after he had contributed a plan to the New York "Tombs" competition. He was therefore, familiar with Haviland's design. However, Mr. Arthur Scully has provided the information that the building was remodelled in its present Egyptian style in about 1897, the year of the destruction of the "Tombs." By 1974 it had been mutilated beyond recognition.

68. Roos, "The Egyptian Style," p. 222; M. M. Hoffman, "John Francis Rague, Pioneer Architect of Iowa," *Annals of Iowa,* 3rd series, XIX (1933–1935), pp. 444–448; Talbot Hamlin, *Greek Revival Architecture in America* (New York, 1944), p. 310; Rexford Newcomb, *Architecture of the Old Northwest Territory,* Chicago (1950), p. 103; *Des Moines Sun-Register* (January 27, 1957), pp. 4–6; B. Woodman, "John F. Rague," (unpublished M.A. thesis, University of Iowa, 1969).

69. Metropolitan Museum of Art, *A. J. Davis Papers,* vol. II, p. 9.

70. *Ballou's . . . ,* XII (February 21, 1857), p. 117.

71. By extension, a form of law court, the customs house might be included in this group. This could be an explanation for the use of the Egyptian style in the original project of A. T. Wood for his New Orleans Customs House of 1847. It was finally executed in a non-Egyptian manner; although the capitals of the entrance columns may be so considered. Eckels, "The Egyptian Revival . . . ," p. 169; Hamlin, *Greek Revival,* pp. 229–230; Zacharie, *Guide,* p. 180. Even James Dakin was called in to work on it at one point. (Arthur Scully, see note 67 above).

72. An interesting use of the Egyptian style in conjunction with the sublime in Europe may be noted in an article in the *Journal of the Warburg and Courtauld Institutes* by Dr. Barbara Stafford. B. Stafford, "Medusa on the Physiognomy of the Earth," *JWCI,* vol. 35 (1972), pp. 308–338. For further information on an architectural theoretician interested in concepts of *l'architecture parlante,* frequently sublime and sometimes Egyptianizing, see the same author's, "Les deux edifices—the New Aeropagus and a Spiritual Trophy: Humbert de Superville's Vision of Utopia," *Art Quarterly,* XXXV (Spring 1972), pp. 49–73; and her "Arena of Virtue and Temple of Immortality: An Early Nineteenth-Century Museum Project," *JSAH,* XXXV, 1 (March, 1976), pp. 21–34.

Conclusion

The Egyptian Revival in America has been discussed in this essay to demonstrate that, although it is not a major architectural movement, it is one that represents a significant pattern of early nineteenth-century formal and iconographic attitudes. It is a well-defined material for the investigation of changing value concepts in architecture, an episode in the history of taste, an effort to identify the sources and nature of some of the romanticisms of the nineteenth century. It has been shown that enough examples were erected or planned to preclude any temptation to dismiss an Egyptian-style monument as an isolated instance of exotic *bizzarria*. It was considered sufficiently important for critics to write about it, characterizing its style and attributes; and for architects to design and build in it domestic, commercial, and public buildings. The interest on the part of these professionals, and their patrons, in the archeological sources further attests to the seriousness of their intent. It is noteworthy that there were no architectural "follies" in the Egyptian style.

As an eclectic movement whose popularity is less obvious than that of the Greek, Roman, and Gothic revivals, it is like them, a descendant of European attitudes which provided it with a pedigree of respectability and tradition. The Egyptian, like the Classical revivals at the time of the Revolutionary architects, provided a vehicle for new attitudes towards architectural organization and arrangement. Although motifs of form and decoration were taken from ancient Egypt, they were composed in consciously new ways. No pharaonic building was slavishly reproduced in its entirety. With the architectural books available through the publications of Denon and the official French commission this could have been accomplished easily enough. Instead, new dispositions of plan, elevation, decorative accent, and space conception were evolved.

The newness of feeling, however, was only one aspect, one which through the similarity of the Egyptian Revival to Romantic Classicism may be studied in Emil Kaufmann's work on the Revolutionary architects. Less familiar is the study of its meaning, the associations and attitudes that the Egyptian style evoked. What were its symbolical connotations? How were its emotional and philosophical values achieved?

The use of the Egyptian style, in some cases, followed pre-nineteenth-century eclectic patterns such as conforming to a preexisting setting, providing an exhibit in an architectural museum, or symbolizing past, but meaningful, forms.

There are more important reasons for the appearance of the style, however, which reflect typical nineteenth-century attitudes. On the one hand, the exploitation of Egyptian motifs may be seen as part of a "Picturesque Rococo" tradition which continues on into the century in the guise of what might be called the "Commercial Picturesque." On the other hand is the concept of the style as a final echo of Romantic Classicism, especially in its evocation of the Sublime. A clear demonstration of the antithetical nature of these two approaches is provided by Piranesi and Quatremère de Quincy. The former who instigated the Picturesque Rococo phase explained that he used Egyptian motifs as "anti-monotony" elements. Quatremère de Quincy who is important for the formulation of the Sublime-Romantic Classical attitude spoke of Egyptian architecture as being too monotonous.

In spite of the fact that both facets of the Egyptian Revival stemmed from principles expressed by the same generation, the earliest manifestations of the style occurred in the Picturesque Rococo guise. The vocabulary was applied to architecture and the decorative arts to achieve variety and novelty (picturesque) for an ornamental effect (rococo). But the use of Egyptian motifs in no way changed the basic style of the monument involved. Tectonically speaking, there was no morphological innovation exerted. Occurring mostly in Europe, this form of the Egyptian Revival did, nevertheless, take place in America, too.

The corollary branch, the Commercial Picturesque, was, however, more popular in the United States. Variety and novelty were still the important qualities, but their purpose was to attract public attention, rather than to achieve aristocratic decoration. Originating in England with the Piccadilly Egyptian Hall, this concept gave a democratic twist to Piranesi's sense of the bizarre. But this corollary was separated from the generating theorem, not only in a social historical sense, but also in a formal aesthetic way. For with the availability of archeological sources through Denon and the *Description . . . ,* the Commercial Picturesque could be, and most often was, most closely allied to the original architectural monuments. In spite of the newness of feeling, certain significant values and principles of the sources were incorporated into the compositions. Thus, if a nineteenth-century Egyptian building was planned for space enclosure, as opposed to the original, its effect was still one of space-displacing mass. Other pharaonic architectural qualities such as simplicity, solidity, and philogeometry were reiterated.

But the Commercial Picturesque, in this aspect, was only a reflection of that other phase of the Egyptian Revival, i.e., the crystallization of Romantic Classical ideals. The Egyptian vocabulary, by presenting a restricted catalogue of forms, emphasized the qualities associated with the principles of the Revolutionary architects, such as clearness, closed composition, planarity, and geometry. As a compensation for the retrenchment in the roster of forms, the shapes themselves could, in the Egyptian manner, be on a tremendously increased scale. Thus, through awesome size, the Egyptian Revival evoked feelings of the Sublime.

But sublime emotions were also achieved by the associations the mode conjured up. Since the Renaissance a tradition of obelisk memorials and pyramid tombs identified the style with the practice of guarding and commemorating the Dead. This funerary affiliation, perhaps the most persistent image ever projected by a culture, also implied agelessness and durability. Egyptian architecture through its sepulchral heritage inspired sublime reactions of fear of death, reverence for the dead, and awe of enduring timelessness. To the feelings of dread and solemn veneration were added those of mystery, foreboding, and doom, all sublime-inducing qualities which are associated with death. It is this funerary tradition which continues in America in public monuments, private tombs, and especially in a new feature, the cemetery gate. Although serious objections were raised that the Egyptian style was symbolic of the most pagan and idolatrous of civilizations, these were met by rearranging the pharaonic emblems to read as Christian symbols, or by incorporating specific Christian motifs and inscriptions upon the monuments. This process produced a kind of architectural *Ovid Moralisé* not unlike the exorcising of reerected ancient obelisks by Renaissance popes.

The other major association called forth by the Egyptian style was that of "the Land of Wisdom and Mystery." Greece, the land of Reason and Logic, had learned first from Egypt. The process had continued with other civilizations, Roman, Renaissance, and the eighteenth century until Egyptian Wisdom appeared as the ancestor of Modern Learning, and Egyptian Mystery became the source for occult sciences and hermetic rites. The latter produced buildings for fraternal orders and undoubtedly contributed to the funerary associations of the style. The former could be applied to a wide range of structures such as those for a school, museum, or library; and even a medical college.

But if sublime awe could be engendered by connotations of Death, Wisdom, and Mystery, it could be equally imparted by enduring timelessness. The civilization that was more ancient than Antiquity produced an architecture that seemed to last forever. Not only was this an idea attractive for sepulchral monuments, but it was also one which appealed to builders and engineers seeking a style to garb structures of the new technology, to give a sense of security to the untried and yet-to-be-proven instruments of progress. Thus it was used to reassure the timid traveller in railway stations, and on suspension bridges. For the latter the Egyptian style also provided a conveniently functional set of forms, which may similarly explain its use for reservoirs and water works, although associations with the Nile probably contributed something. Security and reassurance, further, are associations desired by the merchant of a new building material, iron, or by an insurance company. But Commercial Picturesque ideas may also have been considered. In a like manner, no one reason can be given for the use of the style for synagogues and churches. While it was reasonable for the nineteenth-century mind to think that the Israelites learned architecture from the Egyptians during the Bondage making the Egyptian and Jewish style analogous, the wish of the Jews to symbolize the antiquity of their religion might have led them to the same style. At the same time the spare simplicity of Calvinistic cults could be satisfied by the formal characteristics of the Egyptian style. They might also see in it a symbol of the Rock of Ages, of the primitive state to which in dogma, they wanted to return.

The major Egyptian Revival buildings in America, however, were courthouses and prisons. In these, also, the attitude of the times was that the style was "appropriate." It is significant that the two earliest examples in this category were reform prisons. Here the style became the symbol for humane rectification and human regeneration. If the mode were first employed for practical reasons of economy (vis-à-vis Gothic), it soon became symbolic of the new enlightened prison discipline. To mark the new attitude it was necessary to use a style other than the old Gothic one reminiscent of dungeons and oppressive gaolers. When a courthouse and prison were combined, the same symbolism became reasonable for the court that was to dispense lawful, but enlightened justice. Thus, both building types partook of the "Reform" style.

The element of the sublime should not be overlooked in this connection. For law is not merely man-made, but is inspired from timeless and enduring rights, responsibilities, and principles. Unchangingly objective justice provides the awesome majesty and solemn reverence due to one of mankind's most civilizing forces. The sublime nature of law required that it be given an architectural setting in the most sublime of styles. "L'architecture parlante" became translated as "appropriate architecture." And a major factor contributing to this sublimity was the supra-anthropocentricity of the scale, even as justice is greater than man ("A government of laws, not of men").

The formal development of the Egyptian Revival was one which may be traced in three phases, phases which parallel other styles of the period, and ones which are inextricably involved with the iconography of the movement. The first is the pseudo-Egyptian in which motifs are applied to a core in the picturesque tradition of decoration, variety and *bizzarria*. This Picturesque Rococo, and, later, Commercial Picturesque, are attitudes which continue throughout the movement. The second is the horizontal phase of the 1830s. In it both the form and details are specifically Egyptian with the expressed intent of recreating the qualities associated with Egyptian architecture. The third is the vertical phase of the 1840s in which there is a merging of Egyptian vocabulary with Gothic proportions. It is with this that the movement ends. Egyptian buildings appear afterwards from time to time, but only as isolated examples of the Commercial Picturesque.

Considering the appeal the style exerted for new building types and for ideas concerning meaning in architecture (proto-semiology?), the Revival is not without significance. There are at least eighty monuments in the United States plus numerous examples elsewhere. Almost every major American architect of the period worked in the mode. The style was used in several ways, and for a complex variety of reasons. It extended from eighteenth-century rococo decoration to the beginnings of modern functionalism. It was a form of eclecticism that lent itself easily to symbolism. It was also strongly rooted in picturesque traditions. Above all it was the fullest expression of the Sublime. But even if its most interesting aspect might lie in its iconographic meanings, its greatest significance lies in its formal contributions. One of these is that it did mark a final phase of Romantic Classicism. Within the range of extant styles there was no further statement of that aesthetic to be made.

The second point is more important in that instead of an end, it marked a beginning. What has been called the "Egyptianizing" aspect, that which gives the effect of Egyptian architecture without using the specific archeological details, is a facet of architecture that never has died. Large geometric masses and shapes, spare, simple, and solid, made up of straight lines and angles have been in the architectural vocabulary since the end of the movement that introduced these concepts to America, be they a Richardsonian pyramid in Wyoming or Root's Monadnock in Chicago or Mr. Foshay's tower in Minneapolis or Philip Johnson's atomic reactor. Perhaps even for the young and receptive United States, the specifically Egyptian trappings of the style were too peculiar, too weird, and too alien for easy acceptance. But the underlying formal principles of the Egyptian Revival have continued; once again, "old wine in new bottles."

The middle of the century marked the end of an attitude; that which assumed the validity of symbolic eclecticism. With this ended the popularity of the Egyptian Revival. Too, there were unfunctional aspects such as the problems of fenestration in a windowless architecture, flat roofs in a climate anything but torrid, and the weathering of battered walls. But most of all the propagandizing of Pugin, Ruskin, and the Camden Society, along with the general religious revival betokened by the rise of Methodism, turned popular taste against the heathen associations of Greece, Rome, and Egypt. For the Egyptian style there were no deep cultural values germane to the American sociological psyche; vis-à-vis Gothic, which evoked an entire religious tradition, or Classical Antiquity, which called forth a vital political heritage. It seemed that anyone associating Egyptian architecture with tombs, cemeteries, and prisons would hardly wish to live in it or be surrounded by it. A style which does not take firm root in domestic or religious life is not likely to live long, since it thus remains limited and exotic.

Once the appeal of novelty wore thin, then the Egyptian forms must have seemed as discordant to the mid-nineteenth century as they do to us. Battered, windowless walls are incongruous in a visual world of orthagonal structures, all products of a humanistic tradition. This is the meaning of exotic and applies with equal force to such minor eclecticisms as Moorish and Oriental.

All the values felt in or ascribed to the architecture of Egypt, antique or revived, were not enough to overcome its limited links with Christianity and the steam engine. It was difficult for a Jacksonian democrat to consider himself Pharaoh, even though he owned slaves. But it was easier to identify himself with a knight on a Crusade, or with Cicero and Demosthenes; whereas the literature and civilization of the Egyptians were virtually unknown. And so, one of the most interesting variations of symbolic eclecticism had had its day leaving us a few reminders of a period when architectural forms were loaded with intellectual as well as emotional content.

1. Fireplace design, G.-B. Piranesi, 1769.

2. The English Coffee House, Rome,
G.-B. Piranesi, 1769.

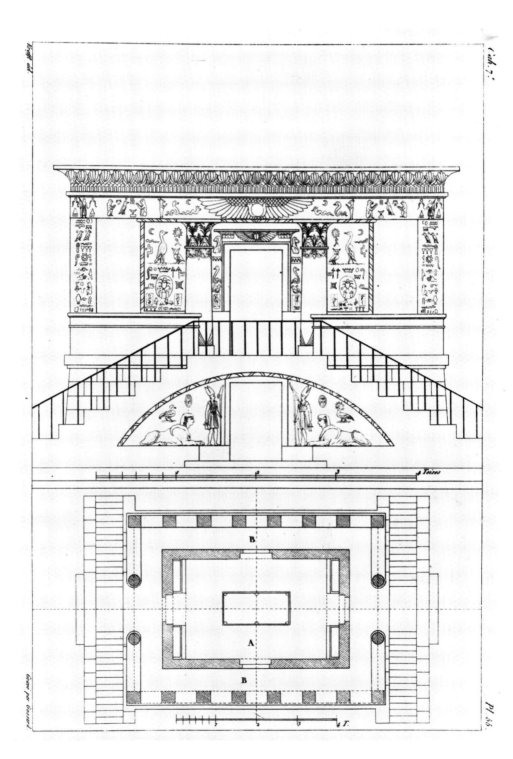

3. Bath House, Château de Montbéliard,
J.-B. Kléber, 1787.

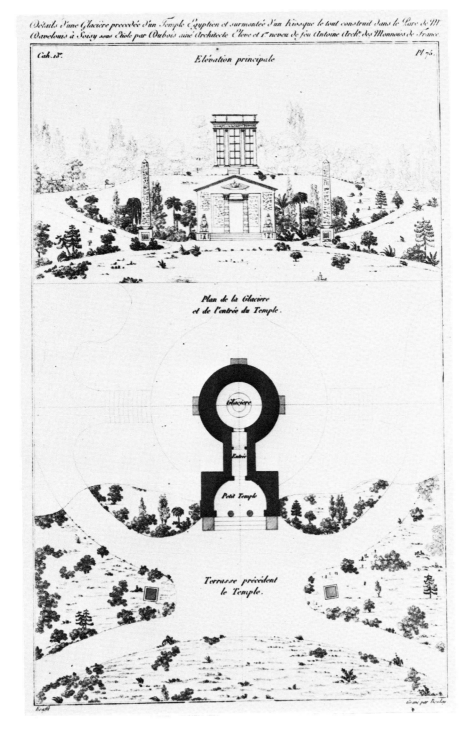

4. Ice House, Château de Davelouis,
P.-F.-L. Dubois, ca. 1800.

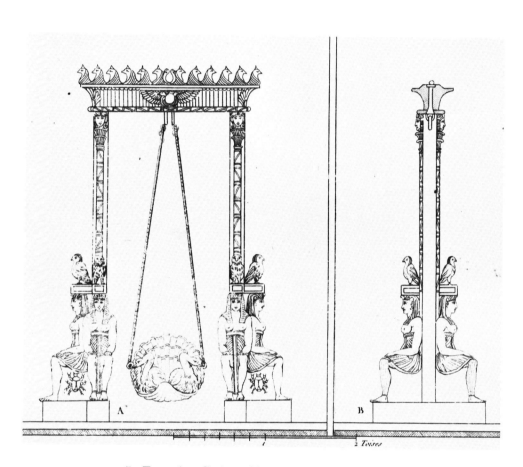

5. Egyptian Swing, Château de Montbéliard,
J.-B. Kléber, 1787.

6. Assembly Room, Château de Bénévant,
J.-A. Renard, 1805.

7. Restoration of an Egyptian Temple,
L.-F. Cassas, 1799.

8. Restoration of an Egyptian Temple (detail of plate 7),
L.-F. Cassas, 1799.

Egyptian Temple.

9. Egyptian Garden Temple, John Soane, 1778.

10. Egyptian Mansion, James Randall, 1806.

11. Egyptian Hall, London, P. F. Robinson, 1812.

OPPOSITE PAGE
12. Canopus Room,
Duchess Street House,
London, Thomas Hope,
1801–1803.

13. Ker Street, Devonport,
John Foulston, 1823.

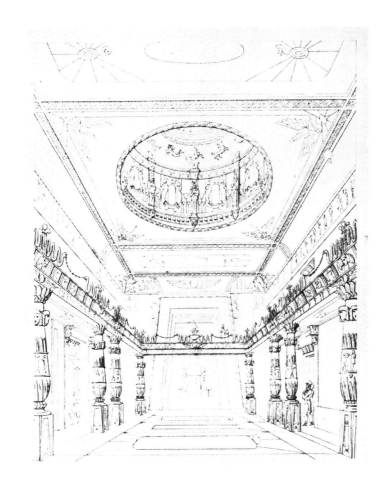

14. Library, Devonport, John Foulston, 1823.

15. Library, Devonport, John Foulston, 1823.

16. The Egyptian House, Penzance,
ca. 1830.

17. Flax Mill, Leeds, Ignatius Bonomi,
1838–1841.

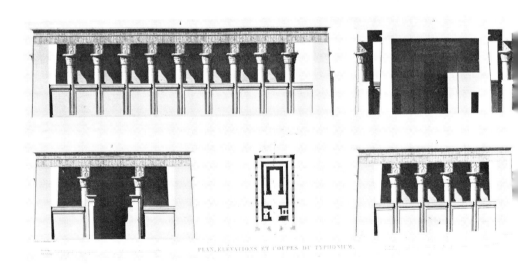

18. Typhonium, Denderah, from *Description*. . . .

19. Flax Mill, Leeds, Ignatius Bonomi,
1838–1841.

20. Temple of Antaeopolis, from *Description*. . . .

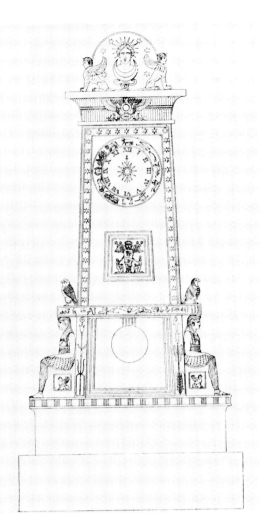

21. Clock, C. Percier,
1812.

22. Table, Italian,
ca. 1815.

OPPOSITE PAGE
23. Secretary, C. Percier,
1812.

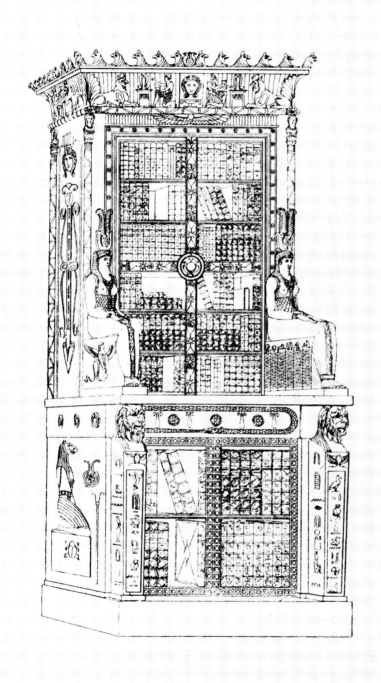

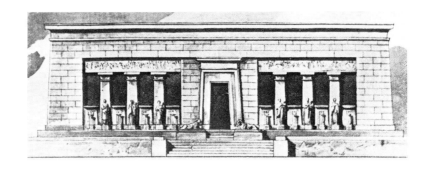

24. Glyptothek (project), Munich,
Haller von Hallerstein, 1814;
with Temple of Denderah.

25. Monument (project), Richmond (?), Benjamin Latrobe, 1812.

26. Egyptian Pyramid, E.-L. Boullée, ca. 1785.

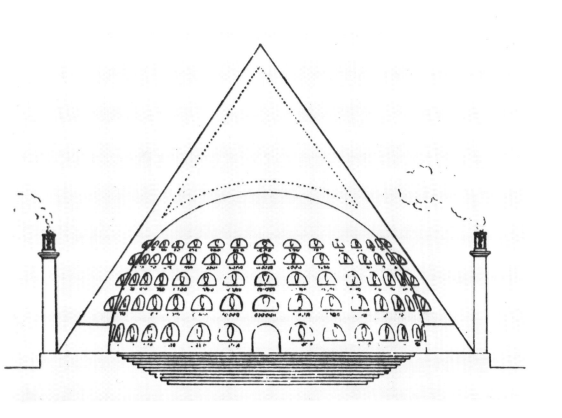

27. Cenotaph, J.-N.-L. Durand, 1805.

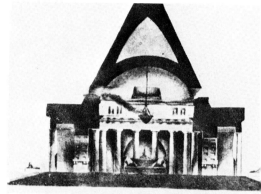

28. Monument (project), Berlin, Friedrich Gilly, ca. 1797.

29. Monument to the defeat of the Tartars,
Kazan, M. Alferov, 1823–1830.

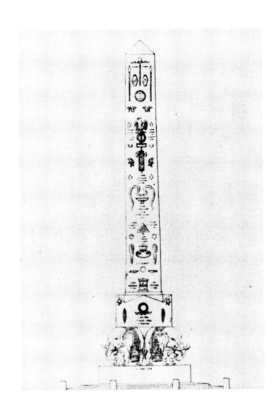

30. Monument (project),
Place des Victoires,
Paris, J.-N. Sobre, 1795.

31. Monument (project), Pont Neuf, Paris, F.-J. Belanger, ca. 1800.

32. Chalmette Monument, New Orleans,
Newton Richards, ca. 1850.

33. Washington Monument (prior to 1884 building campaign),
Washington, D.C., Robert Mills, 1833.

34. Battle Monument,
Baltimore,
Maximilian Godefroy,
1815–1825.

35. Washington Monument (project), New York,
Minard Lafever, 1854.

36. Monument (project), A. J. Davis, ca. 1840.

37. Gatehouse, Woodside Hall,
Cooperstown, N.Y.,
E. B. Morehouse, 1829.

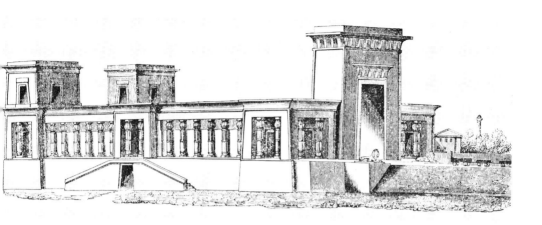

38. Railroad Station (project),
Kensington Common, London,
W. J. Short, 1836.

39. Pearl Street Depot, New Bedford, Mass.,
Russell Warren, 1840.

40. Pearl Street Depot, New Bedford, Mass.,
Russell Warren, 1840.

41. Western Railroad Depot, Pittsfield, Mass., 1840.

42. Pennsylvania Fire Insurance Co.,
Philadelphia,
John Haviland,
1838.

43. Isaac P. Morris Co.(?),
Philadelphia,
Charles B. Cooper,
1847.

44. Pennsylvania Fire Insurance Co.,
Philadelphia,
John Haviland, 1838.

45. Pennsylvania Fire Insurance
Philadelphia,
John Haviland, 1838.

46. Isaac P. Morris Co.(?), Philadelphia,
Charles B. Cooper, 1847.

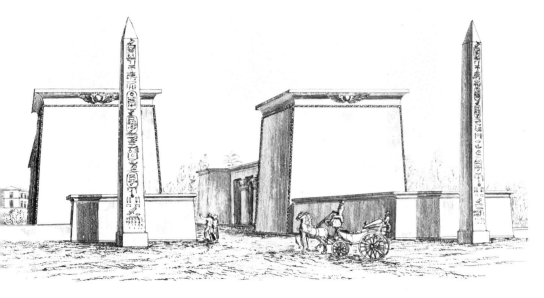

47. Egyptian Pylon Gate, Borghese Gardens, Rome,
L. Canina, ca. 1825.

48. Egyptian Pylon Gate, Borghese Gardens, Rome,
L. Canina, ca. 1825.

49. Rue de Sèvres Fountain, Paris,
J.-M.-N. Bralle, 1808.

50. Karnac, from Denon, *Voyage.* . . .

51. Peristyle, Hôtel de Beauharnais,
Paris, M. Bataille, 1806.

52. Abney Park Cemetery, Stoke Newington, London,
W. Hosking, 1840.

53. Highgate Cemetery, London, S. Geary, 1838.

54. Highgate Cemetery, London, S. Geary, 1838.

55. Cast Iron Gate, Tsarskoe Selo, Adam Menelaws, 1828–1832.

56. Westminster Cemetery, Baltimore,
Maximilian Godefroy,
1813–1815.

57. Mount Auburn Cemetery, Cambridge, Mass., J. Bigelow, 1831.

58. Mount Auburn Cemetery, Cambridge, Mass., J. Bigelow, 1831.

60. North Portal, Temple of Karnac, from *Description.* . . . .

59. South Portal, Temple of Karnac, from *Description.* . . . .

61. Old Granary Burying Ground, Boston, I. Rogers, 1840.

62. Touro Cemetery, Newport, R.I., I. Rogers, 1843.

63. Laurel Hill Cemetery (project), Philadelphia,
W. Strickland, 1836.

64. Laurel Hill Cemetery (project), Philadelphia,
T. U. Walter, 1836.

65. Greenmount
Cemetery (project),
Baltimore,
R. C. Long, Jr.,
1845.

66. Temple of Thebes,
from Denon, *Voyage*. . . .

67. Cypress Grove Cemetery, New Orleans,
F. Wilkinson, 1840.

68. Cemetery
Gate (project),
A. J. Davis,
1828.

1.Tente d'Arabes.   2.Plan du Portique.   3.Portique du temple de Latopolis à Esné.

69. Temple of Esne, from Denon, *Voyage*. . . .

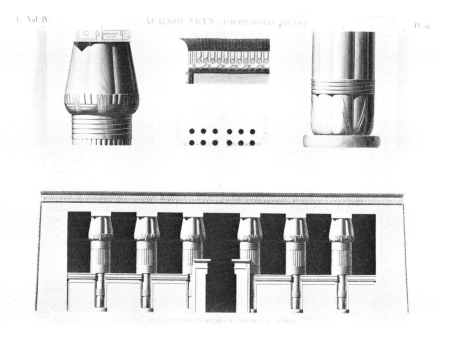

70. Temple of Hermopolis Magna, from *Description*. . . .

71. Grove Street Cemetery, New Haven, H. Austin, 1844–1848.

72. Forest Hills Cemetery, Roxbury, Mass.,
H. A. S. Dearborn, 1848.

73. Old Burying Ground,
Farmington, Conn., ca. 1850.

74. Odd Fellows Cemetery, Philadelphia,
S. D. Button, 1849.

75. Mount Hope Cemetery, Rochester, N.Y.,
J. McConnell, 1838.

76. Mikveh Israel Cemetery, Philadelphia, ca. 1845.

77. Odd Fellows Hall, Philadelphia, 1846–1847.

78. Clifton Suspension Bridge, Bristol, England, I.K. Brunel, 1831.

79. Railroad Bridge,
Harper's Ferry,
West Va.,
B.H. Latrobe, Jr.,
and W. Bollman,
1835–1851.

80. Railroad Bridge,
Harper's Ferry,
West Va.,
B.H. Latrobe, Jr.,
and W. Bollman,
1835–1851.

81. Chain Pier,
Brighton,
England,
Samuel Brown,
1823.

82. Suspension Bridge, St. John, New Brunswick,
E. W. Serrell (?), ca. 1853.

83. Suspension Bridge, Niagara Falls,
J. A. Roebling, 1852–1854.

84. "Egyptian Pavilion" (project), Robert Lugar, 1805.

85. Reservoir, Albany, 1811.

86. Croton Distributing Reservoir, New York, J. B. Jervis, 1842.

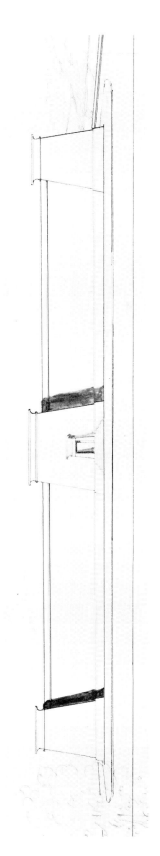

87. Croton Distributing Reservoir, New York, J. B. Jervis, 1842.

88. Northern Liberties
and Spring Green
Water Works,
Philadelphia,
1844–1845.

89. Synagogue, Hobart, Tasmania, 1844.

90. Mikveh Israel Synagogue, Philadelphia,
W. Strickland,
1822–1825.

92. 166 Congress Street,
Troy, N.Y.,
ca. 1845–1850.

91. Beth Israel Synagogue,
Philadelphia,
T. U. Walter, 1849.

93. Downtown Presbyterian Church, Nashville,
W. Strickland, 1848–1851.

94. First Baptist Church, Essex, Conn., ca. 1845.

95. Whalers' Church, Sag Harbor, N.Y., Minard Lafever (?), 1843.

96. Church (project), A. J. Davis, ca. 1845.

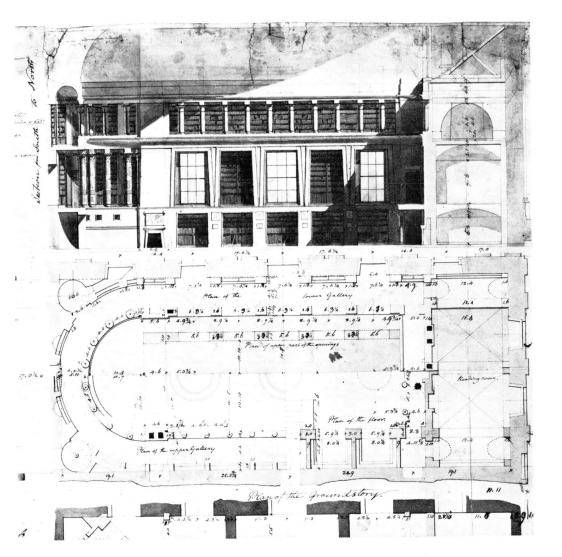

97. Library of Congress (project), Washington, D.C.,
B. Latrobe, 1808.

98. Chapel and School House (project),
A.J. Davis, post–1848.

99. Athenaeum of Natural History (project), New York,
A. J. Davis, 1835.

A DESIGN FOR
THE FRONT OF
BALTIMORE CITY AND COUNTY RECORD OFFICE
BY R.C. LONG ARCHITECT
MARCH 1836

ELEVATION.

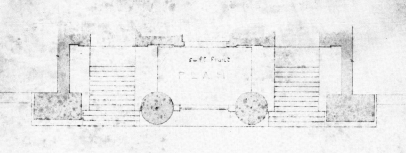

Scale 8 Ft to an Inch

100. Hall of Records (project), Baltimore,
R. C. Long, Jr., 1836.

101. Library and Conservatory (project), Philadelphia,
T. S. Stewart, ca. 1845.

102. Medical College of Virginia, Richmond,
T. S. Stewart, 1844.

103. Medical College
of Virginia,
Richmond,
T. S. Stewart,
1844.

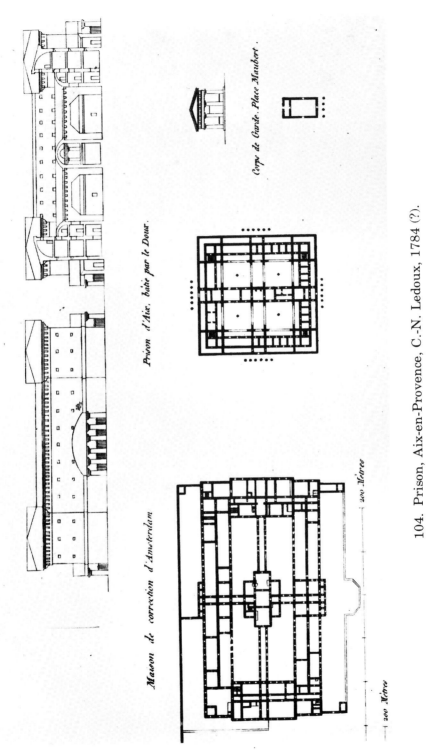

Maison de correction d'Amsterdam.

Prison d'Aix, bâtie par le Doux.

Corps de Garde. Place Maubert.

200 Mètres

200 Mètres

104. Prison, Aix-en-Provence, C.-N. Ledoux, 1784 (?).

105. Moyamensing Debtors' Prison, Philadelphia,
T. U. Walter, 1832–1835.

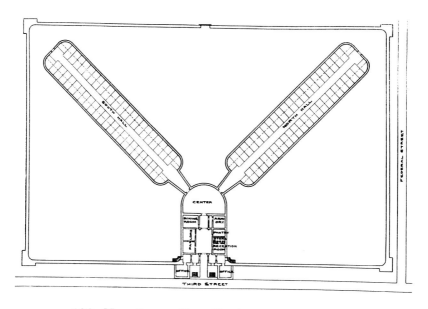

106. New Jersey State Penitentiary, Trenton,
J. Haviland, 1832–1836.

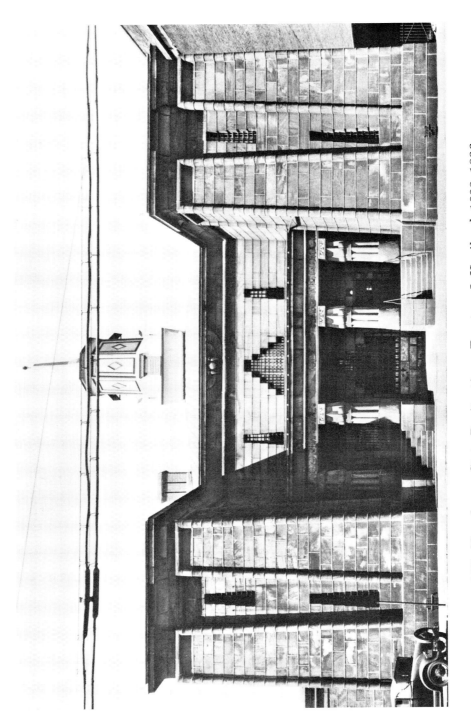

107. New Jersey State Penitentiary, Trenton, J. Haviland, 1832–1836.

108. Lateral View, Medinet Habu,
from *Description*. . . .

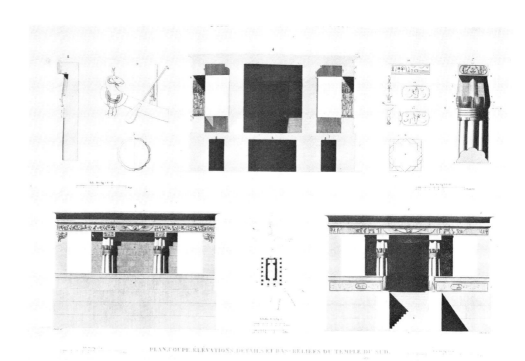

109. "Temple du Sud," Elephantina,
from *Description*. . . .

110. New Jersey State Penitentiary, Trenton, J. Haviland, 1832–1836.

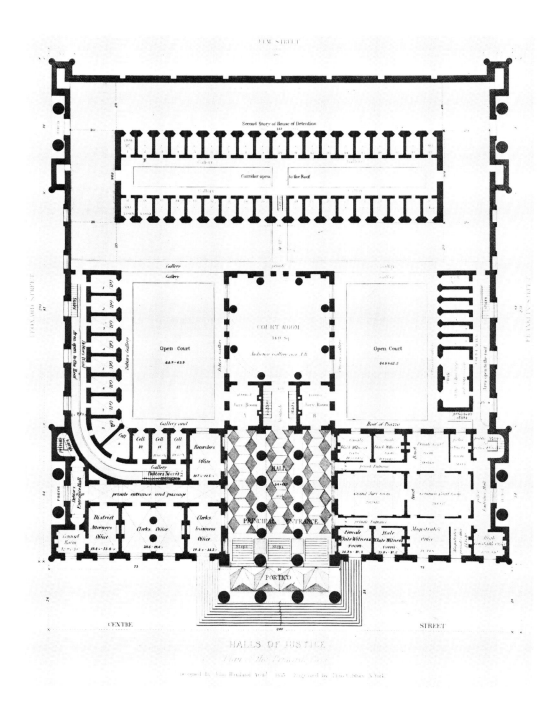

111. The "Tombs," New York, John Haviland, 1835–1838.

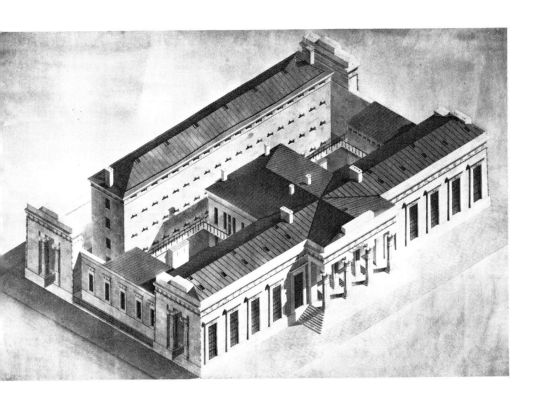

112. The "Tombs,"
New York,
John Haviland,
1835–1838.

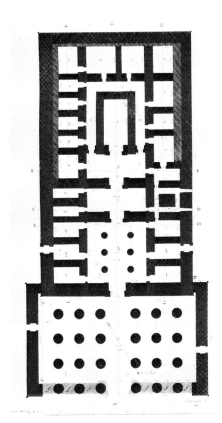

113. Plan of
Temple of Denderah,
from *Description*. . . .

114. The "Tombs," New York, John Haviland, 1835–1838.

115. Entrance Gate (project), A.J. Davis, 1828 (?).

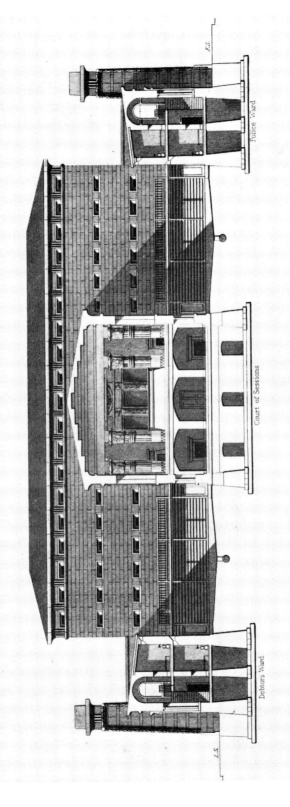

HALLS OF JUSTICE

A Transverse section from Leonard to Franklin St

Designed by John Haviland Arch[t] 1835   Engraved by Tho[s] C. Story   New York.

Police Ward

Court of Sessions

Debtors Ward

116. The "Tombs," New York, John Haviland, 1835–1838.

COURT OF SPECIAL SESSIONS IN THE TOMBS.

117. Main Courtroom, the "Tombs," New York, John Haviland, 1835–1838.

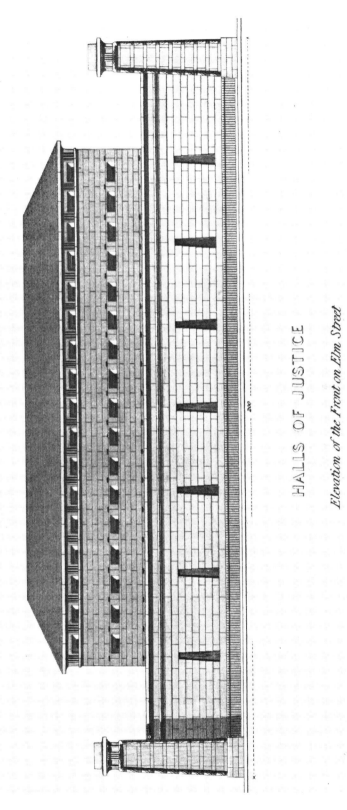

HALLS OF JUSTICE

Elevation of the Front on Elm Street

118. The "Tombs," New York, John Haviland, 1835–1838.

119. "Couvent blanc,"
Deir Beyadh,
from Denon,
Voyage....

120. Unidentified temple,
Fayoum,
from *Description....*

121. Lateral facade,
"Tombs," New York,
John Haviland,
1835–1838.

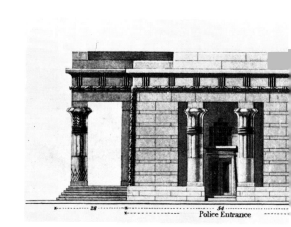

122. The "Tombs,"
New York,
John Haviland,
1835–1838.

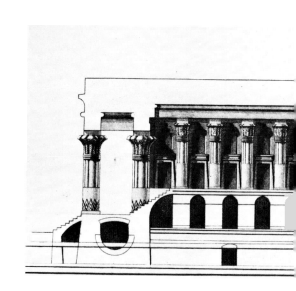

123. The "Tombs,"
New York,
John Haviland,
1835–1838.

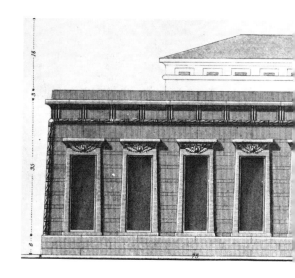

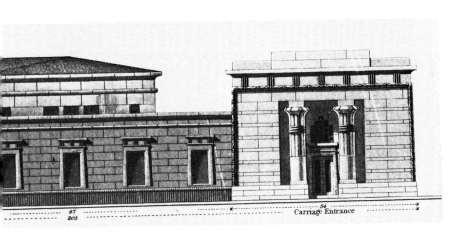

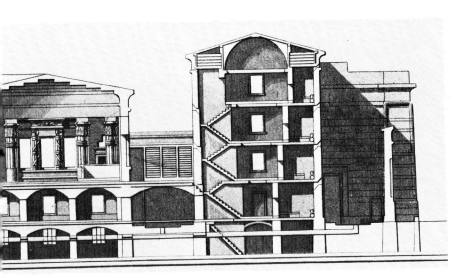

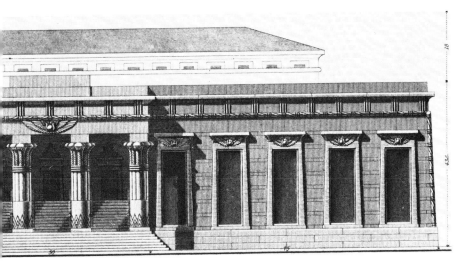

Carriage Entrance

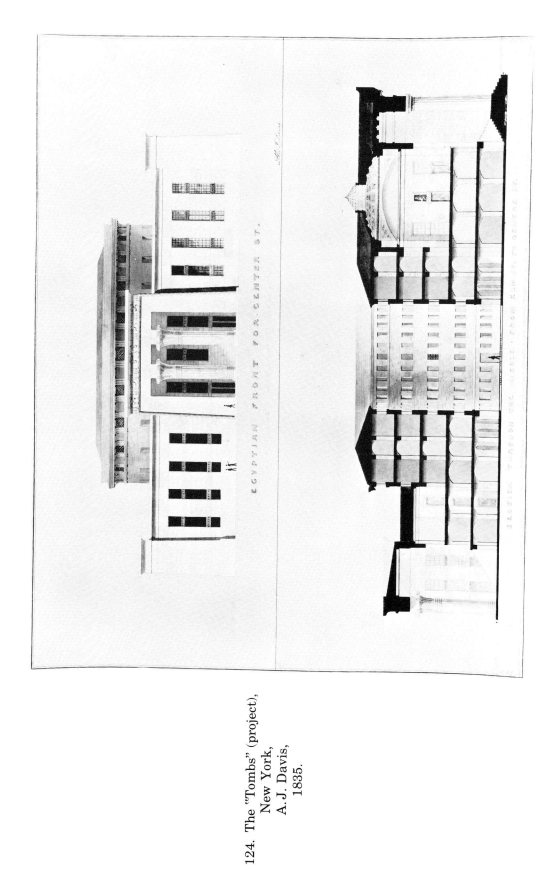

EGYPTIAN FRONT FOR CENTER ST.

124. The "Tombs" (project),
New York,
A. J. Davis,
1835.

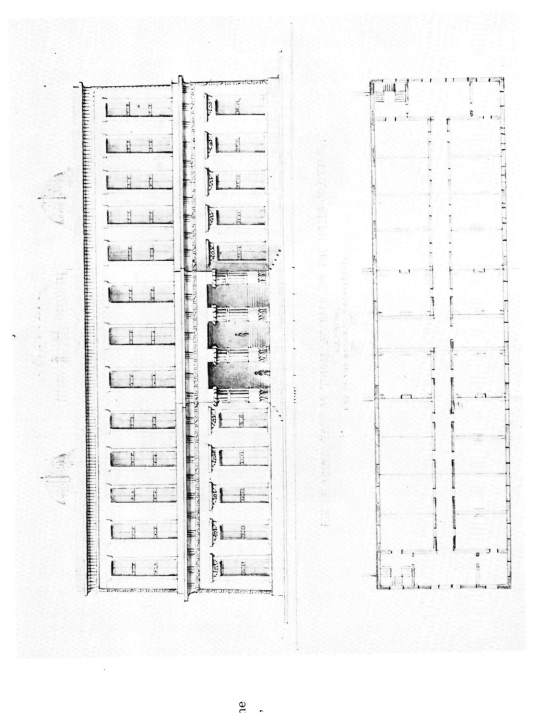

125. Addition to the
"Tombs" (project),
New York,
A. J. Davis,
1878.

126. The Kremlin and government office building,
Moscow, from an early nineteenth-century print.

127. The "Tombs," New York, John Haviland, 1835–1838.

128. The "Tombs,"
New York,
John Haviland,
1835–1838.

129. Essex County Courthouse, Newark,
J. Haviland, 1836–1838.

130. Essex County Courthouse, Newark,
J. Haviland, 1836–1838.

COURT HOUSE AND SQUARE, NEWARK, N J.

131. Essex County Courthouse, Newark,
J. Haviland, 1836–1838.

132. City Jail,
Dubuque, Iowa,
J.F. Rague,
1857–1858.

133. City Jail,
Dubuque, Iowa,
J.F. Rague,
1857–1858.

134. The "Tombs," New York, John Haviland,
1835–1838, from *Ballou's*. . . . .

135. Thorwaldsen Museum, Copenhagen, M. B. Bindesbøll, 1838–1847.

136. Washington Monument,
Washington, D.C., R. Mills, 1833
(designed),
1848–1884 (built).

Obelisks

Obelisks as specific monuments in the United States, 1792–1860:

1. Columbus Monument, Baltimore, Md. By the Chevalier d'Anmour, 1792. C. W. Eckels, "The Egyptian Revival . . . ," p. 164.

2. Battle Monument, Lexington, Mass., 1799. *Gleason's* . . . , II, 19 (1852), pp. 301, 304; Charles Hudson, *History of Lexington* (Boston, 1868), pp. 215–219.

3. Three pairs of obelisks for Washington Family Tomb, Mount Vernon, Va. Designed by William Strickland, 1837. Charles C. Wall, "The Mount Vernon Experience," *Museum News,* XXXVIII, 1 (1959), pp. 18–23; Gilchrist, *Strickland,* p. 95.

4. Battle Monument, mastaba base, Baltimore, Md. (plate 34). By Maximilian Godefroy, 1815–1825. *Gleason's* . . . , IV, 16 (1853), p. 248; Robert Alexander, "The Public Memorial and Godefroy's Battle Monument," *JSAH,* XVII, 1 (1958), pp. 19–24.

5. Battle Monument (project), Philadelphia, Pa. By William Strickland, 1825. *Minutes of the Select Council of the City of Philadelphia* (1821–1830), p. 289.

6. Battle Monument (project), Philadelphia, Pa. By John Haviland, 1824. Pennsylvania Academy of Fine Arts, *14th Annual Exhibition of the Pennsylvania Academy of Fine Arts* (Philadelphia, 1824), p. 15.

7. Monument to Pulaski and Greene, Savannah, Ga. 1824–1829. *Gleason's* . . . , VI, 14 (1854), p. 216; F. D. Lee and J. L. Agnew, *Historical Record of Savannah* (Savannah, 1869), p. 169.

8. Bunker['s] Hill Monument, Charlestown, Mass. By Solomon Willard, 1825. Eckels, "The Egyptian Revival . . . ," p. 165; S. Wil-

lard, *Plans and Sections of the Obelisk on Bunker's Hill* (Boston, 1843), p. 19. Also claimed for Robert Mills; H. Pierce Gallagher, *Robert Mills* (New York, 1935), p. 163; Frank J. Roos, "The Egyptian Style," p. 221. Also claimed for Horatio Greenough; Samuel Swett, "H. Greenough, the Designer of the Bunker Hill Monument," *New England Historical and Geneological Register,* XVIII (January, 1864); definitive discussion in J. Zukowski, "Monumental American Obelisks: Centennial Vistas," *Art Bull.* LVIII, 4 (1976), p. 575.

9. Fort Griswold Monument, Groton, Conn. By Town and Davis, 1826–1830. Davis Journal, vol. I, MS., Metropolitan Museum of Art, pp. 10, 19; *Ballou's . . .*, IX, 13 (1855), p. 201; Zukowsky, "Obelisks," p. 575.

10. Harvard Monument, Charlestown, Mass., 1828. *Gleason's . . .*, III, 24 (1852), p. 372; James F. Hunnewell, *A Century of Town Life: A History of Charlestown, Mass.* (Boston, 1888), p. 74.

11. Donop Monument, Red Bank, N.J., 1829. *Gleason's . . .*, IV, 22 (1853), p. 352.

12. Monument to Gov. Lincoln, Augusta, Me., 1829. *Gleason's . . .*, V, 21 (1853), p. 329; James W. North, *History of Augusta* (Augusta, 1870), p. 498.

13. Castle Island Monument, Boston, Mass., ca. 1830. *Gleason's . . .*, VII, 21 (1854), p. 329.

14. Washington National Monument, Washington, D.C. (plates 33, 136). By Robert Mills, designed 1833, built 1848–1884. Gallagher, *Mills,* pp. 115, 117; Roos, "The Egyptian Style," p. 220; Clay Lancaster, "Oriental Forms in American Architecture, 1800–1870," *Art Bull.,* XXIX, 3 (1947), p. 184; Eckels, "The Egyptian Revival," p. 165; *Gleason's . . .*, IV, 21 (1853), p. 333; VI, 17 (1854), p. 272; VII, 1 (1854), pp. 7, 13; *Ballou's . . .*, VIII, 7 (1855), p. 107; Zukowsky, "Obelisks," p. 576.

15. Bloody Brook Monument, South Deerfield, Mass. By "Mr. Woods of Sunderland," 1825. Edward Everett, *Address Delivered at Bloody Brook, South Deerfield* (Boston, 1835); *Gleason's . . .*, I, 16 (1851), p. 245.

16. Battle Monument, Concord, Mass., 1836. *Gleason's . . .*, II, 23 (1852), p. 353; J.L. Swayne, *The Story of Concord* (Boston, 1939), p. 17.

17. Obelisk, Cairo, Ill. by William Strickland (?), 1838. John W. Reps, "Great Expectations and Hard Times, the Planning of Cairo, Illinois," *JSAH*, XVI, 4 (1957), p. 17.

18. Chalmette Monument, New Orleans, La. (plate 32). By Newton Richards, 1840–1855. Roos, "The Egyptian Style," [incorrect date]; Eckels, "The Egyptian Revival . . . ," p. 165; Lancaster, "Oriental Forms . . . ," p. 184; *The Picayune's Guide to New Orleans* (New Orleans, 1904), p. 53; Zukowsky, "Obelisks," pp. 575–576.

19. Battle Monument (project), Trenton, N.J. By John Haviland, 1843. University of Pennsylvania, Haviland Papers, MS., vol. IV, p. 120.

20. Monument to Gov. Silas Wright, Weybridge, N.Y. By B.M. Underhill, 1850. *Gleason's . . .*, VII, 16 (1854), pp. 249, 252.

21. Clark Monument, Rahway, N.J., ca. 1850. *Ballou's . . .*, XIV, 5 (1858), p. 72.

22. Battle of Concord Monument, Acton, Mass. By C.G. Parker, 1851. *Gleason's . . .*, I, 30 (1851), p. 472.

23. Major Andre Monument, Tarrytown, N.Y., 1853. *Gleason's . . .*, VI, 13 (1854), p. 204.

24. Murray Hill Washington Monument (project), New York City (plate 35). By Minard Lafever, 1854. Roos, "The Egyptian Style," pp. 220–221; Eckels, "The Egyptian Revival . . . ," p. 165; Minard Lafever, *The Architectural Instructor* (New York, 1856), pp. 485–487; Jacob Landy, "Washington Monument Project in New York," *JSAH*, XXVIII, 4 (December, 1969), pp. 291–297; also covered in Professor Landy's *The Architecture of Minard Lafever* (New York, 1970), pp. 140–146; Zukowsky, "Obelisks," p. 576.

Monuments

Major Egyptian Revival Monuments in America 1808–1858:

Albany, N.Y.	Albany Reservoir, 1811 (plate 85).
Baltimore, Md.	Westminster Cemetery Gate, 1813–1815, Maximilian Godefroy (plate 56).
	Project for Baltimore City and County Records Office, 1836, Robert Cary Long, Jr. (plate 100).
	Project for Greenmount Cemetery Gate, 1845, Robert Cary Long, Jr. (plate 65).
Boston, Mass.	295 Washington Street office and store building
	Old Granary Burying Ground Gate, 1840, Isaiah Rogers (plate 61).
Brighton, Mass.	Railroad Station, ca. 1840–1845.
Cambridge, Mass.	Mount Auburn Cemetery Gate, 1831, Dr. Jacob Bigelow (plates 57, 58).
Charleston, S.C.	Vanderhorst Tomb, 1855, Francis D. Lee.
Chester Factories, Mass.	Railroad Station, ca. 1840–1845.
Cincinnati, Ohio	Mrs. Trollope's Bazaar, 1829, Seneca Palmer.
Columbus, Miss.	"Waverly" Egyptian room, 1858.
Cooperstown, N.Y.	Woodside Hall, Gate House, 1829, Eben B. Morehouse (plate 37).
Covington, Ky.	Suspension Bridge, 1854.
Harrisburg, Pa.	Dauphin County Jail (project), 1842, John Haviland.

Dubuque, Iowa	City Jail, 1857–1858, John F. Rague (plates 132, 133).
Essex, Conn.	First Baptist Church, ca. 1845 (plate 94).
Farmington, Conn.	"Old Burying Ground" Cemetery Gate, ca. 1850 (plate 73).
Forest Hills, Mass.	Forest Hills Cemetery Gate, 1848, General H. A. S. Dearborn (plate 72).
Harper's Ferry, W.Va.	Railroad Bridges, I—1835, Benjamin H. Latrobe, Jr.; II—1841-June, 1842; III—1851, Wendel Bollman (plates 79, 80).
Lewiston, N.Y.	Suspension Bridge to Queenstown, Ontario, Can., 1850–1851, E. W. Serrell.
Lexington, Ky.	Receiving Vault, Cemetery, 1857.
Nashville, Tenn.	"Downtown" 1st Presbyterian Church, 1848–1851, William Strickland (plate 93).
Newark, N.J.	Essex County Courthouse, 1836–1838, John Haviland (plates 129–131).
New Bedford, Mass.	Railroad Station, Pearl Street Depot, 1840, Russell Warren (plates 39, 40).
New Haven, Conn.	58 Hillhouse Avenue, ca. 1840–1845, Henry Austin.
	Grove Street Cemetery Gate, 1844–1848, Henry Austin. (Surrounding wall and corner piers, Hezekiah Augur, 1840–1844.) (plate 71).
New Orleans, La.	Cypress Grove Cemetery Gate, 1840, Frederick Wilkinson (plate 67).
	Customs House (original project), Canal Street, 1849, A. T. Wood.
	Methodist Episcopal Church, 1836, James H. Dakin.

Newport, R.I.   Jewish Cemetery Gate, Touro Memorial Gateway, 1843, Isaiah Rogers (plate 62).

New York, N.Y.   Halls of Justice and House of Detention, The "Tombs," 1835–1838, John Haviland (plates 111–114, 116–123, 127, 128).

Croton Reservoir, 1842, James Renwick (supervisor), J. B. Jervis (designer) (plates 86, 87).

Lyceum (Athenaeum) of Natural History, design, 1835, A. J. Davis (plate 99).

Washington Monument, design, 1854, Minard Lafever (plate 35).

Niagara Falls, N.Y.   Suspension Bridge, 1852–1854, J. A. Roebling (plate 83).

Philadelphia, Pa.   Oilcloth Manufacturing Company, 1810, John Dorsey.

Mikveh Israel Synagogue, 1822–1825 William Strickland (plate 90).

Laurel Hill Cemetery Gate, 1836, project by William Strickland (plate 63).

Laurel Hill Cemetery Gate, 1836, project by Thomas U. Walter (plate 64).

Moyamensing Debtors' Prison, 1835–1836, Thomas U. Walter (plate 105).

Pennsylvania Fire Insurance Company, 1838, John Haviland (plates 42, 44, 45).

Engine House of the Northern Liberties and Spring Garden Water Works, 1844–1845 (plate 88).

Library and Conservatory, ca. 1845, design by Thomas S. Stewart (plate 101).

Mikveh Israel Cemetery Gate, ca. 1845
(plate 76).

Odd Fellows Hall, 1846 (plate 77).

138 South Front Street, 1847, Charles
B. Cooper (plates 43, 46).

Odd Fellows Cemetery Gate, 1849,
S. D. Button (plate 74).

Crown Street (Beth Israel) Synagogue,
1850, Thomas U. Walter (plate 91).

Pittsfield, Mass. Railroad Station, 1840 (plate 41).

Richmond, Va. Plan for "Monumental Church," 1812,
Benjamin H. Latrobe (plate 25).

Medical College of Virginia, 1844,
Thomas S. Stewart (plates 102, 103).

Rochester, N.Y. Mount Hope Cemetery Gate, ca. 1838,
John McConnell (plate 75).

Rocky Mountain, Ga. "Cloud's Tower," ca. 1850, Aaron Cloud.

Roxbury, Mass. See Forest Hills, Mass.

Sag Harbor, N.Y. Whalers' Church, 1843, Minard Lafever(?)
(plate 95).

St. John, New Brunswick Suspension Bridge, ca. 1853; E. W. Serrell
(?) (plate 82).

State Line, Mass. Railroad Station, ca. 1840–1845.

Trenton, N.J. New Jersey State Prison, 1832–1836,
John Haviland (plates 106, 107, 110).

Troy, N.Y. 166 and 168 Congress Street, ca. 1845–
1850 (plate 92).

Washington, D.C. Design for "Library on west of Senate,"
1808, Benjamin H. Latrobe (plate 97).

The New York City
Halls of Justice
and House of Detention
(the "Tombs")

The history of the "Tombs" falls into two distinct divisions. The first is concerned with the attitudes leading up to the actual competition for the building. The second deals with the complex itself, and its style. The keynotes of the first are humanitarianism and functionalism, while those of the second are the realization and the iconography of the architecture.

Although today we are not led to consider prisons in this country of particular architectural importance, they were, in point of fact, the first form of American architecture to achieve international fame and influence. In 1831, in part, doubtless, as a result of the Duc de la Rochefoucault's writings on the Philadelphia prison system,[1] Alexis de Tocqueville and the Comte de Beaumont were sent to the United States to inspect American prisons for the July Monarchy's recently established commission to overhaul the French penal organization.[2] William Crawford and Whitworth Russell embarked upon a similar task for the British government in 1834,[3] closely followed the same year by a second French team, this time of architects, the first real "professionals." These were G. Abel Blouet and F.-A. Demetz.[4] Also in that year an official Prussian investigator appeared on these shores in the person of Dr. Nicolas Julius.[5]

It is especially gratifying to realize that the reasons for this European awareness lie solidly within American traditions of the sanctity

146

of the individual and the betterment of society. The genesis came from England; the implementation was purely American.

It is not the purpose here to describe the appalling prison conditions throughout late eighteenth-century Europe which were portrayed in 1777 with such horror by the penal reformer, John Howard.[6] Suffice it to say, in England there were two possible fates for the convicted criminal: execution, or transportation (first to the American colonies, later to Australia; at either end of the world, convicts were worse off than slaves).[7] There were two other categories of prisoners, however: the petit criminals, and those individuals awaiting trial. For the former, as Howard pointed out, workhouses had been "established under Elizabethan Poor Laws as houses of correction for dissolute paupers and idle apprentices." It is with the latter, however, that we shall be particularly concerned. Often these unfortunates were detained for more than a year waiting for the local court to convene. During this time they were treated like any *convicted* criminal, and thrown into a dungeon with all types of convicts from pick-pockets to the most hardened assassins. Thus prisons of the day became breeding grounds for crime (due simply to the associations). But the corruption of the innocent was only the sociological evil. The philosophical one so decried by Howard and his followers was, in the incarceration of those only *accused*—not yet convicted or exhonorated—of a crime, a violation of the assumption that a man is not guilty until so proven.

John Howard's proposed reforms, however, were not to take effect for over two generations. His most recent biographer states: "He started the war for prison reform . . . but most of the battles took place after his death when followers continued the cause."[8] It was the English-born architect, John Haviland, who first designed a prison according to Howard's principles, in Philadelphia in 1821.[9] That this was a radical step for its day we might infer from the following statement describing conditions in England during the second quarter of the nineteenth century, "In 1835 an inspectorate had been created, but its task was to enforce the most elementary standards of hygiene upon recalcitrant local governments, and it often encountered situations described with such displeasure in *The State of Prisons* more than sixty years before."[10]

Among the proposals that Howard published were the following which should be borne in mind when considering the actual material needs of a prison: fireproofing; good ventilation; proper sanitary conditions with safe water and an efficient pump; a bath "to wash prisoners who come in dirty"; an oven "to purify clothes" (by literally baking them); a hospital separate from the main building, as well as both a surgeon and a chaplain in attendance; a workshop for those who want it and for the convicted; a debtors' prison "separate from the main building to preserve cleanliness, morals and health"; and, particularly important, "separate rooms or cabins (i.e., cells) for each man to be alone at least by night for reflection and repentance."[11] In general, these were the prerequisites which Haviland incorporated into his plan, which became the "modern," and model, prison so admired by his European contemporaries.

The unique climate of opinion which made all this possible was that of Pennsylvania in the early days of the Republic. One year before the publication of Howard's book, Richard Wistar formed "The Philadelphia Society for Assisting Distressed Prisoners" in 1776.[12] Out of this humanitarian organization grew, in 1787, "The Philadelphia Society for Alleviating the Miseries of Public Prisons," more familiarly known as "The Philadelphia Society for Prison Discipline." It was this group which strove to implement Howard's reforms in the United States. At about this time a complication developed in that two distinct attitudes arose, not only in America, but also in Europe, as to how these reforms could best be effected according to the type of prison discipline employed. It is thus that we find the two alternatives of the "silent" system and the "separate" system. Briefly, the silent system proposed that convicts work during the day in shops or hired out, being separated into individual cells at night. The crux of this arrangement was that no comment, conversation or other sort of communication, even a glance, was to take place between prisoners at any time. The advantage was that the convicts would, through the workshops, financially support the prisons. The disadvantage was the near impossibility of enforcing the rule of silence under such conditions of continual daily contact.[13]

The separate system called for each prisoner to be in his cell day and night, working, eating, and sleeping there. He was allowed to talk to prison officials, the chaplain, and the surgeon (as well as his family and counsel before the trial) who paid daily visits to his cell. Thus the contagion of crime among inmates could be avoided. It is unfortunate that the word "solitary" came to be employed to describe this method of confinement, for this is decidedly incorrect. It was this separate system which was the Pennsylvania method, the other being championed by New York and Massachusetts. And it was the former which became the accepted model, eventually, for enlightened penal administration. The British, French, and Prussian inspectors all returned to their respective countries to recommend the Pennsylvania System, and specifically Haviland's architectural arrangements. Appearing to bear in mind Howard's suggestions, one admirer wrote of the architect's Eastern State Penitentiary that the cells were "fireproof, of comfortable dimensions with convenient courts to each, built on the surface of the ground—judiciously lighted from the roof—well ventilated and warmed, and . . . [having] a continual supply of water to insure the most perfect cleanliness of every prisoner and his apartment."[14] It was the first prison to be built on the radial cellular system, and was published by Crawford as well as Blouet and Demetz, thus providing "a new functional concept for penal architecture influential abroad."[15]

But, although it would seem that the rest of the world recognized the primacy of the Pennsylvania System, America, in the early 1830s, did not. It was in the middle of this decade at the stronghold of the silent system that the decisive step was taken which marked the triumph of the separate system. In 1835 the complex called the Halls of Justice and House of Detention, later nicknamed the "Tombs," was begun in New York City.[16] As we shall see, the public officials in charge did not blindly follow the arrangements established on the silent system at Auburn and Sing-Sing, the major prisons in the state, but they carefully sought the desiderata for such a project, and then arranged for a nation-wide architectural competition based on these findings. The separate system was the one chosen. Thus the municipal jail and courthouse of the city of New York have a significance which even transcends their architectural importance.

By the second quarter of the nineteenth century the burgeoning city of New York had more than outgrown the physical plant provided by colonial civic services. In the earlier days of the Republic a fine City Hall had been constructed, but in 1830 the provisions for the city jail, debtors' prison, criminal courts, police offices, and city watch were wholly inadequate, and dispersed in a highly inefficient manner. The city jail, for instance, was split into three different locations: the old Bridewell and the cellar of the old almshouse downtown, and parts of Bellevue, considerably "uptown" at that time. Persons accused of offenses were imprisoned to await trial in the cellar of the Bridewell (of which the upper part served as a debtors' prison), or in either of the other two places of detention.[17] In all cases the quarters were crowded, small, damp, poorly ventilated, and dark. Of the above-mentioned needs, it was this one, the necessity of a new jail, which was the most pressing. As we shall see, the other offices and facilities were combined with this to form an efficient and centralized final project.

The first call for a new Bridewell was suggested in a message of Mayor Gideon Lee to the Common Council of New York City on March 4, 1833.[18] This had been urged upon the Mayor by the Board of Assistant Aldermen the year before. The Mayor merely pointed out the need, and suggested that the building be arranged so that the prisoners could be classified into a series of separate rooms according to "degrees of crime, vice, suspicion of crime, age, youth, color and sex."[19]

On June 22, 1834, after waiting more than a year for action, a group of humanitarian and public-spirited citizens numbering 124 altogether, and led by Hugh Maxwell, signed a petition urging that "a Prison should be built in some convenient and healthy place with cells of suitable size, well-lighted and ventilated."[20] Among the suggestions was separate confinement with accessibility to good books which would aid the prisoners' character. The Court was urged to avoid as much as possible public exposure of the charges, and to allow benevolent persons "to visit and instruct." The point was made that of roughly 8,000 prisoners detained during the four years 1822–1825, 5,000 were discharged without trial, no accuser appearing. Thus a large majority of presumably innocent people were subjected to the contagion of crime by the associations contacted in jail. This, then, was the major point in urging the separate system, and one which exerted a heavy influence upon the later deliberations of the architectural committee.

But a new and vigorous mayor had not been idle, and in his annual message to the Common Council hardly a week later (June 30, 1834) C. W. Lawrence, the first popularly elected mayor of New York City, recommended the building of a true house of detention to rectify the current evils. "In the detention of persons charged with crime, their health, morals, and civil rights seem to be greatly neglected. . . . I found in one apartment about forty, and in another twenty-eight persons charged with offenses of different kinds and degrees, from venial errors of disobedience, to crimes of atrocious character."[21]

To study the problem the Board of Assistant Aldermen formed a special committee to work with the committees of Police, Watch, and Prisons; Charity; and the Almshouse. This group was to lay the groundwork for providing a House of Detention as well as a new location for the Court of Sessions and its offices, the Police Office and its appendages. On November 24, 1834 these four committees issued a joint report to the Mayor, running to several pages, and a testimony to the humanitarian and sociological concerns of the municipal public office-holders of the day. (The italics are the author's.)

These are subjects of great interest and are so felt by the Committees. They open for discussion . . . the duty of the Common Council imposed by the *humane principles* of the human heart; some important doctrines of Prison Discipline; the honor and character of the City as connected with its Jails, *its Architecture, its taste* and its humanity. . . . [Those held for trial] by *the humanity of law are presumed to be innocent.* [A further moral danger is that] of confining the innocent with the most hard-ened criminal. . . .

As a site the Public Yard[22] is not too far from City Hall . . . for the Police Office its location is very central to the great mass of crime committed in this city . . . for the Court of Sessions it is convenient to . . . the business section of the town, and well-situated as a center in respect to the quantum of population. . . . The ground is ample; and with streets on four sides of it, *an abundance of air would be obtained* and the building could be made to *appear to advantage.* . . .

The plan and style of the proposed edifice [is to be decided upon by] a small joint committee [three members each from the Board of Aldermen and the Board of Assistant Aldermen] to be charged with these matters. However, it is advised that the House of Detention be so constructed in its interior arrangements as to allow a minute classification of prisoners—if not the separate confinement of the worst criminals, and proper and proportionate comforts and indulgences to offenders of a milder character; to give separate apartments to confined witnesses, apprentices and others, who though *innocent of crime* are subjects of confinement under the policy of law; and still other apartments to vagrants. [The Debtors' Prison should have rooms] of comfortable size for a single individual and the whole connected with a yard to which the prisoners may have *free access* during the day. . . .

As to the architectural character of the building, these committees can say, but in general terms, that it should be *simple in keeping with the uses and objects of its construction.*[23]

Within a month this report had been condensed into a series of resolutions all of which were passed by both boards and approved by the mayor. Among the resolutions was one which stated (author's italics):

That a new building or set of buildings be constructed, comprising a House of Detention, a Debtors' Prison, accommodations for the Court of Sessions and its appendages; . . . That such edifice be constructed with regard to such *architectural proportions and ornaments as will be appropriate to its dimensions and proposed uses* . . . That a Committee of three from each board be raised, and that such committee be charged with the preparation of plans, specifications and details of the proposed building . . . and whereas the *beauty and magnificence* of cities are dependent greatly upon the architecture of their private and public edifices, and the *taste and refinement* of the people judged by their encouragement of Fine Arts, therefore, to draw forth the exertion of men of *architectural science, taste and talent,* and such designs of the proposed building as shall be *appropriate* to its character and most honorable to the city, it is further resolved that said Committee be . . . authorized to offer, by advertisement, a premium of $500.[24]

From both these interrelated documents three basic ideas may be noted. One, is the very conscious feeling for humane prison reform—a sense of civil justice and penal regeneration. The second point is the careful consideration of the practicality of the site—a sense of functionalism that continues throughout the entire building history of the "Tombs." And, finally, there is a strongly accented attitude towards architecture in general, which should be borne in mind. The point is, however, that the public officials were specifically concerned with what the building was to look like. The operative phrase is "appropriateness of the style" that was to be chosen.

Before the New Year of 1835 the Architectural, or "Joint," Committee was appointed by the mayor consisting of Aldermen Bolton, Waters, and Cornell, and Assistant Aldermen Johnson (Chairman), Delamater, and Suydam.[25] No time was lost in getting on with their task. As a matter of fact, from this point until the actual beginning of construction, the swiftness of the proceedings was breath-taking; as if all the years since John Howard's proposals could be compensated for. Among the first actions was the drawing up of a questionnaire, to be sent to various experts, on court and prison matters asking for facts and figures and other vital statistics, as well as general information and knowledge. The questions dealt with arrests, classifications, and ideal physical accommodations for a House of

Detention, Debtors' Prison, Keepers' quarters, Court of Sessions, and Police and Watch offices. With a strangely touching and admirably modest flavor, the questionnaire began, in letter form, stating its purpose, and further: "The Committee feel themselves very ignorant of the matter with which they are charged, and are desirous of obtaining information from every source; and they specially charged me to address you as a person whose studies, experience and reflection qualifies you to instruct them; and to request you to favour them with your views..." The letter was printed and sent out in early January, 1835.[26]

By January 12 the answers began to flow in, the first one bearing that date, and coming from the Hon. Henry Meigs. Statistically, the overwhelming suggestion appears to be a plea for separate confinement. Not one of the letters on file at the New York City Municipal Archives and Records Center suggests the silent, or Auburn, system. Almost all state that if separate confinement is impossible, there should at least be a classification system. Another frequent recommendation is particularly clearly stated in the Hon. Stephen Allen's letter: "Cells should be on the outer walls thus allowing fresh air, good light, and the privilege of looking out on the yard."[27] Thus, the whole concept of good ventilation and light was a paramount one. Another point recorded in the poll was a kind of architectural edition of the "Cleanliness-is-next-to-Godliness" dictum: "All prisons should be so constructed as to admit a daily *washing* of the bodies of prisoners from head to foot—to be done in a comfortable manner ... I have no doubt that the perfect cleansing of the Bodies will, more than any punishment, tend to amend the morals."[28]

Other suggestions which were noted by the committee included: separation of the Debtors' Prison from the rest of the House of Detention "in the name of Decency and Cleanlyness [sic]," (not all public officials could be numbered among the tolerant and understanding humanitarians); each prisoner should be masked (for anonymity); good sanitation; a "chapple"; and a hospital.[29]

Meanwhile the Committee had not been marking time. Acting upon the advice of Samuel R. Wood, the warden of the Eastern State

Penitentiary who had strongly recommended Haviland,[30] the members voted themselves a trip to Philadelphia, not only to inspect the Penitentiary, but also to meet with its architect. A side trip to Haviland's New Jersey State Prison (plates 106–107, 110) was undertaken at the same time. It was the latter which must have particularly impressed the Committee, for among the minutes has been included a thorough description of that penitentiary. This item, from its date, January 13, and from the hasty scrawl of the writing, must have been written "on the spot" during the inspection tour. The noteworthy points that were recorded dealt mostly with the functionalism of the plan in relation to its correctively humanitarian principles. The carriage-way which permitted a van of prisoners to be backed up underneath the portico between two heavy columns to a raised entrance was remarked upon in detail, as was the processing of the newly arrived convicts. In the first room, directly behind the portico entrance, the prisoner was stripped and washed. In the next he was "dressed and blindfolded." From thence he was taken to his cell and unmasked. (Thus he would not be seen by other convicts to be possibly recognized by one of them at a later date.) The size of the individual cells was noted along with their appointments to the health and well-being of their occupants, i.e., windows, ventilators, water taps, and water closets.

But what is interesting about this report on the physical plant is that at least one quarter of its length is devoted to describing the Egyptian style of the unfinished building. There are even rough sketches of the columns, pilasters, and cornices, as well as descriptions of the torus moldings and the degree of the "battle" ("batter", one assumes) of the walls. It would seem that the Committee had been already intellectually predisposed toward separate confinement (there was not even a suggestion of a trip to visit the silent system prisons of Sing-Sing and Auburn in their own state), but their first aesthetic attitudes must have been rather forcefully engendered here upon their initial contact with this most recent example of the Egyptian Revival. There was no such attention given to the architectural style of Haviland's Gothic Eastern State Penitentiary at

Philadelphia. As a matter of fact, the architect's earlier prison was hardly mentioned at all.

With a rapidity which is astonishing in our own day of bureaucratic sloth, the Committee within a week passed a resolution to submit "a short advertisement to architects" in the leading newspapers. The announcement of the architectural competition was run on January 22 and 23.[31] On January 24, an elaborate list of "Instructions to Architects" was drawn up specifying the number of cells, and giving in detail the various chambers that would be needed in the complex which was to contain so many different departments and facilities: e.g., Watch Offices, Police Offices, two prisons, all the accoutrements of a Court of Sessions, District Attorney's Office, Sheriff's Office, wash rooms, kitchens, bakery, ice house, etc. As for the style of the arrangement, the only stricture was a repetition of the earlier statement, "Document No. 29," calling for "appropriateness."[32]

Some sixty architects responded to the advertisement, among them, A. J. Davis, Ithiel Town, William Strickland, Thomas U. Walter, Isaiah Rogers, Minard Lafever, Thomas Stewart, and John Haviland. It would seem that every architect of the first rank in America had expressed interest. The majority of them, however, appear to have become discouraged by the shortness of the time allowed, as the finished drawings were to be in the hands of the Committee by February 14, a scant three weeks from the initial notice! Thomas U. Walter's answer seems typical, as well as being indicative of the attitude of the day upon the subject of prisons. After regretting that he could not enter the competition, there remaining so little time until the deadline, he goes on to say:

> Nothing would afford me greater pleasure than to be able to enter fully into this matter, with me 'tis a favourite theme— The whole subject of prison architecture and prison discipline is one of deepest importance—and one that has been shamefully neglected—Our prisons have heretofore been colleges of vice from whence our land had been overrun by vagabonds well schooled in crime—This ought not to be. Our prisons should not only be "houses of correction," but schools of reform.

It affords me peculiar pleasure to find that New York is awake to this matter—the philanthropic spirit of Prison Reform originated *"down east"*—Pennsylvania commenced the work in earnest, New Jersey has followed and to the praise of our inestimable townsman, Jno. Haviland Esq. be it said she has excelled, and now let New York "cap the climax."[33]

In any case, "the handsome premium offered by the Common Council drew forth a very beautiful display of taste and science in five and twenty designs by as many architects."[34] On the back of one of the sheets of the original of the Instructions to Architects is a rough list organized only by the home city of the individuals noted. That this was a list of the competing architects seems probable in that there are twenty-five of them, and in that the four who, as we shall see, were prize-winners have check marks by their names. One assumes that the arrangement by geography was in the interest of "favorite son" candidates, at least for New York City. Undoubtedly there was pressure to have a New York architect get the commission for a New York building. For the present-day student, this list is particularly helpful in indicating the whereabouts of various early nineteenth-century architects who were known to have travelled extensively for their practice. In the original order they are: New York: John T. Sole, Calvin Pollard (checked), James H. Dakin, William Ross, Charles Friedrich Reichardt (checked), George A. Cobham, Ithiel Town, A. J. Davis (checked), Samuel Dunbar, Isaiah Rogers, Martin Euclid Thompson, Foster Bryant, James Sears, Edward Pilbrow; Philadelphia: John Haviland (checked), Joseph Singerly, Isaac Holden; Providence: Warren and Bucklin; Boston: Dwight and Shaw (former not checked, but should have been); Baltimore: Charles Leves, John Mills Van Osdel; separate listing: Laura, [John H.] Merrill, Bunting.[35]

Between February 15 and March 7 two exhibitions were held in the city of New York; one private, and the other open to the public. The former was in the offices of Town and Davis at 72 Cedar Street. Davis invited the Committee "for the purpose of examining *models,* drawings, engravings and the *Great Work of Napoleon on Egyptian*

Antiquities—preparatory to the adoption of a design for the House of Detention."[36] In light of later developments, it is interesting to note the emphasis on Egypt in relation to the choosing of a plan and style for the new building.

The other exhibit was the public one to view the competitors' projects prior to the judging. Of it, a contemporary newspaper reports:

> *New Public Building or Halls of Justice*—Most of our readers probably are aware that the Common Council having in contemplation the removal of the present buildings which deface the Park, passed an ordinance to erect in some suitable part of the city an appropriate edifice for the courts of justice, house of detention, &c.—It is presumed that this public structure, which, when completed, will be one of, if not the most extensive and important in this city, will occupy an entire block and cost a very considerable amount of money. Accordingly it was desirable to have the architecture and arrangement unexceptionable, for which purpose a premium of $500 has for some time been made public, for the best plan that should be offered. So liberal a prize and reputation it will bring with it to the successful candidate, has naturally brought into the field, a large number of competitors—here, as well as from other cities, in all between 20 and 30 in number.
>
> The plans and drawings of the models proposed, are now being exhibited in the jury room of the building in the rear of City Hall. We have been to look at them, and they are really worthy of the public attention generally, as elegant and ingenious specimens of art, highly honorable to the progress which architectural studies have made in our country. It is a subject of so much importance also to every citizen, that we hope they will be generally visited, as the more information and emulation that can be elicited, the better. Without wishing to prejudice or forestall the decision which the committee of the Council are to make, we may take the liberty to say that we were very favorably impressed with the beautiful Egyptian design, with a magnificent portico by Mr. John Haviland of Philadelphia; the classic finish in the Grecian style of the plan offered by the distinguished Alex.

J. Davis, of this city; one of the Gothic order, by Geo. A. Cobhan [sic] also of this city; another plain Gothic or Saxon by Joseph L. Singerly; a very splendid plan by John T. Sole of this city; and lastly, a plain structure, remarkable for the pure and chaste simplicity of its design, and the felicitous arrangement of its interior, by a young Prussian of this city, of the name of Charles Friedrich Reichardt. Now for the honor of New York, it would be much to be wished, that the design which shall be adopted, should come from one of our own citizens, though we trust this patriotic feeling will not, by any means, act upon either board as a paramount consideration to the disparagement of superior merit, come from what quarter it may. For ourselves, we think it ought to enter as an essential principle into all edifices of this description, that, considering the coerceive purposes to which they are to be appropriated, their exterior aspect should be pleasing, and, at the same time, imposing to the eye—not gloomy and terrific, as they too often are, as if intended to remind us ever of the depravity of our species, and the degraded condition to which it may be reduced.

If our own opinion only were to be consulted we should certainly prefer an admixture of the Gothic and Egyptian styles as represented in two of the drawings mentioned. The Grecian, we think, better adapted to structures intended for halls of justice or deliberative and legislative bodies. It possesses a majesty peculiarly in harmony with the uses of such edifices, and might, if possible be incorporated in the edifice at present contemplated, in that portion of it to be occupied by the courts. The Gothic, by its solemnity and richness, belongs more exclusively to monumental, collegiate and sacred architecture. Nevertheless, it is, in our opinion, when carried out in all its gorgeous details and sublime tracery, the most magnificent combination of proportion, the most impressive in its symmetry and ornaments, of any style that human genius has ever contrived. We see no reason why the porticoes, supposing that there are to be four of them, one on the center of each side of the parallelogram, should not be, two of them, Gothic, and two Grecian or Egyptian, while the remainder of the edifice could be constructed

159

after the more plain and unornamented modes of building which are now much in vogue, both for their durability, economy and beautiful simplicity, as seen, for example, in the great hotel of Mr. Astor.

We hope the committee will have a special regard to the strength of the masonry, and, as a matter of course, presume that the materials to be selected will be of the elegant blue or grey granite of our country, which is coming so much into fashion, and which, we hope, will one day entirely supersede flimsy shells of brick walls, both in our private and public edifices.[37]

A few points might be remarked upon here. First is the idea that the building is an important one whose "architecture and arrangement" are to be "unexceptionable" (i.e., without exception as to being first rank). Thus, the competing architects were also of first-rate quality.

Secondly, as to the specific plans, one might note that the first mentioned is Haviland's "Egyptian design," followed next by the Davis Grecian plan. Thus, in the eyes of the reporter, at least, these two stand out as being the most important. It is unfortunate that we do not have the Reichardt plan today, but from the brief discussion of it, one is reminded of what must have been the Schinkelesque background of the young Prussian. In relation to the critic's ideas of the desirability of "an admixture of the Gothic and Egyptian style," it should be mentioned that within a year this very point was to be realized by Thomas U. Walter when his Egyptian Debtors' Prison (plate 105) was completed alongside the Gothic Moyamensing Prison in Philadelphia in 1836.[38] Finally, one notes rather wistfully that the "durability, economy, and beautiful simplicity, as seen in the great hotel of Mr. Astor" do not seem to have appeared in the architect of that hotel's plan for this building. No mention is made of Isaiah Rogers' design.

But the most telling comments are those which deal with the iconography of the style. The idea that the "essential principle" of buildings of this sort, "considering the coerceive purposes to which they are to be appropriated," should be a "pleasing" aspect of the exterior, as well as an "imposing" one, "not gloomy and terrific," is worth remembering.[39] Thus, in this journalist's apologia for an Egyptian design, we have a direct reflection of the Committee's repeated plea for the appropriateness of the style of the building to its function.[40]

On Saturday, March 7, 1835 the Committee met to decide who should win "the handsome $500 premium." One of the conditions of the contest had been that if the judges could not find any one ideal plan, they could split the premium into a graduated series of prizes. This is precisely what transpired. According to the rough minutes of the meeting, Haviland was given first honors of $200; Reichardt and Davis (mentioned in that order) were each given $100 as second premium; and Dwight and Pollard split the third prize which gave them $50 apiece. Haviland was named supervisor of the building of the complex at a salary of $2500 per annum. Further, he was asked to draw up revised plans incorporating the best features of the various winning designs. It is an unhappy circumstance that there is no trace of the original designs, except A. J. Davis', from which would be found the elements for combination. Actually, according to the minutes, Haviland, the first choice of all six committeemen, was most appreciated for his Prison, Debtors' Jail, Court Rooms, and "general arrangement."[41] Reichardt's strong points were his designs for the Watch, Police, Elevation, and Ventilation. This last item is somewhat of a mystery, for it was in just such practical matters that Haviland excelled, and impressed the Committee upon their inspection tour, as has been noted. Furthermore, in the revised plans which he drew up later, he employed the same method that he had already used at Trenton. Opposite "Davis-Egyptian" are noted the Elevation, Court Room, and Approach. But in this case, too, there is something of a problem, for his Court Room is in the Doric section of his project, and resembles hardly at all the one in Haviland's revised plan. Nor do any aspects of Davis' Elevation and Approach seem to appear in the final version. In point of fact, the elevation of the revised project may perhaps imply a debt to Reichardt (also commended for his Elevation), for it is by far the most horizontalizing of any Haviland facade in the Egyptian vocabulary. In any case, it would not seem out of order to remark a strongly Schinkelesque quality in this revised design which might be traced through the young Prussian, Reichardt.

Dwight is given credit for his "Kitchen, Chappel [sic], Supervision." One wonders how this last feature could be better expressed architecturally than whatever Haviland, the experienced master of this type of building, must have indicated. As for the chapel, there seems to be none in the final plan.

Opposite Pollard's name there is nothing at all.

Upon this admittedly skimpy evidence, it could be proposed that the commissioners must have realized that Haviland was obviously their man, not only because of his qualities as an architect, but also because of his experience, reputation, and recommendations. The revised plan must very closely have followed his original one. Therefore, perhaps it is not without the realm of possibility that the judges, who were, after all, primarily public servants of the City of New York, felt they could not, politically speaking, give this important commission unrestrictedly to an "out-of-towner." Even if most of the architects in New York had been imported, they were at least tax-paying residents. One need only refer to the comment of the newspaper reporter, quoted above, in which "it would be much to be wished that the design . . . should come from one of our own citizens." Even if not verbally expressed, the problem must at least have been implied to Haviland when it was indicated that his own plan be used, and that he would be appointed as the salaried supervisor while the construction lasted.[42] This would in part explain why there were no comments after the commercially and politically important Pollard's name, as well as the seeming discrepancies between the various noted "good points" and the actual revised plan. In any case, Haviland appears to have been given more-or-less carte blanche for his revision. That there was indeed a revised plan, we may be sure of from a letter dated March 29 from Haviland to the Committee telling of "the revised drawings of the plans enclosed."[43] As a final point of this aspect, one might surmise that some sort of "security leak" must have taken place even before the inspection trip to Philadelphia and Trenton. In a letter from the latter city dated December 12, 1834, Haviland wrote to the chairman, W. S. Johnson, asking if there would be a competition, and explaining that he had drawn up plans, elevations, and sections, having already been to New York to inspect the site.[44]

We know that the judging took place on March 7, the results being adopted unanimously. Louis Dwight, in a letter acknowledging receipt of his $50 award and dated March 17, gives us an indication of when the prize money was distributed. It was not until April 20, however, that the Announcement of Winners was published. In this, "Document No. 60," is also a detailed exposition of the specifications by the architect including such items as the proportions of the portico columns (5 ft. × 25 ft., diameter to height), the risers of the entrance steps (1/9 of 66 in., with a 12 in. tread), an ice cellar, 26 marble mantles, a steam pump for "a 50,000 gallon cistern on the roof for baths, water closets, etc." The plans, elevations, and sections of the complex must have been printed at this time.[45] The call for estimates was answered by a wide variety of contractors, some of whom had initially expressed interest in the competition, e.g., Foster Bryant, Seth Gear, and Martin E. Thompson.[46] Haviland's own estimate as to how much the project should cost was for somewhat over a quarter of a million dollars ($257,388) (cf. $14,535,000 in 1957 for "Tombs" III).[47] On April 27, 1835 the Board of Aldermen set a flat rate of $250,000 for the building. At the same time it was officially decided to name the project the "Halls of Justice." Also, to help defray the expenses, materials from the old Bridewell were to be used. In his message to the Common Council on December 7, 1835, the mayor had proposed to raise the necessary funds by a public loan rather than by taxation.[48] Throughout the next three years, however, there were, at various times, requests for extra funds which were granted (e.g., August 2, 1837: $13,500 appropriated for warming, watering, and cooking equipment; November 1, 1837: $26,000 for extra work laying the wood foundations;[49] November 28, 1838: $8,500 "for further finishing the Halls of Justice"[50]).

For our purposes, however, there is a particularly pertinent section of Document 60 in which, upon the announcement of winners, the reasons for the choice of first prize are stated. "The style of architecture which the Committee have selected is the Egyptian, and the design is from one of the most approved examples contained in Napoleon's Egypt. It combines great *beauty* with *simplicity* and *economy* and its *massive proportions* and general characteristics render it peculiarly *appropriate and fit* to the *objects* and intended *uses* of the establishment." (The italics are the author's.)

The mayor echoed these same sentiments in his annual message to the Common Council on June 18, 1835: "Arrangements were completed during the past year for the erection of buildings on the site of the public yard . . . for a House of Detention for persons accused of crime, and for other purposes connected with our criminal and police departments. . . . The contemplated establishment will furnish accommodations for several departments of the public service, and will be so constructed as to combine *economy* in the use of the public means, *utility* in the arrangements, and *beauty* in the style of architecture. . . . [It is] to be denominated the 'Halls of Justice'."[51] (The italics are the author's.)

Over and above what the Egyptian Revival stood for in the minds of these people, one should note that the attribute of "economy" is used with different connotations in these two statements. The first is a formal value, while the second is purely fiscal. That Egyptian architecture is "economical" in the sense of simplicity of form is fairly obvious. That it is economical to build, may not seem so at once, but this was certainly in the air at the time. In an article for *The Architectural Magazine,* entitled "Design for a Termination to a Railway" (plate 38) William J. Short writing in 1835, but published a year later, stated: "I have chosen the Egyptian style which is probably the most suitable for engineering purposes: being massive; having few and bold details; and, consequently, not requiring expensive workmanship or materials."[52]

A second point which might be made from the two quotations above is the reference to "Napoleon's Egypt" in the former. As a source, this must have been the monumental official French publication sponsored by the Emperor, and not the Denon volumes which were privately undertaken. Among the Haviland papers at the University of Pennsylvania there is a syllabus of a proposed book he planned which was to include "several beautiful examples of Egyptian columns and entablatures . . . from Napoleon's Egypt." And in the partial inventory of his books is listed, "Description d'Egypte, 21 vols."[53]

Certainly the later nineteenth-century legend that the source for the "Tombs" came from plates in John Lloyd Stephens' *Incidents of Travel in Egypt*[54] is incorrect. The first edition appeared early in 1837, a full two years after the competition.[55]

The Halls of Justice was finished in August 1838, the ordinance starting the move into the building having been signed on the preceding June 11.[56]

For a description of the Haviland work, which is undoubtedly the most important Egyptian Revival monument in America, one is referred to the contemporary discussion of it in Disturnell's guidebook to New York of 1839 (*cf.* plates 111–128):

> This edifice is now in progress of erection and nearly completed, on an extensive scale, occupying the whole of the block bounded by Leonard, Elm, Franklin, and Centre streets (formerly the Corporation Yard), and is 253 feet 3 inches in length, by 200 feet 5 inches in width.
>
> The interior combines accommodations for the Courts of Sessions, Police, Grand Jury, House of Detention, Records, City Watch, District Attorney, Sheriff, Clerk of the Court, and other officers belonging to the different branches of the Institution, together with the necessary offices for cooking, washing, watering, warming, &c. The whole designed by Mr. John Haviland.
>
> The four Facades, as well as the entrance hall, are executed in the Egyptian style of architecture, with Hallowell granite.
>
> The principal front has a distyle portico of four columns, with palm-leaved capitals. Above the capitals are square dies, upon which rests the architrave, ornamented with a large winged globe encircled by serpents. The architrave, is surmounted by a cornice, composed of a bold Scotia, enriched with reeded Triglyphs and a banded Torus; and which, being of the same height

with that of the similarly embellished wings, form with them one continued line. Moreover, the banded moulding of the cornice descends in the form of a roller on all the external angles of the edifice. Both the wings are perforated with five lofty windows, extending the height of two stories, and finished with diminished pilasters which support a cornice over each, composed simply of a bold Scotia, enriched with a winged globe and serpents.

The lateral fronts of Leonard and Franklin Streets have each two projecting Pylones [*sic*] or Porches, with two columns: the one on Leonard street adjoining the principal front, is the entrance to the Debtors ward, and the opposite one on Franklin street is the entrance to the Police ward; the other two corresponding porches next to Elm street, form the carriage entrance to the House of Detention. These porches are 54 feet wide, and their columns and entablatures correspond with those of the principal front, but the caps and shafts of the columns are less enriched. The recess in both these lateral fronts is six feet, and is relieved by five windows corresponding in character with those of the principal front, but of less proportion and enrichment, the Scotia being finished with reeded Triglyphs only, instead of the winged globe and serpents. The approach to the windows on these fronts is guarded against by a neat railing in keeping with the architecture. The rear or front on Elm street having no entrance or windows, is simply relieved by seven narrow recesses in imitation of embrasures, and a railing in the same style as those on the lateral fronts.

A terrace surrounds the whole enclosure, raised ten feet above the level of Centre street, from which you ascend eight steps of a truncated and pyramidal form, to the platform of the portico, from which you ascend also twelve steps, between the intercolumniation of the rear columns to the entrance hall. This hall is 50 feet square and 25 feet high, supported by eight columns, ranged between two rows with their antae placed on the opposite walls. These columns bear the character o[f] an order taken from the colonnade of the temple at Medynet Abou. Attached to the antes opposite these columns, the architect originally designed to place the Egyptian cariatides [*sic*], so highly spoken of by the French artists in Napoleon's great work on Egypt, published by Paukonche [*sic*]; and he feels assured that the Board will yet be of his opinion, and finally adopt these splendid and imposing figures in this entrance hall, as nothing else will be wanting to perfect the edifice; their capitals are ornamented with the leaves and flowers of the Lotus. The floors are arched and laid in mosaic of an Egyptian character, governed in form by the compartments in the ceiling to which each belongs.

The principal courts, jury, witness, and other business rooms, are connected with, and leading into the entrance hall. On the left side are doors and passages communicating with the grand jury room, offices for register, clerk of the court, district attorney, and sheriff, debtors' ward and witness rooms; and on the right side are disposed the magistrates' offices, court and witness rooms, watchmen's dormitories, police court, officers' rooms, and cells for nightly commitments. The centre leads to the court of sessions (including two jury rooms, and separate gallery capable of containing an audience of 300 persons); the whole well ventilated and lighted, and in a situation the least liable to be disturbed by the noise of the adjoining streets.

The House of Detention is a distinct and isolated building, 142 feet in length by 45 in width. It contains 148 cells, divided into four distinct classes for prisoners, including baths, and rooms for male and female, white and black vagrants. The lower cells are 6 feet 9 inches wide, 11 feet high, and 15 feet long, diminishing 18 inches in length in each story; they are provided with cast iron water closets, hydrant, water cock, ventilators, and are warmed by Perkins' hot water pipes (introduced and now in successful operation in the new Penitentiaries at Philadelphia and Trenton, by J. Haviland, architect.) The floors, and ceilings, and galleries are formed from slabs from the North River flagging; the doors and window jambs of iron; and the entire cells are otherwise finished on the most approved plan for security, seclusion, ventilation, economy of supervision and watching. The corridors are ten feet wide below, and widen at each story to 19 feet at the summit, affording a free ventilation and uninterrupted view of every cell door, from the observatory. A bridge leads across from the House of Detention to the prisoners' seat in the court-house. By reference to the specifications and drawings, it will be seen that every part of the building is calculated to be executed in the most substantial and approved manner, with the best materials of their kind; and that no pains or expense is spared to effect all the desired objects of the Institution, with the aid, experience, and best talent that the country affords.

The building is generally fire proof by ceilings and floors of arched masonry.

The site on which the building is erecting, is formed of made ground, every precaution having been used to render the foundation secure by the introduction of iron ties, inverted arches, and heavy timbering. The whole area was excavated several feet below the water level, large timbers were placed together, and range timbers at right angles with these laid several feet wider than the respective walls.

This edifice was commenced in 1836 [*sic;* it was undoubtedly started in 1835], and finished during the summer of 1838. The several stories of the House of Detention, with their weighty stone floors, have now been completed some time, without showing any appearance of cracks or partial settlement.[57]

In this description it is disappointing not to find a comment as to specific reasons for the style of architecture. One cannot, however, help being struck by the obvious pride in this style and in its workmanship which is exhibited by the author of the guidebook, who had certainly discussed the building with the architect. Also it should be noted that the functionalism of the complex has been carefully worked out and noted by the author; for instance, the fact that the Court Room has been placed "in a situation least liable to be disturbed by the noise of the adjoining streets." This aspect, incidentally, is not so true of the Davis plan (plate 124). Or, one might note the section on the disposition of the cells in the House of Detention "affording a free ventilation and uninterrupted view of every cell door from the observatory." Throughout the entire description there runs a thread of consciousness of sanitation and health: running water,

water closets, hot water pipes, "the whole well ventilated and lighted."

As for the specific drawings themselves, one might point out their overall sense of clear, classicizing geometry (note especially plate 114). Strangely enough, although the architectonic forms are those of trapezoids due to the batter motif, the effect seems as if they are the strictest sort of rectangle. The almost unrelieved system of straight lines combined with a severely restricted use of ornament builds up a rigidly formal rhythm of disciplined order. There is a pervasive sense of the uniform blocular arrangement which contributes to the feeling for a massive effect, perhaps tidier and less monumentalizing than the overwhelming "chunkiness" of antique Egyptian architecture. In relation to this anti-colorist, geometric formalism there are two interesting documents pertaining to the estimates for the building. K. B. Sewall, a contractor in stone, proposed his wares stating: "It [his granite] splits and works as well as Hallowell Granite[58]—is nearly as dark as Quincy and is entirely *free from iron rust and veins*—The jail at Wiscasset in Maine, built of this stone before the State was admitted into the Union, presents the same *uniform appearance* now as when first erected. For a public building such as your advertisement describes, Granite is certainly preferable to any other material. The colour of marble from our best quarries is *not uniform*—it is easily soiled and when exposed to wear it is not much more durable than wood."[59] (The italics are the author's.)

A second bit of evidence towards this "whole-block" concept is to be noted from a letter containing Foster Bryant's estimate of contracting for the work: "The specification requires the joints to be fitted with *putty of the same colour as the stone*. . . ."[60] Thus the viewer was to behold a building comprising static, solid geometric shapes, rather than one of dematerialized, nervous, coloristic effects.

In general, the edifice does indeed present a rational crystalization of Schinkelesque or Ledolcian ideals. This may be specifically noted in the front elevation (plate 123) where the masonry joints parallel to the ground are mildly emphasized (vis-à-vis, the vertical ones which are suppressed). This contributes to the overall horizontalizing effect which is abetted by the absence of terminal accents at each extremity. The individual masonry blocks themselves are laid upon their long sides. Also, the more imposing and higher flight of stairs is inside the portico, thus not disturbing the planar effect of the long, low facade. At the top of these steps are three portals fitted into the block of the structure, and surmounted by a favorite Havilandian motif, corbelled arches above the lintels (cf. New Jersey State Penitentiary, Trenton) (plates 107, 110).

The lateral facades (plate 121) bespeak an unexpected axial arrangement as a contrast to the front. The initial plane presents an opposite organization with the strong terminal point of a pylon portico, modified to *distyle in antis,* at each end. These are joined by a lower wall whose masonry is compensatingly somewhat less horizontalizing than that of the side pylons. The principal building lies in a deeper plane, and contributes towards varying the otherwise rather sterile symmetry of the primary plane. But, as was the case with the main facade, even in this more complex view one is made aware of the militant governing rules of order. The roof line of the main section of the principal building is the same as the top of the side porticoes. The cornices of all the porticoes are at precisely the same level. The iron railing in front of the lower side wall is of the same height as the top of the pseudo-podium upon which the parts of the building appear to sit. The corbel motif above each of these side entrances is echoed more grandly and in reverse by the stepped pedimental arrangements of all three porticoes.[61]

The rear elevation (plate 118) is the most formally abstract of any. Here the clear, simplified geometric statement made by the profile view of the side entrance pylons appears at each end of a long, high wall. This, itself, is unrelieved except for the battered niches echoing the shape described by the torus moldings on the profiled pylons. These recesses in the walls were doubtless inspired by the "flagpole" niches of such Egyptian temple pylons as those found at Karnac and Philae. Behind looms the hipped roof of the rather non-Egyptian cell block of the House of Detention. The precise tempo of horizontal openings punctuates the severe wall of this building. The reeded cavetto cornice does produce a more recognizable Egyptian motif, however. The fenestration is somewhat less obvious. These low, horizontal windows, whose exterior frames are smaller than the interior ones, are cut into the wall at oblique angles. Between the two frames is a distance of twelve inches. The smaller, outer frame measures 5½ in. × 30 in. which would appear to discourage any effort at escaping via that path. Any necessity for iron bars is thus precluded; a feature that doubtless would have appealed to the sensitivities of those who were particularly prison-reform conscious. These windows were at the top of each cell. At the bottom were small rectangular holes which may be seen between and immediately above the windows of the story below. Thus, with these openings at the ceiling and floor of each chamber, there was provided an efficient system of ventilation and light. Strange to say, the window-form here is similar to New Empire temple fenestration. We have seen that the interior columns of the main entrance hall in the Court building have as their source "Medynet Abou." It is exactly at Medinet Habu that this sort of window may be found. But the more immediate source is probably from plate 69, Antiquities, vol. III of the *Description de l'Egypte*. . . . This back view of an unidentified temple in the Fayoum with its similar windows appears almost as a roofless House of Detention (plate 120; also note plate 119).

The disciplined severity is similar on the opposite side of this structure which faces on the courtyard (plate 116). In the drawing of the transverse section this may be noted where the cell block appears as a massive backing for the tripartite, three-storied forward element of which the central member, the Court Room, is higher, larger, and more accented than the flanking separate wings of the Debtors' Prison, and the Police and Watch offices.

In the longitudinal section (plate 122) the truly impressive grandeur of the Egyptian Public Hall and Court Room may be realized when their spaces are compared to the more human module of the cell block and the service areas. The former, placed as a *piano nobile,* present a one-storied effect barely lower than the five floors of the House of Detention. The interior Egyptian palm capitals are upon bundled papyrus shafts which are of a somewhat less ponderous proportion than the similarly styled exterior columns (whose capitals are one-fourth of the height). Again, on the inside (plates 116, 122), the windows and doors of this section are battered and in most cases there are, above, either corbelled openings, or blind corbelled openings. Several of the mantels are also battered. The unique corbel technique is similarly used in the dome of the Court Room. This is marked upon the exterior; that is, contained within the rectangular block.[62] The three basic parts of this complex—Hall, Court, and Cells—are fitted into the two buildings, thus affording more interesting rhythm of ascending spaces than if each increase in height were housed separately (plate 122). This upward movement is presaged by the stairs themselves which are interrupted by the massive main portico. The only richness of surface decoration is to be found in the various capitals; although we know from engravings of somewhat turbulent interior scenes that there were winged orbs above the doors. Otherwise the interiors appear to be simple and severe, relieved by corbelling motifs and coved ceilings.

As to the ground plan of the main building, one should note in the lower floors an acute sensitivity to practical problems such as sewage and drainage, as well as functional ones such as the placement of the various servicing areas, liberal storage space, ample provision for fireplaces, seven separate stairways, and even the Watchmen's Coffee Room. When one considers the number of functions the complex was to provide, it is astonishing to note that more than one-third of the site is given over to out-of-door areas. Perhaps this is not, after all, so surprising when one recalls the definite preoccupation of the Committee with ventilation, fresh air, and light. Surely this happy ratio was only made possible by the skill of the architect in utilizing to good purpose all available space in the building itself. Staircases and offices were provided in the pylon towers. The curious curvature of the corridor of the Debtors' Prison, for instance, can most easily be explained *not* on the basis of supervision, which was relatively unimportant in the case of debtors, but by the fact that the northern portion of the pylon tower could, only in this manner, be used as one of the stairwells.[63] If the entrance and passage on that side were to be of comfortable width, and if each of the cells was to have an outside window onto the courtyard, then this was the only arrangement which would provide for the maximum number of decently-sized cells.

The basic pattern of the plan for the almost square rectangular site is dominated by the main facade of the Court building backed by the parallel cell block to the rear (plate 111). The three back wings of the former, and at right angles to it, serve as a minor motif, which, in turn, provides a relieving aspect to the major disposition. The Portico-Entrance Hall-Court Room unit gives an important balancing axial accent with its rows of columns and walls running straight through the facade block in a strong counter-movement to it, recalling a great hall church. One enters the impressive and shadowy portico, proceeds along the three-aisled entrance hall into the lighter, airier, and more spacious Court Room. This is the axis that interrupts the opposite-running facade plan. As for the two side wings, it might be observed that they are not slavishly symmetrical in their interior organization. This is due to their difference in function; the curving Debtors' wing is imbedded in the main block so organically that one is hardly aware of moving from one part of the building to the other, while the Police and Watch wing is strongly separated from the principal section by a stairway. It is this end of the main building, incidentally, which contains in its inner areas the private court room and the Common Police Court (vis-à-vis the main Court of Sessions).[64]

A brief glance at the Davis plan (plate 124)[65] will show the superiority of Haviland's project. In the first place, the former, with its more elaborate decoration, greater number of stories, higher masonry, and larger size, would undoubtedly have been in excess of the proposed cost.[66] Further, that design allows for an extremely limited amount of open ground, while the proposed height of the building would let little or no direct light upon the courtyard. As we have noted, the main Court Room is virtually on the street. And, whereas the Doric facade in front of the shallow Roman dome seems meticulously archeological, the Egyptian facade which rises before the looming Castel Sant'Angelesque cell block, is strangely ineffectual, probably due to the clash of a certain degree of archeological correctness (the central portion)[67] with elements quite foreign to this (the fenestration). Although it is obvious that Haviland's window disposition is similar to the typical Davis motif of one vertically oriented frame containing more than one story of windows, the former architect, by employing Egyptian detail such as the batter, torus molding, and cavetto cornice manages more successfully to unify the facade elements. Davis' slender, long windows, and his breaking up of the roof-line of the front elevation into three distinct levels, betray a basic verticalizing attitude that is more in keeping with neo-Gothic than with an Egyptian Revival aesthetic. Davis places a flight of stairs between the two central columns only, and not across the entire portico. Furthermore, this stairway leading to the *piano nobile* is uninterrupted from the street level to its apex. In this manner, Davis provides a steep, narrow ascent which again gives a strong vertical sense. It is a feeling different from Haviland's imposing, and also curiously lofty, arrangement.

On the other hand, one should not discount Davis' taste, imagination, and archeological learning. We have seen that he was aware of the Egyptian mode as a valid revival style, having designed several monuments in that manner,[68] and having invited the Committee to inspect his models of Egyptian buildings and to view his copy of "Napoleon's *Egypt*." That he was aware of the symbolic aspects of the style is not beyond the realm of probability. Indeed, in his Egyptian facade for the "Tombs," he has portrayed, in place of cartouches in the central cavetto cornice, a series of "hieroglyphic metopes" which depict such traditional prison accoutrements as a flail crossed with a large key, a ball and chain, and the scales of justice, the first two motifs hardly evocative of the spirit of prison reform.

In this case, however, Haviland's design is the more effective. The Davis project for adding "two or three stories to the Halls of Justice"[69] underlines this (plate 125). He was quite unable to play a Palazzo Farnese Michelangelo to Haviland's San Gallo, for the imposition of his overwhelming personal style upon that of Haviland destroys the building.

There remain two small problems in connection with the "Tombs."

The first is the question of what the actual ground plan was. The second is the apparent presence of an extra element in the building not shown in the plans.

We have noted that there are several sets of plans for the Halls of Justice:

A. The plan for the competition.
B. The plan after the competition, the "incorporating" one, a printed group which belongs with the official published description of the building that Haviland wrote for the city documents, and for the contractors applying for the commission.
C. Another copy is on file at the Royal Institute of British Architects (the two former ones are dated 1835, the latter, 1838).
D. Further, there is among the Strickland papers at Nashville[70] a copy of the ground plan of the principal story, presumably by a draughtsman-student in William Strickland's office. The credit is given to Haviland with the date 1837, and the rendering is signed "Andrew J. Binny, Nov., 1840."

There are minor differences in all of these ground plans, the most notable being the disposition of rooms in the right-hand side of the frontal block. This is the section which contains the two lesser court rooms. The two later plans ("C" and "D") are almost alike, however, and appear to give greater size to the Common Police Court at the expense of a through-running passage from the right side entrance to the main hall. As "B" was the earlier plan published and presumably issued for the benefit of the various competing contractors, it must be supposed to be the second, or "incorporating," Haviland plan, *after* the judging of the competition. Thus, the differences cannot be ascribed to the revisions which the architect was meant to have made following the contest. It might be proposed that the later plans ("C" and "D") were those made of the building as it was actually executed, rather than as it was originally conceived in its final form; the changes being the result of reflection and practical considerations of one sort or another made during the period of construction, which, as we know, lasted for three years. The newer arrangement allows the Common

Court Room to be approximately twelve feet longer. This was made possible by reducing the number of witness rooms from four to two, and eliminating the magistrate's private office, still leaving his official one. Although this also meant that there was no unimpeded passage between the right side entrance and the main entrance hall, the changes do appear to be reasonable and practical ones.

This theory might be reinforced by consideration of another change, which is that in the later plans the entrances to the individual cells are placed at the sides of their corridor walls rather than at the centers of them. As the cells measured either 7 ft. 3 in. × 9 ft. 9 in. in the House of Detention (main floor), or 6 ft. 9 in. × 11 ft. in the Debtors' Prison, it would seem more commodious if the widths were not broken up so awkwardly in the center by a door. Certainly the placement of a bed or cot would be more convenient in the later-designed cells.

That changes did take place during the building program would perhaps partially explain the second problem which is the presence of an octagonal tower of at least three stories that appears to have been erected over the main entrance hall, and which would account for the strange octagonal block that is to be seen on the roof behind the main portico in pictures of the finished building. There is, however, no indication of any of this in the architect's renderings. But from an engraving of the fire which destroyed this element, one sees that its eight sides were battered, as were its openings.[71] Although it cannot be ascertained how it was capped, it does recall similar Haviland motifs on other Egyptian buildings at both the Trenton State Prison (earlier than the "Tombs"), and the Essex County Court House (later) at Newark, a Georgianizing survival to the structures.[72] A later (1871) description of the Halls of Justice relates: "The building as it appeared some thirty years ago contained a high tower which was destroyed by fire on the day appointed for the execution of Colt, and is believed to have been a part of the unsuccessful plan for his escape."[73] This would date the fire November 18, 1842, only four years after the "Tombs" was completed.[74] Actually, David M. Kahn has pointed out in an interesting recent article that this tower served as a fire watch and was built in 1842. Although constructed of wood it is an irony that it burned some six months after the commission was approved by the Mayor.[75] Although there is apparently no proof, it is not impossible that the addition was designed by Haviland, as suggested above.

The distinctive aspects of the complex may be grouped into four categories. First, the building was conceived at a high point in the nineteenth-century tide of humanitarianism. Part of prison reform was involved with the actual discipline; equally important for the treatment and rehabilitation of the convict was the reform of the physical conditions under which he lived. This involved such features as: separate cells, fireproofing, efficient ventilation and light, adequate heating facilities, and effective sanitary provisions. All these features were not only due to an awakening to the fact that prisoners are human beings, but also there was the realization that many of the committed were legally innocent until proven guilty, and thus not deserving of actual punishment.

Secondly, the building was one upon which much attention and effort had been expended to make it an efficiently functioning agent for the public service. This involved, not only the effective installation of the above-mentioned humanitarian "machinery," but also the efficacious laying out of the various offices, chambers, cells, and yards, so that in their day-to-day interrelated uses the optimum of efficiency could be achieved at a minimum of all types of expenditures (e.g., main court room backed up to the cell block and connected with it by the original New York "Bridge of Sighs" thus enabling a swift and secure passage of the accused to his trial).

The third aspect is the source and nature of the formal style itself. The complex was highly original in its organization and arrangement. The inventor of the radial cellular system of penitentiaries here produced another plan independent of predecessors. For, with its involved combination of varied functions, this architectural problem was a new one, as was the case earlier at the Eastern State Penitentiary.

To this solution Haviland applied a studiously archeological Egyptian vocabulary. It has been noted he owned the foremost scholarly publication of the day dealing with the Land of the Nile, and that he took certain of the details from a specific ancient monument, Medinet Habu. In his reinterpretation of the style, Haviland makes a final statement of Romantic Classical ideals. The ancient source (more antique than Antiquity), the solid geometric forms and their inter-relationships, the refined precision of their definition, the accent on volumetric blocks rather than coloristic surface patterns, the extreme severity and simplicity of these forms, the economy of decoration, the monumental additive aspect of the few parts; all these combine to produce a stoically classical, rationally ordered, and evocatively appropriate architecture.

And it is this appropriateness which is the final aspect of these four. In a neighboring state the style had already been used for penitentiary architecture in the most modern, and the most admired jail in the country. Not only had the Committee felt called upon to write a detailed description of this building from the functional standpoint, but also there was a significant interest in its style. No other prison was so remarked upon by those who were to choose the style of the "Tombs." Time and again, from the official documents it can be noted that the appearance was to be tasteful and beautiful, as well as being stylistically apt for the building's purposes and uses. The fact that Haviland's Egyptian design was the choice indicates that in its day Egyptian was considered to incorporate taste, beauty, simplicity, refinement, magnificence, and massiveness, besides being pleasing, imposing, and sublime. If the key phrase of the mayor's statement on its attractiveness were economy of the public means, utility of function, and beauty of style, its most important attribute would appear to be an unnecessary-to-explain, *a priori* appropriateness.

The New York City Halls of Justice, the "Tombs," was, then, a building of distinguished quality, appropriate and meaningful style, serving a utilitarian purpose in a humanitarian and functional manner.

Notes

1. Duc de Liancourt-La Rochefoucault, *Les prisons de Philadelphia* (Paris, 1796). (English translation same year published in London.) Frédéric Alexandre Duc de Liancourt-La Rochefoucault (1747–1827) was a noted philanthropist and agronomist.
2. George Sumner, *The Pennsylvania System of Prison Discipline Triumphant in France* (Philadelphia, 1847), p. vi, 11.
3. William Crawford, *Penitentiaries of the United States* (London, 1834).
4. F.-A. Demetz, *Lettre sur le système penitentiaire* (Paris, 1838).
5. William Crawford, *Extracts from the Second Report of the Inspectors of Prisons for the Home District* (London, 1837), p. 30.
6. John Howard, *The State of Prisons* (London, 1929) (original edition, 1777); D. L. Howard, *John Howard; Prison Reformer* (London, 1958).
7. Between the American Revolution and the "opening up" of Australia for this purpose, convicts were incarcerated in the old prison hulks which formerly had served as depots until enough prisoners were collected to be sent overseas in a shipment.
8. D. L. Howard, *Howard,* p. 83.
9. Haviland had worked in Russia after leaving his master, James Elmes. There he was under the protection of his uncle by marriage, Count Morduinoff, Admiral of the Black Sea Fleet and Minister of Marine. This man had been a close friend and death-bed companion of Howard in 1790. It was quite possibly through this Russian nobleman that Haviland became interested first in prison reform. "Obituary Notice of John Haviland," *Pennsylvania Journal of Prison Reform,* vol. VII, no. 3 (July, 1852), p. 98. The prison was the famed Eastern State Penitentiary of 1823–1828. Haviland also submitted a design for the first Western State Penitentiary at Pittsburgh in 1818, of which we have no trace, although Fiske Kimball in his article on Haviland in the *Dictionary of American Biography* (New York, 1935), (hereafter, *DAB*) indicates that there may be a case for a "reform-type" prison here, even though there appears to be no solid evidence. Haviland did design the second Western State Penitentiary which very soon replaced the first one. H. H. Richardson organized on Havilandian principles his county jail in that city.
10. D. L. Howard, *Howard,* p. 169.
11. John Howard, *Prisons,* pp. 20–25.
12. Richard Vaux, *The Pennsylvania Prison System* (Philadelphia, 1884), p. 3.

13. "In the report of Demetz upon the prisons of the United States he mentions that in that of Sing-Sing, on the silent system, on the second day of his visit, his object and his character were known to nearly all the prisoners." Sumner, *The Pennsylvania System . . .* , p. 17.

14. Vaux, *The Pennsylvania Prison . . .* , p. 13.

15. H.-R. Hitchcock, *Architecture, Nineteenth and Twentieth Centuries* (Baltimore, 1958), p. 77. For a general summary of the two reform systems see David J. Rothman, *The Discovery of the Asylum* (New York, 1971), particularly chapter 4, "The Invention of the Penitentiary," pp. 79–108.

16. It must be admitted that the "Tombs" was not a penitentiary, but it was a prison and was designed to house those waiting for trial, or execution; petit criminals; debtors; in short all those criminals and accused criminals of the city not actually "serving time" for major offenses.

17. The use of the term "Bridewell" to denote a city prison seems to derive from an early London jail donated to that city in 1552 by Edward VI. It had been "formerly a palace near St. Bridget's (St. Bride's) Well; from whence it had the name; which after it became a prison, was applied to other prisons of the same sort." John Howard, *Prisons,* p. 174.

18. Municipal Archives and Records Center of New York City, Filed Papers 1835, Drawer no. T-607, Mayor's Annual Message, March 4, 1833 (Hereafter, MARC, followed by the year and drawer number plus the date of the document, if any. The category "Filed Papers" applies to all the MARC material to be quoted, and so will be omitted in future references.)

19. [New York City] *Documents of the Board of Assistant Aldermen,* vol. I (1832) Document 18 (Hereafter, *Doc., Bd. of Assist.*)

20. MARC, 1835, T-607, Memorial of Hugh Maxwell, June 22, 1834.

21. *Doc. Bd. of Assist.,* vol. I (1834), Mayor's Annual Message, June 30, 1834. (As the printing of official city documents was considered to be a political plum, there were frequent changes of such firms. This explains why there is no logical sequence of volumes in such publications.)

22. The site suggested was the Public Yard, part of a former freshwater pond which, shortly before its being filled in (1808), was the scene of perhaps the first experiment in steam navigation by John Fitch witnessed by both Livingston and Fulton. Charles Sutton, *The New York Tombs* (San Francisco, 1874), p. 47. Before choosing this site, elaborate tests were made, and officially reported as to the possibility of erecting a major stone edifice on the fill of this Collect Pond. Such feasibility was affirmatively recorded, MARC (1835), T-604. The plot was bordered by Leonard, Franklin, Elm, and Centre streets.

23. MARC (1835), T-604, Doc. No. 29, Nov. 24, 1834.

24. [New York City] *Proceedings of the Boards of Aldermen and Assistant Aldermen,* vol. II (1835), pp. 288–289 (Hereafter, *Proc. Bds. Ald. and Assist.*)

25. [New York City] *Documents of the Boards of Aldermen and Assistant Aldermen,* vol. II (1835), p. 288. (Hereafter, *Doc. Bds. Ald. and Assist.*)

26. MARC (1835), T-607, Questionnaire, Jan. 1835. There are roughly twenty answers filed. The suggestions were recorded in the original minutes of the Committee, and filed in the same drawer under "Notes as to principles in construction of Prisons." *Re* separate confinement: "To protect the accused from all unreasonable and unnecessary restraint, and especially from all injurious and corrupt associations . . . for the safety of the accused . . . good for reflection. . . . Desperate bands of rogues are formed out of companions in prison."

27. *Ibid.,* dated Jan. 16, 1835.

28. *Ibid.,* letter from the Hon. Henry Meigs, Jan. 12, 1835; a letter in the same drawer from the Rev. Louis Dwight of Boston dated Jan. 22, 1835, after praising the architectural arrangement of the Eastern State Penitentiary, ends: "In one respect, however, I cannot be to [sic] explicit, nor can you be too resolute, i.e., on the importance of a room, bath, and every convenience for cleansing the men. . . ." Dwight was deeply involved in the prison reform movement.

29. *Ibid.,* letters of Police Capt. I. Swain (n.d.); Joseph Curtis, Jan. 19, 1835; Henry Ramsey, Jan. 15, 1835; and Dr. Smith of Committee on Police (n.d.).

30. "[John Haviland] can give you a better plan than any other man in this or any other country. I know this is strong language, but I am well satisfied and do sincerely believe that he knows more about building prisons and penitentiaries than any Architect living. He is a man of much taste regularly educated in his profession and has for the last 12 years paid special attention to this subject. Besides having created the penitentiary which I have charge of, he has had the pulling down and new modelling of the one in Pittsburgh, has furnished drawings for one now erecting in Missouri; has lately given them drawings and estimates for one in Rhode Island; done the same for a new one in Lower Canada and is super-intending one now erecting in New Jersey which I believe when finished will be the most complete building for the purposes for which it was designed that has ever been built. He associates and consults with those who have had great practical experience in prison discipline and has embodied in his plans views which no Architect can have as an artist alone. Added to his elegant acquirements he is a most amiable excellent man, and too modest to push himself through a crowd. . . ." MARC (1835), T-607, letter from Samuel R. Wood to Joseph B. Collins, Nov. 14, 1834. It ends with the familiar plea: "I do hope you will adopt the plan of separate confinement, its importance is beyond any expense you can incur."

31. "To Architects. $500 PREMIUM—The Common Council of New York have determined to erect a new Public Building and offer a premium of $500 for the best design. The building must comprise a Prison for

two hundred offenders committed previous to trial—a Prison for fifty debtors—a Common Court Room—Grand and Petit Jury Rooms—etc., etc.; a Police Office and Watch House. The land appropriated for the Building has a street on each side, and is 200 feet on the easterly and westerly sides, 253 feet on the southerly side and 233 on the northerly side.

"Architects who may desire to offer designs will be furnished with instructions in detail, and a Plan with profiles of the land free of postage on application by letter to the subscriber. Immediate application is requested, as a very short time can be allowed in which to prepare the drawings. William Samuel Johnson, Chairman Committee. New-York, Jan. 21st, 1835." *New-York American* (Jan. 22, 1835), vol. XVI, no. 4987, p. 3.

32. For a contemporary view on the trials and tribulations of architects involved in competitions (e.g., not enough time, unqualified judges, personal politics) see: Hostis, "Remarks on Competition Plans," *Architectural Magazine,* vol. II (1835), pp. 12–14.

33. MARC (1835), T-607, letter from Thomas U. Walter, June 30, 1835. It is interesting to note in *re* Walter's praise of Haviland that the former in 1838 (Dec. 7) presented a complete set of copies of plans, elevations, and sections of the Halls of Justice to the Royal Institute of British Architects (hereafter, RIBA) where they remain today filed under "Haviland" (plate 112). A manuscript description of the interior (which Fiske Kimball in his *DAB* article attributes to that architect himself) has been lost from that library, unhappily. One might surmise that Haviland gave the plans and description to his friend to present to the newly formed society. At the same time Walter presented an elevation of his Egyptian-style Moyamensing Debtors' Prison. (Walter had been sent to England in 1838 by the Girard College trustees to study British college buildings. [Agnes Addison Gilchrist, "Girard College: An Example of the Layman's Influence on Architecture," *JSAH,* vol. XVI, no. 2, p. 26.]) not only did the Institute welcome such gifts to its repository, but it is also known from an undated copy of a letter Haviland wrote to Crawford that the architect still considered himself a British subject, and was desirous of opportunities and work back in England. "The Halls of Justice have been in successful operation since May 1st [thus the date of this is probably 1838, the same year as the Walter presentation]. . . . [I would] wish to work in England where as a native architect I should not labour as I do here, under the disadvantages of national prejudices." University of Pennsylvania, Haviland Papers, vol. I, pp. 174–175. For a similar, if somewhat softer view see "Z", "Letter *re* Emmigration of Architects to North America," *Architectural Magazine,* vol. I (Dec. 1834), pp. 384–386.

34. MARC (1835), T-607, Document 60.
35. Among the more noteworthy of the group (in the order noted in the minutes):

Calvin Pollard (fl. 1825–1850; died 1850) mostly a minor New York architect, although Hamlin feels he is responsible for the Greek Revival church at Petersburg, Virginia. He may have been involved in the building of the 1833 National Theatre in New York; in any case, he did the 1840 rebuilding of it. He is also responsible for the Dutch Reformed Church in that city. There is a large collection of his plans in the New-York Historical Society, mostly of urban houses. T. F. Hamlin, *Greek Revival Architecture in America* (New York, 1944), pp. 127, 151, 152, 191.

James H. Dakin (1808–1852), in the firm of Ithiel Town prior to 1835. When both Town and Davis were absent from New York in 1833, it was Dakin who was in charge of the office. Although he designed some of the houses in Washington Square in that city, and was possibly involved in the building of the Dutch Reformed Church (see above), he was also particularly adept as a Gothicist. He was one of the founders of the American Institution of Architects, in 1836. Roger H. Newton, *Town and Davis, Architects* (New York, 1942), pp. 61, 103, 119, 140, 171, 231. In 1835 he went to New Orleans to work with his brother Charles. They won the competition for the first State House at Baton Rouge. H. F. and E. R. Withey, *Biographical Dictionary of American Architects* (Los Angeles, 1956), p. 160. The firm of Dakin and Dakin was responsible for the Gothic Revival Church of St. Patrick in New Orleans which had not been completed by 1845. [B. M. Norman], *Norman's New Orleans and Environs* (New Orleans, 1845), p. 95. James H. Dakin also submitted three drawings to the Girard College competition. These were in the Greek Revival style. Gilchrist, "Girard College . . . ," p. 26. But he was not responsible for the former 6th Precinct Police Station on Rousseau Street, New Orleans, which exhibits certain "Tombs"-like features in its details, as the author had once thought. He designed an Egyptian prison for Havana, Cuba, in 1833, and was responsible for the partially Egyptian Methodist Episcopal Church of 1836 in New Orleans. See Arthur Scully, Jr., *James Dakin, Architect: His Career in New York and the South* (Baton Rouge, 1973). The "Tombs" competition plan is discussed on p. 37.

William Ross (fl. 1830–1840) was the English engineer and architect who apparently was called in to execute the dome, in its final version, for the Town and Davis New York Customs House. William Ross, "Plan, Elevation, Section, etc. for the Custom-House, New York," *Architectural Magazine,* vol. II (Dec. 1835), pp. 525–533; also Hamlin, *Greek Revival,* pp. 86, 154–155. For an opposing view, see Louis Torres,

"Samuel Thompson and The Old Custom House," *JSAH*, xx, 4 (1961), pp. 185–190. He was the American correspondent for the *Architectural Magazine* while in this country, 1834–1839(?).

Charles F. Reichardt (fl. 1830–1840) described in the above-mentioned "Document 60" as "late of Prussia," was another founder of the American Institution of Architects in 1836. He should probably, more than Isaiah Rogers, be given credit for the Charleston (S.C.) Hotel of 1839. Hamlin, *Greek Revival*, pp. 60, 115, 199.

Ithiel Town (1784–1844); the fact that this famous New Haven architect's name appears singly in the list of "five and twenty architects and *as many plans*" (author's own italics) would seem to revise Newton's discussion of what was certainly Davis' plan, but which that author gives to both Town and Davis. The plan in question shows a well-integrated scheme, one facade of which is Egyptian, the other, Doric. Metropolitan Museum of Art, Print Room, Davis Papers, acc. no. 24.66.437. He gives the former to Davis, and the latter to Town, although among the Davis Papers there is no evidence to support this theory. Further, in the minutes of the Committee for the House of Detention there is a notation that the Davis *Egyptian* aspect of the plan is what gained second premium, vis-à-vis his Doric part. Newton's date of 1838 for the Haviland plan of the "Tombs" is, of course, incorrect. Newton, *Town . . .*, pp. 175, 177; MARC (1835), T-607, Minutes of the Committee, March 7, 1835.

A. J. Davis (1803–1892); see above.

Samuel Dunbar (fl. 1825–1840); although Newton refers to him as "a minor New York architect . . . more of a builder . . . than architect," Hamlin suggests that he built the Amity Street Baptist Church, and is responsible for the design of the Greenwich Presbyterian Church on West 13th Street. Newton, *Town . . .*, p. 173; Hamlin, *Greek Revival*, pp. 173, 151.

Isaiah Rogers (1800–1869); unfortunately the author has been unable to locate this competitor's solution to the problem here, as it must have been an interesting sideline for the famous "hotel architect" (e.g., Tremont House, 1828–1829; Astor House, 1832–1836; Maxwell House, 1854–1860). He was in New York at the time supervising work on the Astor House. It is, of course, well known that Isaiah Rogers' hotel architecture was the next category of American building (after Haviland's prisons) to attract international attention. H.-R. Hitchcock, *Architecture . . .*, p. 87–88. Rogers resided in New York, 1834–1842. Montgomery Schuyler, "The Old Greek Revival," *American Architect* (May 3, 1911), pt. 4. He designed two noteworthy, almost-identical Egyptian Revival monuments: the gate to the Old Granary Burying Ground, Boston, 1840, and that for the Touro Memorial Jewish Cemetery in Newport, Rhode Island in 1843. He won third prize in the Girard College competition with three drawings in the Greek Revival mode. Gilchrist, "Girard College . . . ," p. 23.

Martin E. Thompson (ca. 1787–1877) had been a partner of Town in 1828–1829, and was also a designer of some of the Washington Square houses, as well as the Second National Bank of the United States, the tower of St. Mark's-in-the-Bouwerie, and the Assay Office of 1826, all in New York City. He later became a partner of Josiah Brady. Newton, *Town . . .* , pp. 55, 91, 140; T. F. Hamlin, *DAB* article on Thompson. Along with Joseph Tucker, Seth Gear and Horace Butler, Thompson certified that Haviland's newly erected Wall Street banking house for J. L. and S. Josephs and Co. was satisfactory and approved it for the bank, Feb. 18, 1837. University of Pennsylvania, Haviland Papers, vol. V, p. 64.

Joseph Singerly (ca. 1807–1878) was "a successful carpenter and builder in Philadelphia" (*DAB*). This could point up the fact that it was not necessary to be a trained architect to aspire to create prize-winning plans. His eldest son (b. 1832) was William M. Singerly, publisher of the *Philadelphia Record.* J. Thomas Scharf and Thompson Westcott, *History of Philadelphia,* 3 vols. (Philadelphia, 1884), p. 2040.

Isaac Holden (fl. 1830–1860), "a British architect" who had been employed by Haviland 1830–1831. University of Pennsylvania, Haviland Papers, vol. III, p. 79; vol. IV, pp. 8, 70. Evidently the student felt he had learned enough to compete with his master. Later he submitted designs to the Girard College competition which included both a gymnasium and swimming pool. Gilchrist, "Girard College . . . ," p. 27. In later life he appears to have returned to England. In 1856 the architectural firm of Isaac Holden & Son of Manchester was awarded a silver medal in the Notre Dame de la Treille et St. Pierre competition held at Lille. H.-R. Hitchcock, "G.E. Street in the 1850s," *JSAH,* vol. XIX, no. 4 (1960), p. 156.

Russell Warren (1783–1860) and *James C. Bucklin* (1801–1890) were the Rhode Island firm which had designed the Providence Arcade in 1828. Hitchcock, *Architecture . . .* , p. 86. The former, of course, was the architect of the New Bedford railway station in the Egyptian style (1840).

Dwight and Shaw. Edward Shaw (1784–1847) of Boston is perhaps better remembered for his publications on architectural theory than for any extant buildings (e.g., *Civil Architecture* [Boston, 1831], *Rural Architecture* [Boston, 1843], *The Modern Architect* [Boston, 1855]). Shaw's association with the Rev. Louis Dwight (1793–1854) seems only to have produced their plan for this competition which shared third premium with Pollard's design. Dwight was particularly interested in prison reform. For many years he was secretary of the Massachusetts Society for Prison Discipline. (See note 28, above; also at MARC [1835],

T-607 there is a second letter from Dwight explaining that Shaw was his partner in the plan. This letter is dated March 17, 1835.) Could the reform-conscious clergyman have just this once dabbled in this species of architecture that was of particular interest to him, asking for technical aid from a "professional"?

John M. Van Osdel (also "Vanosdel") (1811–1891). His early work was done in New York, but he returned to Baltimore in 1831 where he wrote carpentry handbooks. After removing to New York in 1836, he settled in Chicago (post-1840) where he became the foremost architect of the city. His best known early work is, perhaps, the Rush Medical College of 1844. His papers are at the Art Institute of Chicago (*DAB*). He was the author of *The Carpenter's Own Book*. MARC, 1835, T-607, letter from John M. Vanosdel (n.d.). There is further material on this architect's biography in T. C. Bannister, "Bogardus Revisited," *JSAH,* vol. XVI, 1, (March, 1957) p. 18.

"Laura" was the *nom de plume* of *James R. Mount.* MARC, (1835), T-607, letter from James R. Mount (n.d.).

Merrill was *John H. Merrill* of Canandaigua, N.Y. *Ibid.,* letter from John H. Merrill (n.d.)

36. *Ibid.,* letter from A. J. Davis (n.d.)
37. *New-York Evening Standard* (February 24, 1835), II, 28. Another journalistic report appeared in the April 1835 issue of the *American Monthly Magazine,* v, ii new series, p. 160. The "Tombs" was admired for its "novelty" but even more for the archeological "purity of design" as well as its "solidity" and "grandeur."
38. The Egyptian style had already been closely juxtaposed with Saracenic, Greek, and Roman in four closely connected, but separate, buildings at Devonport (on Ker Street) in England by John Foulston in 1823. John Foulston, *The Public Buildings in the West of England* (London, 1838). One is also reminded of Alexander Pope's *Temple of Fame* in which each of the four facades is in a different style, the southern one being Egyptian. This, as early as 1711.
39. Although our journalist champions the Gothic *or* Egyptian style, his criterion would seem to apply more logically to the Egyptian Revival aesthetic than to the other. It is perhaps because of this that he makes such an involved case for the Gothic designs; he reasons that the primacy of the Egyptian is more obvious.
40. In *re* architectural symbolism of the time one need only point to William Ross' project in the competition, of which there remains his description. It was to be in the "Castellated style of the Middle Ages . . . most appropriate for buildings devoted to the purposes for which this is intended." The description of this plan of three towers (octagonal for administration, square for male prisoners, round for females) is introduced by a quotation from Sir Walter Scott's *Marmion,*

The battled towers, the Donjon Keep,
The loop-hole grates where captives weep,
The flanking walls that round it sweep.

MARC (1834), T-602, "Description of a design for a new House of Detention in the City of New York," MS. (This paper has been incorrectly filed, of course.) With sentiments such as these, it is small wonder that the journalist's quest for the "pleasing and impressive, not the gloomy and terrific" skipped over this plan, as did the judgement of the reform-minded committee.

41. It is not without interest to note Haviland's own modest account of his initial plan, taken from his copy of the letter he sent accompanying these plans. He commences by speaking of the difficulty of designing so many departments conveniently and efficiently into one complex. He then continues: "[The basic divisions were] an easy task, but to arrange each of these divisions and their branches in detail so as to give them the most perfect combination in a given space is difficult. Numerous have been the plans suggested in my mind, but all were more or less objectionable. From my long studies and experience in the construction of prisons I am sensible of the objects to be attained, and the difficulties to contend with. I thought myself near to perfection in the construction of the cell fifteen years past, but in every succeeding year have gleaned from experience some new and valued property in its ventilation, light, warming, watering, and security. . . . Those now constructing in the New Jersey State Prison will embrace more of the desired properties of a cell calculated by seclusion with labour to carry this system into effect." University of Pennsylvania, Haviland Papers, vol. III, p. 280.

42. In one of Haviland's record books there is a short notation which would appear to bear out this theory. On March 24, 1835 he received his premium of $200 for the design. At the same day he was given an added $300 (making a $500 total which is what the full prize was to have been) for "extra drawings, estimate, and specifications." *Ibid.*, vol. IV, p. 91. As has been pointed out earlier, Haviland did not send the Committee the revised plans until March 29, almost a week later. There is, therefore, no very obvious explanation for this $300 item at this particular date, other than as a sub-rosa awarding of the "real" prize.

43. MARC (1835), T-607, letter from John Haviland, March 29, 1835.

44. *Ibid.*, letter from John Haviland, Dec. 12, 1834. (This letter has, of course, been misfiled. It should be in drawer T-602.) Actually there are several sketches in Haviland's notebooks which could well have been preliminary plans for the "Tombs" project. One is a magnificent Boullée-esque arrangement consisting of two long *batiments* serving as lofty parallel wings to a dropped central section. University of Pennsylvania, Haviland Papers, vol. VI, pp. 154–155. The facade silhouette recalls the an-

cient Egyptian pylon arrangement of a battered tower on either side of a lower central gate. Haviland's reworking within this vocabulary includes a sphinx in profile atop each pylon tower with a temple portico arrangement for the lower entrance. The latter is made up of four palm-capital columns surmounted by a winged orb in a cavetto cornice which, in turn, is topped by a reverse corbel or step pyramid-attic masking a flat roof. The perspective view shows the pylon towers to be in actuality, long, uninterrupted building blocks which, it appears, would contain the various cells. It would seem that each of these wings would have a long, rectangular skylight to illuminate a through-running light well. No exterior windows are indicated. It is interesting to note that there is no monumentalizing flight of stairs, an archeologically correct aspect. There is, however, a giant obelisk at each of the four corners of the complex, rendering a sense of grandeur and of the sublime that recalls Gilly's similar use of obelisks in his plan for the Frederick the Great Monument. The width of the main portal is indicated as being forty feet, which by projection would make the width of the entire complex a bit over 200 feet. This would indeed fit the dimensions of the plot (235 ft. × 200 ft. × 253 ft. × 200 ft.). The drawing is a rough one on a double page at the back of a notebook containing material of a later date (the early 1840s). As there are several drawings on these fly-leaf pages some of which recall the cupola disposition of the final version of the "Tombs," one might surmise that the journal had first served as a sketchbook.

While the evidence is not conclusive that the above was a project for the "Tombs," there is one sketch which certainly may be identified. Not only do the stated dimensions fit (200 ft. × 204 ft.), but the names of the appropriate streets are indicated on each of the four sides of the plan: "Elme" [sic], "Centre St.," "Leonard," and "Franklin." *Ibid.*, vol. III, p. 98. Alongside the plan is a rough elevation of the principal facade (on "Elme" street, rather than Centre which was later specified by the Committee). The style would appear to be Egyptianizing rather than Egyptian Revival, with a long colonnaded porch of eight columns between two gable-roofed projecting end pavilions. Above the colonnade is a sloping roof. This is roughly the disposition Haviland planned for the United States Naval Hospital at Norfolk, Va. in 1831. The Egyptianizing features in this first "Tombs" project would be the battered walls and the cavetto cornices. In back of the facade, and at right angles to it is a central block flanked by open courts. Beyond is a walled yard with the cell block in its center.

As we shall see in the final plan, our architect not only changed the plan to out-and-out Egyptian style, but also reorganized the main facade accenting the center, and abolishing the two end pavilions which had contained the building at each side. In addition to the perpendicular middle wing, two side ones were projected. The cell block was maintained within a walled court.

In the journal three pages previous to this plan the date of Nov. 15, 1834, is noted. The next date mentioned comes eight pages after the drawing, April 25, 1835. Between the drawing and this last date are four pages of estimates for the "Tombs." It thus seems that the plan, and probably the estimates were done between the Nov. 15 date and the Dec. 12, 1834 letter to Johnson. In his diary Haviland noted that he started on a "model of the New York prison" on Jan. 7, 1835. On Jan. 12 he was still working at it. *Ibid.,* vol. IV, pp. 88–89.

45. The document was printed, a copy of which is at MARC (1835), T-607. The plans, sections, and elevations are discussed, but are not included, nor are they in the bound edition at the New-York Historical Society. *Proc., Bds. Ald. and Assist.,* vol. II (1835), p. 399. In the former there is, however, a double sheet containing a variety of details of both practical and aesthetic nature; e.g., water closets, steps, cell doors, torus mouldings, cavetto cornices, etc. In the Map Room of the New-York Historical Society there are to be found under "Halls of Justice" the various unbound printed drawings of the complex.

46. MARC (1835), T-607. It is interesting to note that Thompson, basically an architect, also had a contracting firm. The work was actually awarded to the partnership of Wells and Butler at the request of Haviland in a letter to the Committee dated April 24, 1835. University of Pennsylvania, Haviland Papers, vol. III, p. 107.

47. [New York City], *Invitation to the Ceremony to Mark the Start of Construction* (New York, 1957).

48. *Ibid.,* T-607, Mayor's Message of Dec. 7, 1835. Also mentioned in earlier 1834 communications of the mayor. *Proc., Bd. of Assist.,* vol. VIII (1835), p. 253.

49. *Proc., Bd. Ald.,* vol. XIX (1837), pp. 292, 483.

50. *Proc. Bds. of Ald. and Assist.,* vol. VI (1838). This was posterior to the actual opening of the building. The general rebuilding after the great fire of 1835 in New York must have been, in part, responsible for the length of time it took to finish.

51. MARC, T-605, Mayor's Annual Message, June 18, 1835.

52. W. J. Short, "Design for a Termination of a Railway," *Architectural Magazine,* vol. III (1836), p. 219.

53. A prototype for Haviland, at least as to a courthouse and jail with the Egyptian style applied to it, may stem from the design by his teacher, James Elmes, for the Sheriff's Court House and Gaol at Thanet (England), exhibited in 1805. Hugh Honour, "The Egyptian Taste," *The Connoisseur,* vol. CXXXV (1955), p. 244. Elmes' source in turn could be an interesting hypothesis if one notes the following quotation from

the article on "Prisons" in his *Dictionary of the Fine Arts* in which he cites a third and most recent example of great world prison architecture, "We find likewise a representation of the prison of Aix [1784?] built by M. Ledoux in a style which savours somewhat of that of the Egyptian, but simple in its details." James Elmes, *Dictionary of the Fine Arts* (London, 1826), no pagination.

54. J. L. Stephens, *Incidents of Travel,* 2 vols. (New York, 1837).

55. Sutton, *Tombs . . . ,* p. 48. The author asserts that the "Tombs" owed its nickname to an illustration of an ancient Egyptian tomb in Stephens' book from which it had been copied. The few plates in the book portray views that look nothing like our building, and, contrary to Sutton, there are no tombs shown. He confuses the issue further by referring to the author as "John L. Stevens of Hoboken." There was a famous John Stevens (with a *v*) of Hoboken who lived in the early part of the century and was a rival of Fitch (of Collect Pond fame), Fulton, and Livingston in the field of steam navigation. He also was the founder of the Stevens Institute. Our tourist in Egypt, John Lloyd Stephens (with a *ph*) did come from New Jersey, but from Shrewsbury, not Hoboken.

56. I. N. Phelps-Stokes, *The Iconography of Manhattan Island* (New York, 1926), vol. VI, p. 535; *Proc. Bds. Ald. and Assist.,* vol. VI (1838), p. 21. More than a half-century later demolition began on May 24, 1897 followed by the erection of "Tombs II" in a not particularly original Renaissance style. Phelps-Stokes, *Iconography . . . ,* vol. VI, p. 535. The building was opened on Sept. 29, 1902, to be torn down by 1948. New York Public Library, Transfile, #16065. "Tombs III," the present structure in the rather boxy vernacular of the 1950s, is undistinguished public architecture of our century par excellence. The cornerstone was laid February 14, 1957. This is the courthouse, not the prison.

57. [Disturnell] *New York As It Is* (New York, 1839), pp. 24–27.

58. The building was eventually constructed in Hallowell granite (*ibid.,* p. 24), a type of Maine white granite. J. F. Richmond, *New York and its Institutions* (New York, 1871), p. 515.

59. MARC (1835), T-607, letter from K. B. Sewall, (n.d.)

60. *Ibid.,* letter from Foster Bryant, (n.d.)

61. This same combination of motifs is to be found in P. F. Robinson's famous Egyptian Hall at Piccadilly in London of 1812. Granting that the arrangement here may, of course, have been pure Havilandian invention, he could have noted it in Robinson's building before he left London. (He arrived in America in 1816.) In any case, it is to be remarked that in his inventory of his library there is one entry dealing with "views of London" which would probably have pictured the Egyptian Hall, also known as the London Museum, at some point among its pages. And it

would seem unlikely that Haviland was not aware of his master, James Elmes' *Metropolitan Improvements* (London, 1827) (if, indeed, this was not the book of "views on London" that he did have). In that book is a plate of the Hall with a description on page 157.

Ultimately, the reverse step, or corbel, motif as applied to Egyptian revivals, can be traced to Piranesi chimney designs. G. B. Piranesi, *Diverse maniere d'adornare i cammini* (Rome, 1769), especially plate 36.

62. As one may see from ancient blurred photographs, and admittedly faulty engravings, this dome was, when actually executed, indicated by a small, flat-topped octagonal campanile of rather Georgian proportions, but with seemingly battered openings. Doubtless its purpose, other than being a belfry, must have been to provide better ventilation for the Court Room as it does not give any real manifestation of the dome beneath. The strange flat octagonal element in front of it which is much larger and appears over the entrance hall marks the base of the incinerated watch tower, discussed below.

63. The Debtors' Prison became the Female Prison upon the repeal of the Debtor Laws. Richmond, *New York . . .*, p. 515. A similar disposition was made in the case of Walter's Egyptian Debtors' Prison at Moyamensing, "after the abolition of imprisonment for debt in 1841." Scharf and Westcott, *History of Philadelphia,* p. 1836.

64. From engravings of this interior one should note that here, too, the Egyptian vocabulary was used; *e.g.,* battered door frames and winged orbs. *Gleason's . . .,* IV, 4 (Jan. 22, 1853), p. 49.

65. Metropolitan Museum of Art, Print Room, Davis Papers, acc. no. 24.66.437.

66. "W. L." of Yorkshire in that year wrote of the unfairness of competitors who often produced a plan which would have far exceeded the supposed price, but which dazzled the untrained judges. "Remarks on Competition Plans with another Instance of Partial Decision," *Architectural Magazine,* vol. II (1835), pp. 483–485.

67. Newton traces this portion to Karnac and Philae which is certainly questionable. Newton, *Town . . .,* p. 176.

68. Metropolitan Museum of Art, Print Room, Davis Papers. Here one may see such Davis Egyptian projects as: a Proscenium (acc. no. 24.66.442) which Newton (*Town . . .,* p. 87) implies is to be dated ca. 1816 (Davis dated it, on the drawing, 1825); a Portico to a Military Academy (Virginia Military Institute?) (24.66.439) (plate 115); Cemetery Gate (24.-66.441) (plate 68); Church (24.66.443) (plate 96) (Newton, on p. 176, assumes this is the Sag Harbor Church, but Davis, a man not noted for his modesty, says nothing about this); a School (24.66.799) (plate 98); monuments (24.66.1605,—1610) (plate 36); tombs (24.66.1603,—

1607,—1608); and the New York Lyceum, or Athenaeum, of Natural History (24.66.438) (plate 99). This last was an alternate plan to the one actually executed in 1835.

69. Metropolitan Museum of Art, Print Room, Davis Papers, acc. no. 24.66.1131.
70. Archives of the State of Tennessee, Nashville, Strickland Papers.
71. Sutton, *Tombs,* p. 80.
72. That Haviland was adept at working in the Georgian vocabulary may be seen from his commission to restore parts of Independence Hall in early 1831. University of Pennsylvania, Haviland Papers, vol. II, p. 170. He was asked to restore rooms in "the State House, recently vacated by Mr. Peal [*sic*] as a museum." *Ibid.,* p. 101, probably 1829. Most significant for this point, he submitted an estimate and a plan for erecting "a spire similar to the old one" for the same building on March 7, 1828. *Ibid.,* p. 22.
73. Richmond, *New York . . . ,* p. 516.
74. Sutton, *Tombs,* p. 155.
75. David M. Kahn, "Bogardus, Fire, and the Iron Tower," *JSAH,* xxxv, 3 (1976), p. 190.

Bibliography

A bibliography or catalogue can never, probably, be exhaustive. In the notes, however, may be found a reasonably complete roster of references for each monument, for the movement in general, and for correlative information. Critical evaluations have also been included. This bibliographical essay is not, therefore, an attempt to repeat, in alphabetical form, such a listing. It is intended to give some idea of where both background and specific material contained in this work may be found. It is also designed to give a brief critical commentary on the various items. It is divided into current or modern sources, and the ones contemporary with the period covered. Both primary and secondary sources are included in the latter. As a rule, only entries on architecture have been included. The general works have been mentioned first, followed by specific ones. Because of the nature of the subject, a differentiation between books and articles seemed arbitrary. When not inconvenient, items have been listed according to date of publication.

I. Current Sources

A. *The Egyptian Revival.* The pioneering work on the American Egyptian Revival is Frank J. Roos' "The Egyptian Style" which appeared in 1940 volume XXXIII, *Magazine of Art,* pp. 218–223, 255, 257. It is an excellent article mentioning most of the major monuments, their architects, dates, and sources. Indeed, after thirty-five years there is little that needs correction, and nothing has been published since which amplifies in a major sense its scope and ideas. The amount of material covered and the wealth of scholarly information is astonishing for such a short essay.

Bibliography

In 1947 Clay Lancaster's "Oriental Forms in American Architecture, 1800–1870," *Art Bulletin,* XXIX, 3, pp. 183–193 devoted one third of its length to the Egyptian Revival. Egypt's being considered oriental may be questioned, but in any case, it is a disappointing article in that it contributes little that was not already mentioned by Roos. The same author's "The Egyptian Style and Mrs. Trollope's Bazaar," *Magazine of Art,* XLIII (1950), p. 95 ff. makes a more valid contribution in its discussion of one early example which, ironically, turns out to have little that is Egyptian about it. C. W. Eckels "The Egyptian Revival in America," *Archaeology,* III (1950), pp. 164–169 is unreliable.

The English Egyptian Revival has been nicely covered by Hugh Honour in his "Curiosities of the Egyptian Hall," *Country Life,* CXV (1954), pp. 38–39, and "The Egyptian Taste," *Connoisseur,* CXXXV, 546 (1955), pp. 242–246. These contain a wealth of references. K. J. Bonser's "Marshall's Mill, Holbeck, Leeds," *Architectural Review,* CXXVII, 758 (1960), pp. 280–282 is an excellent monograph on one Egyptian Revival monument which, although known, had never been adequately published. G. B. Wood's "Egyptian Temple at Leeds," published the same year in *Country Life,* CXXVIII, 3326 (1960), pp. 1363–1365, on the same subject, is unreliable.

The first article on the Egyptian Revival anywhere was Hans Vogel's "Aegyptisierende Baukunst des Klassizismus," *Zeitschrift für Bildende Kunst,* LXII (1928–1929), pp. 160–165. Cautious about calling it the Egyptian Revival, the author, nevertheless discusses the movement intelligently with interesting concepts, analyses and descriptions. It should be used with caution for non-German monuments, however.

By far the best publication on pre-nineteenth-century Egyptianisms is N. Pevsner and S. Lang, "The Egyptian Revival," *Architectural Review,* CXIX (1956), pp. 242–254, now published as chapter thirteen in Nikolaus Pevsner, *Studies in Art, Architecture and Design,* I (New York, 1968). Packed with a wealth of solid information, it is provocative and stimulating in its ideas. Little need be added to it although the following are all useful, reliable, and interesting:

194

A. Blunt, "The 'Hypnerotomachia Poliphili' in XVII Century France," *Journal of the Warburg and Courtauld Institutes* (hereafter, *JWCI*), I (1937–1938), pp. 117–137; William Heckscher, "Bernini's Elephant and Obelisk," *Art Bulletin,* XXIX, 3 (1947), pp. 154–182; Erik Iversen, "Hieroglyphic Studies of the Renaissance," *Burlington Magazine,* C, 658 (1958), pp. 15–21, expanded later as *The Myth of Egypt and its Hieroglyphs* (Copenhagen, 1961); Karl H. Dannenfeldt, "Egyptian Antiquities of the Renaissance," *Studies in the Renaissance,* VI (1959), pp. 7–27. An excellent catalogue of Made-in-Egypt artifacts found in ancient Rome, as well as items made in Rome under Egyptian inspiration (including architectural monuments) is to be found in Anne Roullet's *Egyptian and Egyptianizing Monuments in Imperial Rome* (Leiden, 1972). A parallel to the Pevsner and Lang article, with much new material, may be found in Jurgis Baltrusaitis, *La quête d'Isis* (Paris, 1967). I am indebted to Mark Leach for this reference.

The essential publications are, in short, those of Roos, and Pevsner and Lang.

B. *General Works on Architecture Mentioning Egyptian Revival.* There are two books particularly helpful in dealing with nineteenth-century architecture. H.-R. Hitchcock, *Architecture, Nineteenth and Twentieth Centuries* (Baltimore, 1958), is a monumental undertaking discussing general trends while providing an incredibly detailed encyclopedia of information. More specialized is C. L. V. Meeks, *The Railroad Station* (New Haven, 1956), which, especially in the first chapter, provides a clear discussion and survey of nineteenth-century architecture as well as presenting a provocative thesis. Other works should be mentioned by country. All are useful, some excellent, and have been so indicated.

Italy and France. Emil Bourgeois, *Le style Empire* (Paris, 1930), essential, giving the clearest, most interesting account. Louis Hautecoeur: *Rome et la renaissance de l'antiquité* (Paris, 1912); *L'art sous la Révolution et l'Empire en France* (Paris, 1953); *Histoire de l'architecture classique en France,* 7 volumes (Paris, 1943–1957). Although these contain an enormous wealth of material with plentiful notes and bibliographies, there is unfortunately much incomplete, as well as incorrect, information. To be used with caution, and never to be trusted. Emil Kaufmann, *Architecture in the Age of Reason* (Cambridge, 1955). Indispensable for the understanding of Romantic Classicism. Fully documented and annotated, it is excellent for factual information and stimulating for ideas. Note also his earlier *Three Revolutionary Architects* (Philadelphia, 1952). For Italy note C. L. V. Meeks' ambitious *Italian Architecture, 1750–1914* (New Haven, 1966).

As to specific architects, for Piranesi, H. Focillon, *Giovanni-Battista Piranesi* (Paris, 1928), is the standard work, but H. Mayor's *Giovanni Battista Piranesi* (New York, 1952), is excellent, and should be consulted. Also note R. Wittkower, "Piranesi's 'Parere su l'architettura,'" *JWCI,* II (1938–1939), pp. 147–158; W. Körte, "Giovanni Battista Piranesi als praktischer Architekt," *Zeitschrift für Kunstgeschichte,* II (1932), pp. 16–33. For Selva, E. Bassi, *Gianantonio Selva* (Padua, 1936). For Canina, Luigi Canina, *Le nuova fabbriche della Villa Borghese denominata Pinciana* (Rome, 1828); G. Bandinelli, *Luigi Canina, le opere i tempi* (Alessandria, 1953). For Jappelli, N. Pevsner, "Pedrocchino and Some Allied Problems," *Architectural Review,* CXXII (1957), pp. 212–215; R. C. Mantiglia, "Giuseppi Jappelli, architetto," *L'architettura,* I (1956), pp. 538–551. For Ledoux, M. Raval, *C.-N. Ledoux* (Paris, 1945). For Boullée, H. Rosenau, *Boullée's Treatise on Architecture* (London, 1953); Jean-Marie Pérouse de Montclos, *Etienne-Louis Boullée (1728–1798)* (Paris, 1969) (English abridgement [New York, 1974]). Also helpful, especially for Kléber, are the various publications by J. C. Krafft, especially his *Productions de plusieurs architectes Français et étrangers* (with P.-F.-L. Dubois) (Paris, 1809); and *Recueil d'architecture civile* (Paris, 1812).

Germany. Max Osborn, *Die Kunst des Rokoko* (Berlin, 1929), and G. Pauli, *Die Kunst des Klassizismus und der Romantik* (Berlin, 1925). These old standbys from the Propyläen Series are still helpful especially for German monuments and have good photographs. The new version of the Series done in Berlin in the 1960s is considerably reorganized. Also useful: H. Schmitz, *Berliner Baumeister von Ausgang des Achtzehten Jahrhunderts* (Berlin, 1914); E. Hempel, *Geschichte der Deutschen Baukunst* (Munich, 1949); H. Beenken, *Schöpferische Bauideen der Deutschen Romantik* (Mainz, 1952). There is also an excellent article, Alfred Neumeyer, "Monuments to 'Genius' in German Classicism," *JWCI*, II (1938–1939), pp. 159–163. For specific architects working in the style: A. Oncken, *Friedrich Gilly* (Berlin, 1935); A. Rietdorf, *Gilly, Wiedergeburt der Architektur* (Berlin, 1940); W. van Kempen, "Die Baukunst des Klassizismus in Anhalt nach 1800," *Marburger Jahrbuch für Kunstwissenschaft*, IV (1928), pp. 1–88 (for Bandhauer). H. Bramsen's monograph, *Gottlieb Bindesbøll* (Copenhagen, 1959), although on a Danish architect gives much useful information on the von Klenze circle and is especially helpful for ideas on primitivity in Romantic Classicism and on "Egyptianizing." In this connection the chapter entitled "Toward the Tabula Rasa," pp. 147–150, in Robert Rosenblum, *Transformations in Late Eighteenth Century Art* (second edition) (Princeton, 1967), should be cited, while its superb documentation should be applauded.

England. By far the best work is from the Pelican Series, J. Summerson, *Architecture in Britain, 1580–1830* (Baltimore, 1953). Written with a felicity of style, it is stimulating to read, and essential to use. Note also his *Sir John Soane* (London, 1952). Other works: C. Hussey, *The Picturesque* (London, 1927), pioneering essay, but short on architecture, and dated; H. A. Tipping, *English Homes,* 9 volumes (New York, 1920–1937), dated, but useful; D. Pilcher, *The Regency Style* (London, 1947), pleasant, but not especially profound; R. Turner, *Nineteenth-Century Architecture in Britain* (London, 1950), thin; H. S. Goodhart-Rendel, *English Architecture since the Regency* (London, [1953]), helpful, but not essential; C. Hussey, *English Country Houses,* 3 volumes (London, 1955–1956), handsomely presented, if little that is new; T. S. R. Boase, *English Art, 1800–1870* (Oxford, 1959), helpful and anecdotal. Interesting and useful in a more specialized sense: E. de Maré, *The Bridges of Britain* (London, 1957); L. T. C.

Bibliography

Rolt, *Isambard Kingdom Brunel* (London, 1957); F. Saxl and R. Wittkower's excellent and fascinating catalogue, *British Art and the Mediterranean* (London, 1954). The best guidebook series since Karl Baedeker is N. Pevsner's *The Buildings of Britain* (London, 1951 *et seq.*). H. M. Colvin's *Biographical Dictionary of English Architects* (Cambridge, 1954) is indispensable (the American counterpart, H. F. and E. R. Withey, *Biographical Dictionary of American Architects,* [Los Angeles, 1956], is unreliable). Also extremely useful, Architectural Publications Society, *Dictionary of Architecture,* 8 volumes (London, 1853[?]–1892).

America. The standard work for the Egyptian Revival period is Talbot Hamlin's *Greek Revival Architecture in America* (New York, 1944). It is excellent with a large scope and much information including comments on the Egyptian Revival. His *Benjamin Henry Latrobe* (New York, 1955), is of course extremely useful. At times it is annoying to find sources omitted where clear scholarship would have called for them. There are countless other books on American architectural history, but for this period they add little to the above. J. Burchard and A. Bush-Brown, *The Architecture of America* (Boston and Toronto, 1961), contributes some minor points, but also some incorrect ones. More interesting is Alan Gowans' *Images of American Living* (Philadelphia and New York, 1964). The most unreliable of all books in this bibliography is R. H. Newton's *Town and Davis, Architects* (New York, 1942). Hardly a page can be turned without finding some glaring error of fact, or flight of fancy based on nonexistent or incorrect information. More useful are the following, which are either monographs or give information about Egyptian Revival monuments (as the list is rather a long one, it would seem more advantageous and convenient to give it alphabetically by author): R. Alexander, "The Public Monument and Godefroy's Battle Monument," *Journal of the Society of Architectural Historians* (hereafter, *JSAH*), XVII, 1 (1958), pp. 19–24, a careful documentation of architectural memorials in late-eighteenth-century France as a background for American examples with good material on Maximilian Godefroy, also note that author's *The Architecture of Maximilian Godefroy* (Baltimore, 1974); Glenn Brown, *The History of the United States Capitol* (Washington, 1900), the standard work still, includes Latrobe's Library of Congress plan; "Biographical Sketch of Stephen Decatur Button," *American Architect and Building News* (July 16, 1892), p. 37; Cambridge Historical Commission, *Survey of Architectural History in Cambridge,* 4 vols. (Cambridge, 1966–1973); A. C. Clark, "Robert Mills, Architect and Engineer," *Records of the Columbia Historical Society,* XL-XLI (1940), pp. 1–32, supplements Gallagher (see below); A. Downing and V. J. Scully, *The Architectural Heritage of Newport, Rhode Island* (Cambridge, 1952); H. Gallagher, *Robert Mills* (New York, 1955), competent; A. A. Gilchrist, *William Strickland* (Philadelphia, 1950) (Da Capo reprint, 1969), attractive, and standard work on the architect; "Obituary Notice of John Haviland," *Pennsylvania Journal of Prison Discipline,* VII, 3 (1852), pp. 97–107, the earliest published discussion of the work of this major architect; see also Matthew Baigell, "John Haviland in Philadelphia, 1818–1826," *JSAH,* XXV, 3 (October, 1966), pp. 197–208, and A. A. Gilchrist, "John Haviland before 1816," *JSAH,* XX, 3 (October, 1961), pp. 136–137; H.-R. Hitchcock, *Rhode Island Architecture* (Providence, 1939); M. M. Hoffman, "John Francis Rague, Pioneer Architect of Iowa," *Annals of Iowa,* XIX (1933–1935), pp. 444–448, only published source for this architect, and by an amateur; also an unpublished M.A. thesis by Betsy Woodman, "John Francis Rague: Mid-nineteenth-century revivalist architect (1799–1877)," (completed in 1969 for the University of Iowa, Iowa City, Iowa); R. H. Howland and E. P. Spencer, *The Architecture of Baltimore* (Baltimore, 1953); Joseph Jackson, *Early Philadelphia Architects and Engineers* (Philadelphia, 1923), an early work with nineteenth-century monuments, has been superseded; N. Johnston, "Pioneers in Criminology, John Haviland," *Journal of Criminal Law and Criminology,* LXV, 5 (1955), pp. 509–519, penology rather than architecture; W. Kilham, *Boston after Bulfinch* (Cambridge, 1946); Jacob Landy, *The Architecture of Minard Lafever* (New York, 1970), excellent; T. A. Markus, "Pattern of Law," *Architectural Review,* CXVI (1954), pp. 251–256, prisons, well documented; R. Newcomb, "Thomas U. Walter," *The Architect* (August, 1928), early work on this underpublished architect; R. Newcomb, *The Architecture of the Old Northwest Territory* (Chicago, 1950), nice illustrations, but not particularly helpful; B. St. J. Ravenel, *Architects of Charleston,* (Charleston, 1945); W. S. Rusk, "Thomas U. Walter and his Work," *Americana,* XXXIII (1939), pp. 151–179, more complete than Newcomb, but not satisfactory for this architect's importance; Robert C. Smith, *Two Centuries of Philadelphia Architecture* (Philadelphia, 1953); D. B. Steinman and S. R. Watson, *Bridges and their Builders* (New York, 1941), and D. B. Steinman, *The Builders of the Bridge* (New York, 1945), interesting accounts of nineteenth-century engineering feats but no architectural sense; George B. Tatum, *Penn's Great Town; 250 Years of Philadelphia Architecture illustrated in Prints and Drawings* (Philadelphia, 1961), is extremely valuable for that city; R. Wischnitzer, *Synagogue Architecture in the United States* (Philadelphia, 1955), combines new material with earlier publications by the same author, scholarly, imaginative and informed; for a thoroughly documented discussion of a specific "building type" closely related to the Egyptian Revival see John Zukowsky, "Monumental American Obelisks: Centennial Vistas," *Art Bulletin* LVIII, 4 (1976), pp. 574–581.

II. Contemporary Sources

A. *Guidebooks.* While the W. P. A. guidebooks can be helpful, their quality varies, and they are not particularly useful for a movement such as the Egyptian Revival which has not been generally recognized until recent years and many of whose monuments have been demolished. Far more serviceable have been the earlier nineteenth-century guides to the various major cities written when the examples were new and admired. For Boston and environs: T. S. Homans, *Sketches of Boston* (Boston, 1851); N. B. Shurtleff, *Topographical and Historical Description of Boston* (Boston, 1871), more complete and accurate than Homans; N. Dearborn, *A Concise History of and Guide through Mount Auburn* (Boston, 1843); C. W. Walter, *Mount Auburn Illustrated* (New York: 1847); *Forest Hills Cem-*

etery (Roxbury, 1855). For New York: J. Disturnell, *New York as It Is* (New York, 1839), with several later editions until 1876, good, although a much later source book must be mentioned here, I. N. Phelps-Stokes, *The Iconography of Manhattan Island,* 6 volumes (New York, 1926), a magnificent monument to archival research and absolutely essential; J. F. Richmond, *New York and its Institutions* (New York, 1871), helpful with several illustrations; Charles Sutton, *The New York Tombs, Its Secrets and Its Mysteries* (San Francisco, 1874), an American Ainsworth novel; it is a joy to read and a windfall to find with complete description and numerous engravings. For Philadelphia, the various editions of *The Stranger's Guide to Phila-delphia* published in that city are useful and reliable. The best for Egyptian Revival monuments which are so numerous there is the one of 1854. For New Orleans: [B. M. Norman] *Norman's New Orleans and Environs* (New Orleans, 1845), several engravings and careful factful information. A more recent, and excellent guide to New Orleans architecture is Samuel Wilson, Jr., *A Guide to the Architecture of New Orleans, 1699–1959* (New York, 1959). Diaries of the period such as Philip Hone's, edited by A. Nevins (New York, 1927), and Samuel Rodman's, edited by Z. W. Pease (New Bedford, 1927) can also provide useful information and attitudes.

B. *Books on Architecture Written in the Period.* The most important for America is Mrs. Laurie C. H. Tuthill, *History of Architecture* (New York, 1844). This is the first book on architectural history published in America. Clearly written and in a serious manner, it is surprisingly accurate. Most helpful is the insight it provides on attitudes and tastes of the time. Earlier non-American sources, extremely valuable, are: James Elmes, *Lectures on Architecture* (London, 1821); and Thomas Hope, *An Historical Essay on Architecture* (London, 1835), published posthumously. Also of interest is F. L. Hawks, *Monuments in Egypt* (New York, 1849), possibly the earliest American attempt at a history of Egyptian architecture. Although there are countless builder's guides, handbooks, and publications of architectural designs, not many mention the Egyptian style. Among the more important ones which do are the following, arranged chronologically after a listing of similar English publications important for the movement: John Soan(e), *Designs in Architecture* (London, 1778), this, Soane's earliest work, is extremely rare, most copies having been bought up and destroyed by the architect in his old age; John Soane, *Plans, Elevations, and Sections of Buildings* (London, 1788), includes useful essay on the history of architecture; Robert Lugar, *Architectural Sketches for Cottages, Rural Dwellings, and Villas* (London, 1805); and James Randall, *Architectural Designs for Mansions, Villas, Lodges, and Cottages* (London, 1806), both discuss the picturesque use of Egyptian; H. W. Inwood, *Of the Resources of Design in the Architecture of Greece, Egypt, and other Countries* (London, 1834), discussion of sources for Egyptian architecture; John Foulston, *The Public Buildings Erected in the West of England* (London, 1838), essential for a major concept of the picturesque and its relation to the Egyptian style.

America. Although the earliest guides appear to be Owen Biddle, *The Young Carpenter's Assistant* (Philadelphia, 1805), and Asher Benjamin, *The American Builder's Companion* (Boston, 1806), there is nothing on the Egyptian Revival in them. Haviland's revision of the former as *The Young Builder's Assistant,* 3 volumes (Philadelphia, 1818–1821), is curiously reticent about the Egyptian style which would indicate that he did not become interested in the mode until after 1830, the date of his second edition in four volumes in which there is still no mention of Egypt. The interest generated by the Croton Reservoir in New York City is indicated by two publications which include it: J. B. Jervis, *Description of the Croton Aqueduct* (New York, 1843), and F. B. Tower, *Illustrations of the Croton Aqueduct* (London and New York, 1843). In the same year another monograph on an Egyptian structure was published in Boston, S. Willard, *Plans and Sections of the Obelisk on Bunker's Hill.* A building guide which did discuss the Egyptian style was H. G. Hatfield, *The American House Carpenter* (New York and London, 1844). Among other works which give attention to the style: A. J. Downing, *A Trea-*

tise on the Theory and Practice of Landscape Gardening (New York, 1841), shows little enthusiasm for Egyptian Revival architecture; Thomas U. Walter and J. Jay Smith, *Two Hundred Designs for Cottages and Villas,* 4 volumes (Philadelphia, 1846), crudely illustrated and virtually without text, there is an interesting bath house in an Egyptianizing fashion; Robert Dale Owen, *Hints on Public Architecture* (New York, 1849), not especially enthusiastic about the style, but recognizes certain values therein; Oliver P. Smith, *The Domestic Architect* (New York, 1854), mentions the appropriateness of the style for prisons; Edward Shaw, *The Modern Architect* (Boston, 1855), gives an essay on the history of architectural styles including Egyptian (Shaw's first publication, *Civil Architecture* [Boston, 1830], did not discuss the style); Minard Lafever's *The Beauties of Architecture* (New York, 1835), is less important for the movement than his *Architectural Instructor* (New York, 1856); William Brown, *The Carpenter's Assistant* (Worcester, 1857), the most enthusiastic of any, it appeared, ironically, at the end of the movement. Also to be mentioned as of interest for the style: Robert Cary Long, Jr., *The Ancient Architecture of America* (New York, 1849), discussion of Egyptian and Mayan styles; D. H. Mahan, *Civil Engineering* (New York, 1851), not architectural, but valuable for new technological ideas; Horatio Greenough, *Form and Function* (New York, 1853), published posthumously, an interesting discussion of the style as an example of the sublime.

C. *Publications.* The Egyptian Revival occurred immediately prior to the publication of the more familiar nineteenth-century periodicals which serve so richly the needs of architectural historians of the era. Items on Egyptian archeology, history, architecture, and even the Revival, however, may be gleaned from the pages of such literary and topical magazines as: *The North American Review* (Boston and New York, 1815–1881); *The American Quarterly* (Philadelphia, 1827–1837); and *The American Monthly Magazine* (New York, 1833–1838). Even more helpful because of the copious illustrations is *The Penny Magazine* (London, 1832–1845). This was published by the Society for the Diffusion of Useful Knowledge, but it included other kinds of "knowledge" as well. There was an American Edition which was subscribed to by at least one of the Egyptian Revival architects. Somewhat less elevating (or pretentious), but very similar were *Gleason's Pictorial Drawing/Room Companion* (Boston, 1851–1854), and its continuation as *Ballou's Pictorial Drawing-Room Companion* (Boston, 1855–1859). It is the best source of this type for pre–Civil War American architecture because of the profusion of engravings. Ultimately, however, the most valuable publication with many illustrations, and packed with articles about the current architectural scene throughout Europe and America, was J. C. Loudon's *Architectural Magazine* (London, 1834–1839). These were the critical years of the Egyptian Revival. The publication was well known in the United States, and printed many essays and news items about American architectural matters. This, plus his encyclopedia and other publications on landscape architecture, make Loudon an essential figure in the understanding of the "picturesque," and the "appropriate" (Loudon was the popularizer of ideas in Archibald Allison's *Essays on Principles of Taste* [London, 1780], which dealt with expressionism in buildings, and the necessity of design, fitness, and utility in architecture).

D. *Archives*. While the published reports of various committees to state legislatures, and municipal councils on the particular building of interest—penitentiary, courthouse, cemetery—are valuable, in the same way that directors' reports to stockholders of railroads can be helpful; archival material is essential, and the most rewarding. Current newspapers, minutes of meetings, letters, petitions, diaries, and journals are among the many documents to be investigated. The following archives have provided vitally necessary information: Archives of the State of New Jersey at Trenton for minor material on Haviland; Archives of the State of Tennessee at Nashville for material on Strickland; New Haven Colony Historical Society for documents on the Grove Street Cemetery; the Royal Institute of British Architects, London, for designs by both Haviland and Walter;

the New-York Historical Society for the complete set of plans of the "Tombs"; the Museum of the City of New York for illustrative material on the "Tombs" and the Reservoir; the Print Room of the Metropolitan Museum of Art for a large collection of Davis material, and the plans of the Renwick-supervised Reservoir. Most rewarding of all has been the material on the "Tombs" and its competition at the New York City Municipal Archives and Records Center; and the Haviland Papers on loan to the University of Pennsylvania from the Somerset Archaeological and Natural History Society at Taunton, England. The latter must have been brought to England by Haviland's son, Edward, who repatriated.

Finally, it must be recalled that there could have been no Egyptian Revival without the two great Napoleonic works that have been discussed throughout the text: Dominique Vivant Denon, *Voyage dans la Basse et la Haute Egypte pendant les campagnes du général Bonaparte,* 3 volumes (Paris, 1802). The following year a three volume translation appeared in London, and a two volume one, with many fewer plates, in New York. There were several re-editions in America, three by 1807. Less hastily done, and more scholarly was [Commission des monuments d'Egypte] *Description de l'Egypte, ou Recueil des observations et des recherches qui ont été faites en Egypte pendant l'expédition de l'armée française, publié par les ordres de Sa Majesté l'empereur Napoleon le Grand,* 9 volumes text, 11 volumes plates and an atlas (Paris, 1809–1828). The following year, 1829, the second edition was commenced. This was the one in Ithiel Town's library, and that of Haviland. The first edition had already been presented to Harvard. One of the largest publishing efforts ever undertaken in both scope and physical size, it is a fitting monument to the grandiose civilization of ancient Egypt. (For the vagaries of the numbering of the volumes in this publication, see note 19 in chapter two.)

Index

207

Index

Barnum, Phineas Taylor, 48

Baroque style, 7

Baskerville, H. Coleman, 111

Bataille, M., 28, *pl. 51*

Bath (England), Barker House, 33

Baton Rouge, La., State House, 183 n.35

Bavaria. *See* Germany

Bayfordbury (England), library, 33

Beaumont, Comte de, 146

Beauvallet, P. -N., 12, 24, 39 n.14, *pl. 49*

Beckford, William, 52

Belgium, prisons, 113, 114

Belzoni, Giovanni Battista, 39 n.7, 46 n.69, 48, 124 n.20

Bénéman (or Benneman), Guillaume, 24

Bénévant, Prince de, 27

Bennington, Vt., First Church of, 55

Berlin (Germany): Altes Museum, 117; Frederick the Great Monument project), 30, 188 n.44, *pl. 28*

Bernini, Giovanni Lorenzo, 11, 82, 90

Berry Hill, Va., 6

Bible, 109

Biennais, L., 24

Bigelow, Jacob, 31, 87, 97 n.10, 142, *pl. 57, 58*

Bindesbøll, Michael Gottlieb, 78 n. 28, 111, *pl. 135*

Binny, Andrew J., 175

"bizarre" *(bizzarria),* 23, 26, 29, 130, 135

Blackburn, James, 18 n.4

Blouet, Guillaume-Abel, 146, 149

Bollman, Wendel, 105, 143, *pl. 79, 80*

Bologna (Italy), Egyptian Institute, 32; San Petronio, 11

Bolton, Alderman, 153

Bonomi, Ignatius, 35, *pl. 17, 19*

Bonomi, Joseph, 35

Book of the Dead, 48

Book of Mormon, 48

Borghese, Prince Camillo, 14, 16

Boston (England), Masonic lodge, 46 n.74, 110

Boston, Mass., Bunker['s] Hill Monument. *See* Charlestown, Mass.; Castle Island Monument, 140; Massachusetts General Hospital, mummy, 48; Old Granary Burying Ground, 90, 94, 95,

142, *pl. 61;* 295 Washington Street, 78 n.28, 142; Tremont House, 184 n.35

Boullée, Etienne-Louis, 11, 24, 27, 33, 52, 54, 61, 117, 187 n.44, *pl. 26*

Bourgeois, Emil, 22

Brady, Josiah, 185 n.35

Bralle, J. -M. -N., 12, 19 n.18, 28, *pl. 49*

Brighton (England), Chain Pier, 123 n.11, *pl. 81*

Brighton, Mass., railroad station, 122–123 n.5, 142

Britain. *See* England; Scotland

Brockbank and Atkins, 45 n.56

Brongniart, Alexandre, 24

Brooklyn, N.Y.: Brooklyn Bridge, 124 n.19; Greenwood (Green-Wood) Cemetery, 84, 89

Brown, Sir Samuel, 123 n.11, *pl. 81*

Brunel, Isambard Kingdom, 101, 104–105, 123 n.15, 124 n.16, *pl. 78*

Bryant, Foster, 157, 163, 169

building types; assembly room, 27; asylum, 81; atelier, 46 n.69; banks, 78 n.28, 83; bath house, 26, 78 n.28; billiard room, 33; boudoir, 55; brewery, 35; bridges, 26, 27, 29, 101 n.49, 103–105, 123 n.11, 123 n.15, 124 n.16, 124 n.17, 124 n.19, 133; canon foundry, 27; cemeteries and cemetery gates, 7–8, 30, 31, 50, 53, 74, 81, 82–96, 100 n.49, 108, 133, 136; cenotaph, 33; churches, 38 n.5, 39 n.11, 70, 71–73, 77 n.22, 78 n.25, 78 n.28, 88, 109, 126 n.32, 134, 183 n.35; colleges: *see* institutions of learning and technology; commercial buildings, 35, 56, 57, 68–69, 74, 78 n.28, 134, 136; courthouses, 2, 6, 8, 16, 54, 64, 66–68, 69, 108, 112, 115–118, 121, 129 n.71, 134–135, 146–178, 189 n.53; customs house, 129 n.71; dairy, 33; domestic architecture, 33, 34, 55–56, 60 n.46, 63, 78 n.28, 102; fraternal lodges, 46 n.74, 71, 108; furnishings: *see separate listing under* furnishings; garden pavilions, 26–27, 33, 62, 80; gates, 38 n.7, 53, 101 n.49; *glacières: see* ice houses; hotels, 60 n.46; ice

Index

Index

Index

Index

Index